CAMPAIGN FOR PRESIDENT

CAMPAIGN FOR PRESIDENT

The Managers Look at 2004

Edited by
THE INSTITUTE OF POLITICS
JOHN F. KENNEDY SCHOOL OF GOVERNMENT
HARVARD UNIVERSITY

ROWMAN & LITTLEFIELD PUBLISHERS, INC.
Lanham • Boulder • New York • Toronto • Oxford

ROWMAN & LITTLEFIELD PUBLISHERS, INC.
Published in the United States of America
by Rowman & Littlefield Publishers, Inc.
A wholly owned subsidary of The Rowman & Littlefield Publishing Group, Inc.
4501 Forbes Boulevard, Suite 200, Lanham, Maryland 20706
www.rowmanlittlefield.com

P.O. Box 317, Oxford OX2 9RU, UK

British Library Cataloguing in Publication Information Available

Library of Congress Cataloging-in-Publication Data

Campaign for president : the managers look at 2004 / edited by the Institute of
Politics, Harvard University.
  p. cm. — (Campaigning American style)
  Includes index.
  ISBN 0-7425-3969-5 (cloth : alk. paper) — ISBN 0-7425-3970-9 (pbk. :
alk. paper)
  1. Presidents—United States—Election—2004—Congresses. 2. Political
campaigns—United States—Congresses. 3. Campaign management—United
States—Congresses. 4. United States—Politics and government—2001—
Congresses. I. John F. Kennedy School of Government. Institute of Politics.
II. Title. III. Series.
E905.C36 2006
324.973'0931—dc22   2005013135

Printed in the United States of America

♾ ™ The paper used in this publication meets the minimum requirements of
American National Standard for Information Sciences—Permanence of Paper for
Printed Library Materials, ANSI/NISO Z39.48-1992.

CONTENTS

THE PARTICIPANTS

Theresa Amato
Campaign Manager
Nader-Camejo Campaign

Rick Berke
Associate Managing Editor for News
The New York Times

Nick Baldick
Campaign Manager
Edwards for President

Gloria Borger
Political Columnist
U.S. News and World Report

Mary Beth Cahill
Campaign Manager
Kerry-Edwards Campaign

Stephanie Cutter
Communications Director
Kerry-Edwards Campaign

Nicole Devenish
Communications Director
Bush-Cheney Campaign

Tad Devine
Media Consultant
Kerry-Edwards Campaign

Matt Dowd
Chief Campaign Strategist
Bush-Cheney Campaign

Tom Edsall
Political Reporter
The Washington Post

David Gergen
Professor of Public Service/Director,
    Center for Public Leadership
Kennedy School of Government

Ben Ginsberg
Partner
Patton Boggs LLP

Josh Gottheimer
Strategic Advisor and Speechwriter
Clark for President

Charles Halloran
Campaign Manager
Sharpton for President

Mark Halperin
Political Director
ABC News

Brian Hardwick
Deputy Campaign Manager
Lieberman for President

John Harwood
National Political Editor
The Wall Street Journal

Gwen Ifill
Moderator and Managing Editor
Washington Week

Patricia Ireland
Campaign Manager
Moseley Braun for President

Chris LaCivita
Senior Advisor
Swift Boat Veterans for Truth

Charles Lenchner
Assistant Campaign Manager
Kucinich for President

Brian McCabe
Executive Director
Progress for America

Ken Mehlman
Campaign Manager
Bush-Cheney Campaign

Mark Mellman
Pollster
Kerry-Edwards Campaign

Steve Murphy
Campaign Manager
Gephardt for President

Adam Nagourney
Chief Political Correspondent
The New York Times

Terry Nelson
Political Director
Bush-Cheney Campaign

Steve Rosenthal
Chief Executive Officer
America Coming Together

Phil Sharp
Acting Director
Institute of Politics

Bob Shrum
Media Consultant
Kerry-Edwards Campaign

Erik Smith
President
Media Fund

Tommy Thompson
Political Director
Graham for President

Joe Trippi
Campaign Manager
Dean for President

Judy Woodruff
Anchor
Judy Woodruff's Inside Politics

THE OBSERVERS

Anne Aaron
Director, Profiles in Courage Award
John F. Kennedy Library Foundation

Graham Allison
Director, Belfer Center for Science
  and International Affairs
Kennedy School of Government

Jeff Amestoy
Fellow, Institute of Politics, Fall
  2004

Susan Blumenthal
U.S. Assistant Surgeon General

Chuck Campion
Chairman
Dewey Square Group

Heather Campion
Senior Executive Vice President
Citizens Bank

Ceci Connolly
National Political Reporter
The Washington Post

Ken Cooper
National Editor
The Boston Globe

Rosemarie Day
Chief of Staff, Office of the Dean
Kennedy School of Government

Vicki Divoll
Fellow, Institute of Politics, Fall
  2004

Frank Fahrenkophf
Co-Chairman
Commission on Presidential Debates

Kirsten Fedewa
Republican Political Consultant
Kirsten Fedewa & Associates

Bob Giles
Curator
Nieman Foundation

Joshua Green
Senior Editor
The Atlantic

Jeff Greenfield
Senior Political Analyst
CNN

Tony Halmos
Director of Public Relations
Corporation of London

Chris Henick
Giuliani Partners

Karen Hicks
National Field Director
Democratic National Committee

Fred Hochberg
Dean
Milano Graduate School at the New
    School

Maxine Isaacs
Adjunct Lecturer in Public Policy
Kennedy School of Government

Alex Jones
Director, Shorenstein Center on the
    Press, Politics & Public Policy
Kennedy School of Government

Elaine Kamarck
Lecturer in Public Policy
Kennedy School of Government

David King
Associate Director
Institute of Politics

Joe Klein
Columnist
TIME Magazine

Dotty Lynch
Senior Political Editor
CBS News

Joe McCarthy
Senior Associate Dean and Director
    of Degree Programs
Kennedy School of Government

Mark Merritt
President and CEO
The Pharmaceutical Care
    Management Association

Nick Mitropoulos
The Monitor Group

Beth Myers
Chief of Staff
Massachusetts Governor Mitt
    Romney

Betsy Myers
Executive Director, Center for
    Public Leadership
Kennedy School of Government

Bonnie Newman
Former Executive Dean
Kennedy School of Government

Marty Nolan
Former Editorial Page Editor
The Boston Globe

Nancy Palmer
Executive Director
Shorenstein Center on the Press,
    Politics & Public Policy

Jon Rotenberg
Treasurer
Robert F. Kennedy Action Corps

Kit Seeyle
Political Correspondent
The New York Times

Jeanne Shaheen
National Chairperson
Kerry-Edwards Campaign

Graham Shalgian
Deputy Press Secretary
Office of Senator Edward M.
    Kennedy

Walter Shapiro
Columnist
USA Today

John Shattuck
President and CEO
John F. Kennedy Library Foundation

Roger Simon
Political Editor
U.S. News & World Report

Lynn Sweet
Washington Bureau Chief
Chicago Sun-Times

Karen Tumulty
National Political Correspondent
TIME Magazine

Elizabeth Wilner
Political Director
NBC News

Richard Wolffe
Senior Diplomatic Correspondent
Newsweek

David Yepsen
Political Columnist
Des Moines Register

Jeff Zeleny
National Correspondent
Chicago Tribune

Jim Zigler
Managing Director
UBS Financial Services

INTRODUCTION

THE 2004 PRESIDENTIAL ELECTION revived the American belief that elections do matter and that campaigns can influence the outcome. There was a significant upsurge in citizen participation and a resurgence of two dominant political parties—defying early speculation from pundits.

The searing events of 9/11 and the policies that followed undoubtedly intensified voter interest and certainly were central to the campaigns of 2004.

Americans in larger numbers and with greater intensity than we have seen in recent elections engaged as volunteers, as contributors, and as voters.

Volunteers swarmed into battleground states to champion their candidates. One conference participant said his organization dropped plans to pay 12,000 election-day workers because 17,000 people had voluntarily signed up for action.

There was a renewed focus on old-style organizational politics—the so-called ground war—where by phone, on foot, or via the Internet, campaign workers identified potential supporters, registered them to vote, and pushed them to cast ballots. Historically, this had been the classic work of party precinct workers, but for years it had been declining in many parts of the country. Democrats had especially emphasized this approach to past campaigns, but Republicans aggressively pursued a ground-war strategy from the outset of President Bush's first term. Many observers believe the Republicans carried out the most effective grassroots effort in memory.

This classic organizational work was transformed as the Internet was exploited to dramatic effect by all camps—to raise funds, to engage volunteers, to spread campaign messages, and to combat criticism from opponents or media. During the Democratic primaries, Governor Dean's campaign was particularly creative and effective in using the Internet. Deciding to forgo public financing (and its attendant restraints) could have been a damaging move, but in doing so, the governor gave supporters an opportunity to vote via the Internet and thus lent his decision legitimacy while forestalling public criticism.

The Internet was not simply a tool in the hands of campaign organizers. Individual citizens and groups independently sought and generated information and opinions, and, in some instances, they effectively compelled the campaigns and established news media to respond to their initiatives. "Blogging" and "bloggers" joined the American lexicon.

When it came to money, both parties seemed to find bottomless wells. The surprise was in the Democrat camp, where expectations were substantially exceeded. Indeed Senator Kerry's campaign ended with a sizeable surplus.

2004 was the first campaign to operate under the reforms of McCain-Feingold. "Soft money" was to have been a thing of the past. But critics of President Bush aggressively pursued another path, creating so-called 527s, which they claimed could legally spend unlimited sums so long as they were not coordinated with or directed by the official campaigns. President Bush and the Republicans first denounced this retreat from reform, but soon thereafter similar organizations sprang up to attack the Democrats and Senator Kerry. The "Swift Boat Veterans for Truth" became the most controversial, if not notorious, of the 527s.

Much more about the campaigns of 2004 can be found in this volume, which is a lightly edited transcript from two days of discussions among the key campaign decisionmakers.

Following each presidential election since 1972, the Institute of Politics (IOP) has convened campaign leaders of the various primary and general election candidates. Prominent political journalists have led the participants through an examination of the decisions, the challenges, and the ups and downs of these incredibly dynamic and complex enterprises we call campaigns.

The Institute is grateful for the continued willingness of the victors, the vanquished, and the journalists to sit together and share their experiences and insights. More importantly, all of us should be grateful to them for their contributions to making our democratic system work.

The conference and this book could not have happened without the hard work of so many at the IOP. I would especially like to thank Catherine McLaughlin, executive director of the Institute of Politics for the overall supervision of this project, including countless hours of editing. I would like to thank Christian Flynn for managing the complex logistics of the conference and the production of this book, and Kathleen McGlynn for all of her assistance in making the conference happen. In particular, the Institute is grateful to Amanda Fuchs for taking the lead on editing the transcript; to Adam Katz, a sophomore at the college, for assembling the time line both on paper and online; and to Illan Graff, president of the Student Advisory Committee, who assisted in the editorial process.

Phil Sharp, Acting Director
Institute of Politics
March 2005

EDITOR'S NOTE

O N December 15 and 16, 2004, the Institute of Politics brought to Harvard University campaign managers, senior advisors, political analysts, and journalists to discuss the 2004 presidential campaign. The following is a transcript of the five sections of the conference. The transcript has been slightly edited to make it easier to follow for those who were not in attendance, but for the most part, the text is a verbatim transcript so that readers can appreciate the conversational nature of the discussions. At the end of the book, there is an abridged time line of key events from the 2004 election cycle. For a more in-depth time line of the campaign, please visit the Institute of Politics website at www.iop.harvard.edu. We hope that as you read the transcript of the conference, you will think about what you saw as you watched the 2004 campaign unfold on television and read about it in the newspapers and that you gain an in-depth understanding of the decisions that were made that led to the events you witnessed.

Amanda Fuchs

The Decision to Run for President 1

"There's a little in all of the stories about us that is deeply true and I think John Kerry always wanted to be president. He always looked to where the nation ought to go and what role he could play in that. Looking at the field, looking at who was running, looking at the year, he knew that it was going to be a very tough go but he had as good a chance as anyone."

—Kerry-Edwards Campaign Manager Mary Beth Cahill

"I always thought the President would win reelection. I always thought he would win because the nature of the challenges the country faced meant the public was going to look for someone who they thought was a strong leader who would take on what needed to be taken on."

—Bush-Cheney Campaign Manager Ken Mehlman

PHIL SHARP: Ladies and gentlemen, welcome to our Campaign Decision Makers Conference 2004. I'm delighted to turn our program over to our first moderator, Judy Woodruff of CNN's *Inside Politics*. Judy has a long-standing relationship with the Institute of Politics and the Kennedy School of Government and she is a member of the Kennedy School Visiting Committee. Tonight, Judy will go around the room and talk to some of the people that ran the campaigns and get a brief introduction as to what happened.

JUDY WOODRUFF: This is really a reporter's dream—to get to go around the room and stick a microphone in the face of campaign managers and inject a little truth serum. (Laughter.) Seriously, that's not what we're going to do. There is no truth serum and I don't have a hypodermic needle. What I do have is the full force of your colleagues in the world of campaigning and the media who will be listening and looking very hard at you as we begin tonight and go into tomorrow.

All we're going to do tonight is get a sense of why each one of these candidates got into the race in the first place. What were they thinking? What did they think their little part of the universe was? What in the world made them think that they had a shot? We're going to do all this with five minutes for each one so I'm going to be cracking the whip even more than I do on the air.

• HOWARD DEAN •

JUDY WOODRUFF: Bend your mind back to early 2002. September 11 had obviously happened—the country was still very much shaken by that. It was May 30, 2002, when none other than Howard Dean, the little-known governor of the State of Vermont, announced that he was forming an exploratory committee. We are very fortunate to have his campaign manager Joe Trippi with us tonight. What made Howard Dean, who is from a tiny state in New England with a small population, think he had a prayer? You didn't have the Iraq war yet as an issue. He had governed, some would say, as a moderate conservative in the state, at least by Vermont standards. What made him think he had a chance at the presidency?

JOE TRIPPI: I don't think any of us thought he had a chance. (Laughter.) I'm serious. He got into the race very late. In Howard's mind, he wanted to raise health care as an issue. He felt very strongly about that. And he wanted to raise early childhood development as an issue. He really thought there were things to say. He was definitely angry about the deficit at that point—he really wanted to do something about the deficit. I think he just wanted to add his views to the debate.

Something like sixty-three Democrats have run for president since 1968 and two have won. I remember us having this meeting early on where we said we knew that the odds were two in sixty-three—we were probably not going

Gephardt campaign manager Steve Murphy and CNN anchor Judy Woodruff listen to Howard Dean's campaign manager Joe Trippi talk about running a different type of campaign.

to make it. But that gave us the freedom to run a totally different kind of campaign. If we did that, our goal was to win. If we failed, we hoped to do it in a way that the country would never forget that Dean for America had been on the playing field for 2003 and 2004.

JUDY WOODRUFF: Did you have a model going in? Was it a Jimmy Carter model or a George McGovern model?

JOE TRIPPI: It was a totally different model. I guess a little bit Jimmy Carter—get out there early and visit Iowa and New Hampshire as much as possible early on. In the very beginning, we had 98,000 bucks in the bank, seven staff people and, at that point, 432 known supporters nationwide. So, for a lot of different reasons, we decided that we were an insurgent. We had to run a totally different, decentralized campaign to get any oxygen into the campaign. We had an internal goal. If we lost, we really wanted to change things. That made us try things that other people hadn't tried.

JUDY WOODRUFF: That was May of 2002. In February of 2003, Howard Dean made a speech in which he talked about representing the "Democratic wing of the Democratic party."[1] When did that idea come along?

JOE TRIPPI: We're now jumping towards the war. Howard Dean strongly opposed the war in Iraq. He showed tremendous courage. We were reaching a point where upwards of 80 percent of the American people were in support of the war and 20 percent were against it. He felt the party leadership had gone the wrong way.

That comment was a very spontaneous thing. It was not planned. I was in his hotel room at 10:45—I think he went on at 11:15—and he looked at all of us and said, what am I supposed to say down there? He did. He had red-eyed in from California. He walked downstairs and totally winged it. That whole speech was spontaneous. It was not written. It hadn't even been thought out, which I think is pretty amazing actually.

JUDY WOODRUFF: On the war, was that something that came on gradually or was it something that one night at midnight he said, this is going to be my issue?

JOE TRIPPI: We never thought it was our issue. We just thought we had a responsibility to say that it was wrong. There were other people—Dennis

---

1. Howard Dean delivered the speech at the Democratic National Committee's winter meeting on February 21, 2003.

Kucinich and other candidates—out there saying that. We just had more wind underneath our sails and had a platform that we could build on.

JUDY WOODRUFF: When did you really think you had a shot at the nomination? Can you put a date on it?

JOE TRIPPI: Yes. The end of June 2003, in that unbelievable three or four days when millions of dollars came in over the Internet and $829,000 came in on Monday, the FEC deadline day. We had raised more money than Kerry and Edwards for that quarter.

• JOHN KERRY •

JUDY WOODRUFF: On December 1, 2002, six months later, John Kerry announced that he was going to form an exploratory committee. Mary Beth Cahill, you weren't around at that point, but we're going to give you a chance to answer and maybe you want to bring in some of your colleagues.[2]

How did John Kerry rationalize that he could beat history? He was a sitting senator. It had been forty some years since a sitting senator had gotten elected president. He was from New England. It had been that long as well since a non-southerner had been elected president. What was the rationale?

MARY BETH CAHILL: There's a little in all of the stories about us that is deeply true and I think John Kerry always wanted to be president. He always looked to where the nation ought to go and what role he could play in that. Looking at the field, looking at who was running, looking at the year, he knew that it was going to be a very tough go, but he had as good a chance as anyone. Plus, several of his colleagues got into this race.

He had a record, as we all know now, of coming from behind in tough races and he believed deeply in his ability to do that. He thought that what was critical, as the primary went back and forth, was that he'd always stay focused on the general election. Even during the height of the Dean moments, when there was huge pressure to go to the left on the war, Kerry was talking about building a stronger America. He stuck to that despite huge amounts of pressure from supporters, and to some degree from the press, that he move to the left on this.

JUDY WOODRUFF: Back in late 2002, who did he think was going to run? What was the calculus in terms of other senators? At that point, [Sena-

---

2. Jim Jordan served as Senator Kerry's campaign manager from the first days of the primary campaign until November 10, 2003, when Mary Beth Cahill was brought on to replace him.

*John Kerry's campaign manager Mary Beth Cahill discusses
John Kerry's motivation for running for president.*

tor] Joe Biden was still thinking about it. Certainly, [Senator] Tom Daschle
was still thinking about it. What was the thinking?

MARY BETH CAHILL: And Joe Lieberman and John Edwards got in. So
it is not as though senators have suddenly stopped thinking that they can win.
From all of my experience with senators, that's not the case.

Senator Kerry felt confident in his background and interest in military
power and security and felt he would have something to talk about that
would make him different from his colleagues that were running. That would
be something that would be part of his message throughout the entire campaign. In addition to that, he put forward very detailed plans on health care
and the economy. He felt like he had done all the homework necessary to
talk about the future of the country.

JUDY WOODRUFF: The October war vote—did he or anyone around
him anticipate at all the extent to which that might be a negative down the
road?[3]

---

3. Senator Kerry voted for Senate Joint Resolution 45 on October 11, 2002, to authorize
the President to use force in Iraq to defend American national security and ensure the
enforcement of relevant UN resolutions. The measure passed the Senate by a vote of
77-23.

MARY BETH CAHILL: Seeing as I started in November, I wasn't present when he made that decision.

JUDY WOODRUFF: Bob Shrum?

BOB SHRUM: I wasn't either, actually, because we're talking about 2002. But I think he understood from the beginning, and believed all the way to the end of the campaign in the fall, that that vote was a vote he was going to have to live with, but that the President ought to be given the authority to use force, as he said in the debates, if necessary, to get Saddam Hussein to disarm. He did not think at any point that that was inconsistent with saying, in the absence of evidence of weapons of mass destruction, you shouldn't go forward, and you should give enough time to build the alliances and build the coalition. I think he went into the vote eyes wide open.

I talked to him at the time, as I talked to several other senators, and when I was asked, what's the political implication of this, I said, I don't think anyone knows. This is a vote you've got to make on the basis of what you believe is the right thing to do. And that's what he did.

One other thing I would add and I don't know what Joe [Trippi] would say about this. Being a senator with some serious foreign policy experience was, at least in the primaries and, I believe, ultimately in the general, probably a necessary qualification for being the Democratic nominee in the year 2004. September 11 had transformed the world. I believe that if Bill Clinton had tried to run for president in 2004 with the résumé he had from Arkansas, he could not have been a serious candidate for president. People would have said, what does he know about foreign policy?

The conventional wisdom that a senator is inherently weak or inherently has got problems because they cast two or three thousand votes was wrong at a very profound level. In Iowa, what happened after January 1 was people woke up and said, okay, who do I really think can and should be president of the United States? The kind of background Kerry had actually made him the answer to that question.

JUDY WOODRUFF: The one campaign that would maybe take issue with what you said about having extensive foreign policy experience is the one campaign that's not represented here tonight—the John Edwards campaign.

BOB SHRUM: I don't speak for John Edwards, who is a good friend of mine and who was a very effective vice presidential candidate with us. It was hurtful to him that he did not have a greater depth of experience, going into the primaries, in foreign policy. I think that hurt him in this election. He is a different person today than he was going in.

JUDY WOODRUFF: You're saying the whole national security piece was part of the calculus for getting in, no question?

BOB SHRUM: Mary Beth said the most profoundly important thing, which was John Kerry, and this is quite honest, had thought about being president of the United States for some time. He had very strong feelings about the Bush Administration's foreign policy and about what it was doing to the country. He had surprisingly strong feelings, as you talked to him, about issues like health care, which he had not necessarily spent a huge amount of time on in the Senate but had thought a lot about. He knew why he wanted to run for president and being a senator was an advantage.

JUDY WOODRUFF: Joe Trippi, Bob mentioned your campaign. Do you want to come back on that?

JOE TRIPPI: I agree with Bob. In the end, Senator Kerry's record in the Senate on foreign policy and intelligence helped him tremendously. It was always something that the Dean campaign had a hard time dealing with—not just in Iowa but around the country. The best example of this is when Dean was asked about Wes Clark as a vice presidential pick. He said, I've got a hole in my résumé on foreign policy and defense and I'm certainly going to have to plug that with my vice president. It was a very honest statement. But it also tells you how much it weighed on us in terms of not having that.

I agree with Bob, too, that Iowans woke up and then were really focused. We made some mistakes in our campaign—I take responsibility for that—but we made mistakes at the same time John Kerry's sitting there fitting the bill. That's what happened.

• JOE LIEBERMAN •

JUDY WOODRUFF: John Kerry announced that he was forming an exploratory committee on December 1, 2002. A month later, John Edwards announced that he was not only forming a committee, he was a candidate. Only a few days after that, Joe Lieberman, having been freed from the pledge he made to Al Gore when Gore announced on December 14, 2002, that he wasn't running, announced that he was running.[4]

Brian Hardwick, why Joe Lieberman? Did he regret the pledge that had been hanging around his neck?

---

4. Shortly after the 2000 election, Senator Joe Lieberman publicly declared that he would not challenge his former running mate, Vice President Al Gore, for his party's nomination for president in 2004.

Joe Lieberman's deputy campaign manager Brian Hardwick discusses the effect of Lieberman's pledge not to challenge former running mate Vice President Al Gore for the Democratic nomination.

BRIAN HARDWICK: He felt very strongly about the pledge. But, in terms of a campaign, as we got started, it definitely handcuffed us. That first quarter of fundraising, there was a high expectation that Senator Lieberman would raise tons of money coming off the 2000 campaign as the vice presidential nominee. We came up extremely short as a campaign. There was a sense that we really hadn't been running. He did stay true to that pledge and there's no question that it hurt the campaign early on.

Why Joe Lieberman? First of all, it was reasonable for him to believe he could win a Democratic primary—that, after his experience in 2000, there was real residual goodwill within the party. He had a positive impact on the ticket in 2000. He had helped financially and with votes. It was reasonable that he thought there was residual goodwill. It was also reasonable for him to believe he would have the resources to do it.

He had a strong message combining his long progressive record on the environment, civil rights, and a woman's right to choose, with strong views on foreign policy. Nobody was ever confused about his position on the war. He felt strongly about it and he felt strongly about removing Saddam Hussein. He thought that, combined with his values and being a man of faith, was a nice balance and there was room in our party for a centrist to run. It had been proven in history—Bill Clinton, Jimmy Carter—that there was a constituency in a Democratic primary for president for somebody running from the center.

JUDY WOODRUFF: Who was encouraging him to run?

BRIAN HARDWICK: I wasn't around at the time—I joined the campaign in August—so I'd just be speculating who encouraged him. I presume supporters from 2000.

JUDY WOODRUFF: One of the raps on Joe Lieberman, when he got in, was that this man is too nice to go very far in politics.

BRIAN HARDWICK: He is an extremely nice guy and a great guy to work for. But he's also somebody who has a long history in public service and he feels strongly about his views. He felt there was room in the race for somebody to get in there and to speak their mind, that there was a chance for somebody to be the independent, straight talker in the Democratic party, and that style wouldn't necessarily rule the day.

JUDY WOODRUFF: What about the fact that he is Jewish and a huge supporter of Israel? A lot of people talked about that being a factor. To what extent was that discussed?

BRIAN HARDWICK: It was something that people knew about Joe Lieberman in 2000. I don't think there was a big feeling in 2000 that it hurt the ticket. In fact, there were parts of the country where Joe Lieberman was extremely helpful. The Jewish community was extremely generous financially to the ticket in 2000, so we thought it was a net plus. To know what voters think in their own mind when they walk into a voting booth, and how that affects their vote, I'd have to read their mind and I can't do that.

JUDY WOODRUFF: Just to wrap up, when did you join the campaign?

BRIAN HARDWICK: I joined in August on the day that we gave a speech at the National Press Club, which I'm sure Joe [Trippi] remembers well.[5] We talked about Howard Dean taking us to the wilderness. This was right in the middle of the Dean campaign's "Sleepless Summer" tour—their impressive tour where they went around the country and had huge crowds. Lieberman felt strongly that somebody needed to stand up and be the alternative to Dean.

---

5. Senator Lieberman delivered his speech to the National Press Club in Washington, D.C., on August 4, 2003.

JUDY WOODRUFF: So that became a big part of the rationale?

BRIAN HARDWICK: From that point forward, yes. We didn't think that Ken [Mehlman] and Karl Rove had a strategy against Joe Lieberman.[6] We didn't think they could say that we were a flip-flopper. We didn't think they could say that we were weak on defense. We didn't think they could say we were weak on values. We really felt we would create somewhat of a problem for them. That was what our mantra was from that point forward.

JUDY WOODRUFF: Ken, was that something on your mind?

KEN MEHLMAN: I think Joe Lieberman would have been a very strong candidate. He would have helped overcome a disadvantage Democrats had on some cultural issues. He certainly had foreign policy credentials. I think the President would have won. Ultimately, I don't know that people would have seen him as strong a leader as they saw the President, but I do think he had those attributes.

JUDY WOODRUFF: At this point in the campaign—when Howard Dean has been in there running hard, John Kerry said he's going to run, John Edwards is in, Joe Lieberman's in—what was your campaign thinking? What were you worried about, or were you worried?

KEN MEHLMAN: A couple of things. One, we were trying to raise a lot of money. Obviously, that was our focus at the beginning. The things you saw in terms of the Election Day ground game, in terms of voter registration, the way we were able to target people, all of that was occurring in 2003. That's not something you build in six months. That's something that you spend a lot of time building. We spent four years building it. We particularly spent 2003 building it a lot.

We were getting as much information and putting together different scenarios on the different candidates. Certainly, if either Gephardt or Lieberman had been nominated, we would have had to deal with the fact that they were people who had a proven ability—both on national security issues and on cultural issues—and have a more moderate approach. Now, there would have been other arguments we would have made.

JUDY WOODRUFF: So you were more worried about them?

KEN MEHLMAN: I personally think they would have both been strong candidates. But I totally agree with what Bob Shrum said. The fact is that a

---

6. Karl Rove served as President Bush's senior political advisor during his first term.

senator, or a person that has foreign policy experience and defense experience, particularly a veteran, was a real asset in this campaign and we watched that going forward.

If you had said to me, in the beginning, at this time who will be the nominee, I would have said Kerry. Kerry made the most sense if you looked at his ability to raise resources, the team he put together, and the fact that he had a big state with a base that allowed him to continue to raise those resources. Also, the fact that he had New Hampshire nearby and that he was a veteran. He was the establishment, safe candidate for the Democrats to choose.

JUDY WOODRUFF: This was before Dean started to move?

KEN MEHLMAN: Yes.

• AL SHARPTON •

JUDY WOODRUFF: A few days after Joe Lieberman, Al Sharpton announced that he was running.[7] Charles Halloran, what was the rationale? Why?

CHARLES HALLORAN: There's probably two rationales. There was my rationale, which made my wife and family and friends like Brian [Hardwick] question my sanity, and there was the reverend's rationale.

My rationale, as a life-long Democratic supporter and operative who ran statewide campaigns and worked in presidential campaigns, was that I was concerned that the Sharpton campaign could take one of two directions. I thought if I had the opportunity to get involved, make a positive impact on it, keep him doing the kind of things that he could do well, run a positive race, and embrace the eventual nominee, that was the right thing to do for the party.

JUDY WOODRUFF: What were you worried about?

CHARLES HALLORAN: We had just seen the Mark Green fiasco in 2001.[8] So, quite frankly, a lot of people were worried that a Sharpton candidacy would be problematic for the Democratic primary. Everyone in this

---

7. Reverend Al Sharpton filed papers for an exploratory committee on January 22, 2003.
8. In November 2001, Republican Michael Bloomberg narrowly defeated Democrat Mark Green in New York City's mayoral race. Green had been weakened by a difficult Democratic primary in which Reverend Sharpton's endorsement of Bronx Borough President Fernando Ferrer contributed to a highly polarized vote that divided sharply along racial lines.

Al Sharpton's campaign manager Charles Halloran answers CNN anchor Judy Woodruff's questions about whether Sharpton had a chance at winning a state.

room probably was worried about that, except our friends from the other side.

I took the job and told Sharpton, I'm here to run a traditional campaign and I know what you're here to do—broaden his civil rights work, put up important issues, and grow the base of the party. He needed me to do that and I needed him to do what he did well, which was to be Al Sharpton, in order to run an effective campaign.

JUDY WOODRUFF: It almost sounds like you were there as a babysitter.

CHARLES HALLORAN: To keep him from being the candidate he wanted to be. Not out of control, that's not the right term, but to keep him doing things he said he wanted to do, which was grow the party, grow the base, and endorse the eventual nominee.

JUDY WOODRUFF: Did he have to persuade you to come on board? How did that work?

CHARLES HALLORAN: Yes. He took my passport. (Laughter.)

JUDY WOODRUFF: Were you modeling the campaign after Jesse Jackson or another African American?

CHARLES HALLORAN: There was a lot of pressure to model it after the Jackson campaign, but it was nothing of the sort. It wasn't groundbreaking like the Jackson campaign was. America needed to have Jesse Jackson run and get past that so we could say an African American can run and win delegates and be a part of this process. We proved that so there wasn't as much pressure for the African American community to embrace him.

We had our own model, which was to get out there, call attention to issues, do well in debates, and work a free media strategy, since we had not a dime of money to spend on any paid media.

JUDY WOODRUFF: Did you think you had a prayer at winning a state? South Carolina, maybe?

CHARLES HALLORAN: No. No. (Laughter.)

JUDY WOODRUFF: So obviously you didn't have a prayer of winning the nomination?

CHARLES HALLORAN: Absolutely not. Let's not kid ourselves. (Laughter.)

JUDY WOODRUFF: Charles is setting a model for everybody else here.

CHARLES HALLORAN: You said be honest. Actually, Sharpton's strategy was problematic with the delegate selection plans and the threshold level needed in the congressional districts. He wanted to run, for instance, South Carolina statewide—in places he didn't have a chance of getting the threshold and getting votes. Some of us in the campaign wanted him to run solely in [Congressman] Clyburn's district—stay right there, don't move out of Clyburn's district, get your 15 percent. He said, I'm running a statewide and a national campaign. I'm going to go everywhere, I'm going to meet everybody, I'm not going to hide, I'm going to be everywhere. So let Sharpton be Sharpton. I think if we'd stayed in Clyburn's district, we would have gotten delegates out of South Carolina. It worked in Michigan. We did stay in Detroit the whole time, practically. We had to handcuff him. We almost tied with Kerry in the two Detroit Congressional districts.

JUDY WOODRUFF: It's no secret that Sharpton has had tense relations with some other leaders in the African American civil rights community. How much of a problem was that?

CHARLES HALLORAN: Everyday. No. (Laughter.) It was a big problem. My first day on the job was Frank Watkins' last day on the job.[9] The very next day, Sharpton was supposed to be on an airplane with Howard Dean and Jesse Jackson Jr., so that obviously didn't play very well with the Reverend.

Actually, Reverend Sharpton and Jesse Jackson have a mutual respect for each other. And, from what I've heard from people that have worked for Jesse Jackson, the baton is never passed—it's grabbed from one leader to another. (Laughter.)

The two have a healthy respect for grabbing that baton and no one lays it out for you. (Laughter.)

• DENNIS KUCINICH •

JUDY WOODRUFF: That was January 22, 2003. On Valentine's Day of 2003, Dennis Kucinich went to Iowa and announced that he was a candidate for president. Charles Lenchner was the assistant campaign manager. Charles, was it all about the war? Why?

CHARLES LENCHNER: Yes. I think Dennis [Kucinich] correctly estimated just how damaging the Bush Administration would be and just how divisive and destructive the war in Iraq would be. He wanted to sound the alarm, not only about that particular war, but about what it meant for the United States to be a country that engages in unilateral wars, that sees the threat of terrorism, not as a way of addressing serious problems in the globe, but as creating a situation where America is seen as trying to enforce its dominance by any means necessary.

JUDY WOODRUFF: Were you with the campaign from the beginning?

CHARLES LENCHNER: I joined in September 2003.

JUDY WOODRUFF: At that point, did anyone around Dennis Kucinich think he had a chance at winning the nomination?

CHARLES LENCHNER: I have met his supporters around the country and up until March—Super Tuesday—everyone assumed that he would win. (Laughter.)

---

9. Frank Watkins served as the campaign manager for Reverend Sharpton's campaign from April 2003 until his resignation in September 2003, during a leave of absence from his role as communications director for Congressman Jesse Jackson Jr. (D-IL). Watkins worked for Reverend Jesse Jackson for nearly three decades.

Dennis Kucinich's assistant campaign manager Charles Lenchner discusses why Kucinich stayed in the Democratic primary race.

JUDY WOODRUFF: Everyone?

CHARLES LENCHNER: I did not meet any supporters of Dennis who said that they're in it and don't think he will win—not a single one!

JUDY WOODRUFF: We appreciate your candor. (Laughter.)

CHARLES LENCHNER: You think I'm joking.

JUDY WOODRUFF: Charles, when did you get a sense that Howard Dean was stealing your issue from you?

CHARLES LENCHNER: It was after the great speech Dean gave at the DNC that winter. Before then, there was a situation where, among the peace community, Dennis was a bigger name. I'm talking about those hundreds of thousands of people who went and demonstrated against the war in February. Dennis's name had more recognition than Dean but, after that speech, there was a huge wind in the Dean campaign's sails. Of course we were angry. We thought that belonged to us. But we had to contend with a lot of the marginalization that Kucinich got, in part because of some of his other views and his background and the fact that he's short. (Laughter.)

JUDY WOODRUFF: Are you serious about that? Was that an issue?

CHARLES LENCHNER: Among the people who were not going to vote for Dennis, that was an issue.

JUDY WOODRUFF: How do you know? Did you poll on that?

CHARLES LENCHNER: We didn't poll, but it was mentioned in some press articles and when we spoke to people. I think one of the reasons why John Kerry did well is that people in Iowa and New Hampshire wanted to vote for someone who they thought could defeat Bush and they wanted someone who looked more presidential. They wanted someone who the pundits would pre-nominate as the one who could win and Dennis didn't fit a lot of the criteria that were being set. I don't think he was being judged on the merits of his ideas and policy proposals.

JUDY WOODRUFF: So you think if he had been taller, he might have had a better shot?

CHARLES LENCHNER: We'll never know, but I think that we could have gotten a number of percentage points for each inch. (Laughter.)

JUDY WOODRUFF: Seriously, why did Dennis Kucinich stay in after it was clear that Howard Dean had run away with the war issue?

CHARLES LENCHNER: We made a commitment from the very beginning to allow every single American who wanted to vote against the war to be able to do so at the ballot box. That meant continuing to campaign in all fifty states, including states like New Jersey, just to make sure that everyone had that opportunity. When we got 17 percent in Washington state, we felt very proud of ourselves for being able to keep the debate focused on some of the issues that we and, of course, the Dean campaign had raised. We wanted to make sure that when the nominee was selected at the convention, when we were running against Bush, that we would have a Democratic team that included as many of the 2.4 million Nader voters as had gone his way the last time. That would include people who were marching in the streets against the war. We felt that our participation until the very last minute was the very best strategy to expand the party's base towards the left.

JUDY WOODRUFF: Did you ever get tired of people not taking your candidate seriously?

CHARLES LENCHNER: The people who cared strongly about the war generally did take his candidacy seriously—not in the sense that he could win, but in the sense that his participation, and this would go for Sharpton and for Dean, did wonderful things for the party. They energized the base. They brought wonderful organizations after the election, like Democracy for America and Progressive Democrats of America. They've helped revitalize groups like Progressive Majority, and that's a wonderful contribution that you're going to see the effects of over the next two and four years.

• CAROL MOSELEY BRAUN •

JUDY WOODRUFF: That was Valentine's Day. Four days later, the former senator from the state of Illinois, Carol Moseley Braun, announced her exploratory committee. Patricia Ireland was her national campaign manager. Why was she running?

PATRICIA IRELAND: I think that principally it's a cliché but—she really did want to serve the country. She had been in positions where she was able to do that and wanted to do it again. She liked being in public service. The other aspect was to change the face of power in the country. One of her big applause lines was, "Take the men-only sign off the White House door."

We looked at the 22 million single women who did not vote in 2000 and

Carol Moseley Braun's campaign manager Patricia Ireland discusses why Moseley Braun felt it was time to "take the men-only sign off the White House door."

found, through polling and focus groups, that the best message for them to get them to vote was that there was power in their numbers. They thought nobody was hearing their voice, that nobody cared about their issues. It's extremely significant that more than 90 percent of the women, married and single, said that neither presidential candidate in the general election understood their issues.

My belief is she cared about the issues that she wanted to raise. There is this theory that lightning sometimes does strike twice. She was not supposed to win her senate race and yet, after Anita Hill, a very surprised Alan Dixon woke up after the primary in Illinois to find himself the former U.S. Senator from Illinois.[10] So I think all of those went into the mix.

JUDY WOODRUFF: But that was the senate race. This was the presidency.

PATRICIA IRELAND: Yes, ma'am.

JUDY WOODRUFF: Was the main rationale that she was a woman and there wasn't a woman in the race?

PATRICIA IRELAND: No. I think that there was a desire, as Kucinich's assistant campaign manager said, to strengthen the party and to keep the party from being pulled too far away from its natural constituency, which does include women and people of color.

At the time that she actually got into the race, in September,[11] the truth of the matter is that, in terms of fundraising, all of the oxygen had been sucked out of the air by the anybody-but-Bush thrust of some of the Democrats who were just desperate to find somebody who could win. People would come up to us in airports or anyplace and say, oh, it's so important that you ran, you're so good in the debates, I'm so glad to see you up there on the stage. Finally, I, in frustration, started saying to them, oh, does that mean we can count on you for a campaign contribution? Oh, well, um-uh, um-uh. And they would start backing away.

It was important that she was raising issues. The biggest applause line she got in the debates was talking about equal pay, which had not been raised.

---

10. In March 1992, Carol Moseley Braun defied conventional wisdom by defeating incumbent Illinois Senator Alan Dixon to become the Democratic party's nominee for the United States Senate. Dixon was hurt by his perceived insensitivity to Anita Hill following her allegations of sexual harassment during Clarence Thomas's Supreme Court confirmation hearings.

11. Carol Moseley Braun formally announced her candidacy for the Democratic nomination on September 21, 2003.

She felt very strongly about decoupling universal health care from employment, which would have an impact on our international trade by taking that cost off of U.S. goods. Many of the ideas she brought were important ones and she wanted to get them out there.

JUDY WOODRUFF: There was the matter of some of the controversies associated with her service in the Senate. The person who was on her staff, her former Senate manager, and the issue with the trip to Africa and all of that, weren't you concerned about that, to say the least?[12] Quite frankly, what I would hear from some people, in a very cynical way, was that Carol Moseley Braun was just in this to raise her speaking fees. How do you deal with that kind of skepticism?

PATRICIA IRELAND: That was clearly a hurdle that hurt us in the campaign in many ways. At the same time, when she was confirmed by the Senate as ambassador to New Zealand, or, as she said, ambassador to paradise—because after six years in the Senate, it seemed like paradise—[Senator] Jesse Helms ordered reports from virtually every possible level, anyplace she had ever served or worked, and every one of those charges was disproven. Yet, we would still have reporters coming up and saying the equivalent of, when did you quit kicking your dog? Or, I've heard it said that you are into cannibalism, would you like to comment? It was difficult. We finally ended up putting all the documents from her confirmation hearing into a briefing book. When reporters would ask that, I just passed out that fifty pound briefing book and said, can we talk about something current? That is old news.

JUDY WOODRUFF: Did you ever think she could win the nomination?

PATRICIA IRELAND: I got in a lot of trouble with our other staffers, although the ambassador never said anything about it, because I tend to be truthful with the press and I don't like to sound like a fool. Somebody said to me, do you think she has a chance of winning? I said, no. Apparently, you're not supposed to say that because she was saying, I'm in it to win it.

I was, on the other hand, looking at the books. She had always paid off all of her campaign debts, so a lot of vendors were willing to extend us credit. It made me very nervous to run up a huge debt. When the debates were

---

12. Senator Moseley Braun was the target of criticism pertaining to her perceived misuse of campaign funds, allegations of sexual harassment directed against her then-fiancé and campaign manager Kgosie Matthews, and a much maligned post-election trip to Africa with Matthews and her son during which she met with Sani Abacha, the former brutal dictator of Nigeria.

finished in the primary, I pulled her out before the votes were taken, before we ran up too big a debt.

JUDY WOODRUFF: Did you get paid? Did the people who worked for her get paid or was it voluntary?

PATRICIA IRELAND: Yes, ma'am. There were sixteen people in four cities and I would say half of us were paid. I was paid.

• DICK GEPHARDT •

JUDY WOODRUFF: The very next day, in a different corner of the country, Dick Gephardt announced that he was forming an exploratory committee. Steve Murphy, his campaign manager, is here. You already had all these other people in, another member of Congress running, what did you think?

STEVE MURPHY: There wasn't any calculation on our part in terms of winning or not winning. As a matter of fact, most of Dick [Gephardt]'s advisors—I didn't get involved until December 26, 2002—had told him how difficult it would be.

Dick wanted to be president. He believed strongly that he could make a difference, especially on the issue of health care. He was determined to run, thought it was on his shoulders to win in Iowa, and believed that he could

Steve Murphy, Dick Gephardt's campaign manager, talks about Gephardt's labor strategy.

raise the money. Dick made one miscalculation and that was that he did not have a hard money fundraising base. He'd been raising money for the Democratic Congressional Campaign Committee (DCCC) for ten years. It was soft money. He raised a total of hundreds of millions of dollars over four or five cycles. But he had a hard money fundraising base of a million and a half dollars a cycle out of Missouri. He thought, in his mind, that he could translate that soft money base that he had—those contacts, million dollar and multimillion dollar contributors to the DCCC—into a hard money base as a presidential candidate.[13]

JUDY WOODRUFF: He was good friends with much of organized labor. What were the expectations going in about what labor could do for your candidacy?

STEVE MURPHY: We knew that labor could do a lot if we could win an AFL-CIO endorsement. We thought that was a reasonable prospect if we could develop momentum in the race. That was part of our strategy. We had one huge problem with voters, an insurmountable problem at the end. Along with Dick's position as a Democrat who orchestrated the resolution allowing use of force against Iraq, voters thought that Dick had been around forever, had run for president three or four times, was a loser that couldn't beat George W. Bush, was yesterday's news. We went after that problem by trying to get a real early start, by demonstrating his competence as a candidate with a great announcement, by rolling out his health care plan. We wanted to develop some momentum financially as well and to use all of those accomplishments to persuade his friends in labor, who were part of the naysayers, about his ultimate prospects. If we could demonstrate to them that we could win, we thought it was reasonable that we could get the AFL-CIO endorsement. We could count up privately the two-thirds percentage that we needed to get the endorsement.[14]

JUDY WOODRUFF: There were no early signals that labor might not be there for you when the crunch came?

STEVE MURPHY: Oh, absolutely. When we went to international federation presidents and sought to get them to fulfill their commitment to Dick

13. "Soft Money" refers to contributions made by individuals in excess of campaign finance limits and donations from corporations or unions. "Hard Money" is all campaign contributions by individuals and Political Action Committees (PACs) made within the federal limitations on giving.
14. The AFL-CIO only endorses presidential and vice presidential candidates once they have been approved by a two-thirds vote of the organization's general board. The board is comprised of a variety of union affiliates including the principal officer of each affiliated national or international union.

that he thought he had from 2002 or before, there were many that didn't come aboard. Even some of those who did endorse us eventually—the Teamsters and the Steelworkers—took their time doing it.

JUDY WOODRUFF: Early on, any worry that Congressman Gephardt had not bargained hard enough with the President over the war resolution?

STEVE MURPHY: No. From a political standpoint? Yes, obviously when the war went bad. When the Iraqis weren't like the French and didn't greet the Americans as liberators, it was obvious that we were going to have a political problem. Dick told us that he just dealt straight up with the President. Dick had been telling the President, you've got to go to the UN, you've got to build up an international alliance if you're going to do this. Dick thought there were weapons of mass destruction and that Saddam Hussein presented a threat. He certainly was on board in terms of the ultimate threat to the United States. Bush came back to Dick and said, I'm going to go to the United Nations, but I need a resolution in order to do so, I need a resolution from Congress, they're not going to give me what I need if you don't give me what I need. Dick said, if you're going to do that and you're going to try to build up an international alliance, I'm with you.

• THE WAR VOTE •

JUDY WOODRUFF: I just want to get a little reaction here. Joe Trippi, when you and your candidate heard this rationale, what was the reaction?

JOE TRIPPI: We were absolutely flabbergasted that Dean, Kucinich, and Sharpton were the only folks saying this and that they were leaving this vacuum just sitting there. Particularly if you talked to people in Iowa or any of the early states that had great doubts about the war as it was building up. I remember in Linn County at the first event that Kerry and Gephardt and Dean were at—this was after the DNC meeting—Howard went in and did this railing against the war and the doctrine of preemption.[15] I remember the looks on Gephardt's and Kerry's faces. It was like, this guy's not going to go anywhere with that. It was before we really started picking up steam. I think people quickly realized we were going to go somewhere with that, but we never really could figure out the calculation.

The one thing Kerry and Gephardt people would always say about the Dean campaign was that Howard Dean didn't have to vote—he wasn't part

15. Governor Dean, Congressman Gephardt, and Senator Kerry appeared together at the Linn County Democratic Sustaining Club banquet on January 18, 2003.

of the negotiation with the President, we didn't know what was going on, they had very good reasons to do what they did, we just didn't understand because we weren't part of that.

JUDY WOODRUFF: Do you want to react to that?

STEVE MURPHY: Dick recognized the threat from Howard Dean. He came back from that Linn County speech and said two words to me, Howard Dean. As a matter of fact, I went on to tell our [Iowa] state director John Lapp, who was talking about the threat posed by John Kerry, not to worry about John Kerry—he was in the same demographic box, we get the same 22, 23 percent of the vote that Mike Dukakis got in 1988—Howard Dean was the threat.

JUDY WOODRUFF: I want either Bob or Mary Beth to comment. At this stage of the campaign, we're still in the middle of 2003. Mary Beth, you're not on board yet.

MARY BETH CAHILL: Let me just start this. In every conversation about Iraq, it's impossible to overstate the degree to which Kerry's military experience and his concern for the troops in the field was part of his calculation. It was something that he came back to again and again in every conversation about Iraq.

BOB SHRUM: As I said earlier, I think Kerry understood at the time that the political calculus of this was unpredictable, that what was popular today could become unpopular tomorrow. He agreed with the proposition that, in order to get the weapons inspectors back in, you had to give the President the authority to use force. He believed that. He said it at the time. But it was obvious in May, June, July of 2003, and maybe even a little bit before that, that this was really fueling the Dean campaign. I don't think, by the way, that it was simply Iraq. I think Iraq was the metaphor for the anger Democrats felt at George Bush about very many things. Iraq was the simplest, easiest way to express it.

I actually think there were two primary campaigns. There was the 2003 campaign, which Howard Dean won, which was who dislikes Bush the most or who can express, most fervently, opposition to Bush. Then there was the 2004 campaign which was, who do I think might beat Bush and who do I think should be president. We were conscious of what was happening with the war.

JUDY WOODRUFF: Ken Mehlman, how sensitive were you to this building of what Bob describes as anti-Bush feelings in the Democratic Party and maybe bigger?

KEN MEHLMAN: We were aware of it and I think that, frankly, it can be harmful. We saw a little of that ourselves in 1996 with an anti-Clinton feeling—it could blind you and make you view things in a way that otherwise you wouldn't view them. We were very aware of it. I think one of the weaknesses our opponents had was that they were so blinded by anger, and by hatred in some cases, that what it did was gave them a myopic view of the world.

JUDY WOODRUFF: Do you want to be specific about who or what?

KEN MEHLMAN: We were just targeting the kind of fervor with which people embraced conspiracy theories or the Michael Moore theories about things.[16] I remember when Governor Dean talked about the fact that President Bush may have known about 9/11. Throughout 2003, there was a one-upmanship that continued to occur on issue after issue, particularly on the question of the War on Terror in Iraq. Ultimately, the average person sitting at home watching and listening to this kind of angry rhetoric looks around and says, do these guys reflect me? We did a Web video that we used to raise some money. It had Kerry, Dean, and Gephardt all yelling and screaming. Then it panned down to, "Heard enough? Give money to the Republican National Committee." We were certainly very aware of it. We were watching it. Sometimes we enjoyed watching it. It was sometimes very useful for us.

JUDY WOODRUFF: Was any Democratic campaign at that point worried that maybe there could be too much negativity? (No response.) Okay, let's move on. I take that to mean nobody was worried about that.

• BOB GRAHAM •

JUDY WOODRUFF: A few days after Dick Gephardt, Bob Graham, the Senator from Florida, announced. He had been through heart surgery and there had been concern about his health. Tommy Thompson, political director, you already had four members of Congress in the race—John Kerry, John Edwards, Dick Gephardt, and Joe Lieberman. What in the world made Bob Graham think he could win?

TOMMY THOMPSON: The wrong direction that he saw the administration going towards Iraq was the defining moment in his mind. He really did

---

16. Michael Moore is a controversial, liberal filmmaker whose popular films have included *Roger & Me*, *Bowling for Columbine*, and, in the summer of 2004, *Fahrenheit 9/11*, which offered numerous attacks on the Bush Administration.

Bob Graham's political director Tommy Thompson talks about Graham's belief that the Bush Administration was taking the country in the wrong direction.

believe that it was "Osama bin Forgotten." He thought that our full attention should have been on Afghanistan and trapping al qaeda, getting Osama bin Laden and hauling him in to justice. He thought that the Saudis played a larger role in it than the administration was willing to admit. And he thought that going into Iraq was the wrong way to go.

The heart surgery put him back some. There's no question. His physical going into New Year's that determined he had heart problems set us back.

JUDY WOODRUFF: But you already had Howard Dean. Wasn't Howard Dean making the case?

TOMMY THOMPSON: I agree with much of what everybody here said. Bob Graham felt like it was his time. There was a time for the calling, much like Senator Kerry, of his service in the Senate. He had the résumé. He had the chairmanship of the Intelligence Committee. He also was a very popular two-term governor of Florida, a big southern state with a lot of electoral votes. That was something else he brought to the table. He was known for his initiatives on education and on the environment. Along with his record and service in the Senate, he thought that made him better qualified. I would argue that it did.

JUDY WOODRUFF: When you say he thought it was his time, what do you mean?

TOMMY THOMPSON: Well, three terms in the Senate, two terms as governor. Was he going to stand for reelection to the Senate or was there more for him? I think he thought this was the way he wanted to go.

JUDY WOODRUFF: Did you think he could win the nomination?

TOMMY THOMPSON: Absolutely. I wouldn't have gone to work for him if I didn't. He's a wonderful person.

JUDY WOODRUFF: Did everybody around him think that? I assume they all think he's a wonderful person but did they think he could win?

TOMMY THOMPSON: We would have all loved to have had another year to put this together. The post-surgery and recuperation, getting the entire infrastructure put together, staff hired, that sort of thing, was a big undertaking that late and we would have liked to have had more time. No question. But we had a strategy and we were going to try to execute it. We came up a little short in the fundraising, but we felt like we had a very credible candidate to run for the presidency.

JUDY WOODRUFF: Fundraising was tough at that point?

TOMMY THOMPSON: Yes. We had eight other great candidates—eventually nine other great candidates—out there. Everybody's beating the bushes trying to get the same money. Senator Graham never really had to raise money for office before. Whenever he'd had hotly contested elections, he'd been able to put up the money himself and raise a couple of million dollars. We thought we could do better in Florida than we did and we thought we'd do better nationally.

JUDY WOODRUFF: You thought he could win up until what point—the day he got out or was it before that?

TOMMY THOMPSON: Frankly, fundraising started bothering me in June. We didn't get out until October. Too many of our national trips and too many of our pledges were just not funding to the level that I was comfortable with. Our goal was to raise eight to ten million dollars in 2003 and I started wondering, at that time, if we could do that. If we couldn't, could we successfully pull off a full-blown ground campaign in Iowa and a ground campaign in New Hampshire, as well as media in Iowa and New Hampshire?

• WESLEY CLARK •

JUDY WOODRUFF: That's the end of February. You skip all the way ahead seven months to September 17 when none other than Wesley Clark, the retired general, jumps in the race, making an announcement in Little Rock. Josh Gottheimer, strategic advisor and speechwriter, what was going on? Were you with him at that point?

JOSH GOTTHEIMER: I didn't join for another two weeks, until the famous "Mary help" on the airplane on the first trip out, which dogged us the rest of the time.[17]

JUDY WOODRUFF: Why did he think he had a shot? He had no political experience.

JOSH GOTTHEIMER: For some of the reasons that others have mentioned. He was a general. He was different. I think he was sexy to a lot of Democrats, especially because he was more moderate. He had probably been a recovering Republican. Because he had the military experience, he could speak about the issues that some of the other candidates couldn't with as much genuine background. Because of all those things, he was very attractive to a lot of people. The problem was he had never done it before and that dogged him a lot.

JUDY WOODRUFF: How much encouragement did he get from either former President Clinton or Hillary Clinton?

JOSH GOTTHEIMER: I wasn't there for those private conversations. I think President Clinton called everybody and I think a lot of the candidates called President Clinton. I think that was overblown but he did talk to Clinton. Campaign staffers heard that around the country, which was good for Clark because it drew a lot of the more experienced people out of the box to run the Little Rock campaign because they thought it was a Clinton-endorsed presidential candidate. I think that did affect a lot of people.

JUDY WOODRUFF: For a lot of people, it was the anti-Dean candidacy.

JOSH GOTTHEIMER: Clark was against the war. But he was a little more moderate and he was more against the way they went into the war. He also felt, as Mary Beth [Cahill] said before about Senator Kerry, a very deep connection to the troops themselves. He was always torn between denigrating his military that he had served for so many years and standing up against the way the war was fought. That was a big conflict for Clark.

---

17. On General Clark's first day of campaigning, he called out to his press secretary for help when asked a question about his position on the Iraq war.

Josh Gottheimer, advisor and speechwriter to Wesley Clark, explains the campaign's decision not to participate in the Iowa caucuses.

JUDY WOODRUFF: Was there much discussion early on that he should have gotten in sooner?

JOSH GOTTHEIMER: It was really late for a guy who had never done it before, besides the fact he was under six feet tall. (Laughter.)

JUDY WOODRUFF: We get the height issue again.

JOSH GOTTHEIMER: In December, we made a strategic decision not to go to Iowa based on the union endorsements, how much money was being poured into Iowa, and the organization that other candidates had. They were going to spend $5 million each in Iowa and we had to raise a lot of cash.

We went with the strategy that Dean would win Iowa and would probably win New Hampshire. We'd come in a very strong second in New Hampshire and then, on February 3 and so on, we would do very well down South after the others were knocked out. That was our thinking. Obviously, it didn't work.

JUDY WOODRUFF: Did the candidate think he could win this?

JOSH GOTTHEIMER: Yes. We all thought he'd win, based on our strategy, if it played out. We thought we could win, if, based on our strategy, all the cards were dealt a certain way. Once they weren't, we knew we were in trouble.

• RALPH NADER •

JUDY WOODRUFF: It was early 2004 when a man who had run four years earlier, Ralph Nader, made it official. Theresa Amato, why Ralph Nader? You had so many Democrats begging you not to get in. What was he thinking?

THERESA AMATO: Begging, threatening, all kinds of things.

JUDY WOODRUFF: Literally threatening?

THERESA AMATO: Oh yeah.

JUDY WOODRUFF: For example?

THERESA AMATO: Everything from bribes to threats. Ralph has been around for forty years. His philosophy is that the forces of injustice don't take a holiday so why should the forces of justice take a holiday? He really didn't believe that the Democratic party, left to its own devices, would beat the Bush Administration. He wanted to open up a second front and he told a lot

Ralph Nader's campaign manager Theresa Amato talks about why Nader got in the 2004 presidential race despite pleas from Democrats.

of Democrats he was going to open up a second front on the Bush Administration.

JUDY WOODRUFF: At the same time, you had Democrats worried that he was going to have the same effect that many of them believed he had had in 2000.

THERESA AMATO: Absolutely. People that agreed with him most on the issues were blaming him for the demise of western civilization. It was amazing to see his base saying don't run. They were absolutely furious with the Bush Administration and were extremely worried that a Nader campaign would enable another Bush Administration.

JUDY WOODRUFF: Literally, there were bribes? People offered him what not to run?

THERESA AMATO: Bribes. Money.

JUDY WOODRUFF: Can you name any names? It's off-the-record.

THERESA AMATO: No. Those were people who don't know Ralph Nader. Especially after Mr. Kucinich was not getting traction, Al Sharpton wasn't getting traction, and the Dean campaign was over, there was a lot of oxygen for an antiwar message, somebody who was going to stand up and talk about health care for all and living wages and Ralph's main issue of corporate pull on the political system. Every four years, the corporate wing would pull the Democratic party more to the right and nobody would be pulling from the left.

JUDY WOODRUFF: Did you think that he could win the presidency?

THERESA AMATO: No. But third parties define winning another way. When you looked around, the third-party scene was in shambles. The Reform Party had imploded in 2000. The Natural Law Party had dissolved at the national level. The Green Party was, how shall I put it charitably, a house divided in at least three parts—one wing that was becoming the apologist wing for the Democratic Party, another part that went back to movement building and local elections, and another part that wanted to run hard but weren't going to make the decision until June. It was already really late by February.

JUDY WOODRUFF: What about the candidate himself? Did he believe he could win?

THERESA AMATO: Win? Ralph defines winning as keeping the progressive agenda alive.

JUDY WOODRUFF: Win the presidency?

THERESA AMATO: No. The system is stacked against third-party and independent candidates.

JUDY WOODRUFF: So what did he want to accomplish?

THERESA AMATO: Unless it's the nineteenth century, it's very hard for a third-party candidate to ever break through, even in terms of something as simple as getting on the ballot.

JUDY WOODRUFF: How would he have defined winning and does he think he did that?

THERESA AMATO: Keeping the progressive agenda alive. The fear being that generations would grow up without hearing a cogent defense of Social Security or universal health care or having a candidate in the general election who was not going to promise to out-Fallujah Fallujah.

JUDY WOODRUFF: And he thinks he did that?

THERESA AMATO: Absolutely.

• THE BUSH PERSPECTIVE •

JUDY WOODRUFF: Ken Mehlman, the Bush campaign was watching all this. What was your biggest worry going into this campaign? Who were you worried about?

KEN MEHLMAN: The fact is that the country was and is closely divided. We had always assumed from the beginning that this would be a close election decided by about three points or less—no matter who the Democrats nominated.

JUDY WOODRUFF: You're just saying that.

KEN MEHLMAN: No, we absolutely thought that. We would not have started when we did, raised the resources we did, done all the things we did in terms of voter registration and all that blocking and tackling, which is criti-

President Bush's campaign manager Ken Mehlman
discusses his views on the Democratic primary.

cal in a close election. We didn't do it because it was fun. We did it because we assumed this would potentially be a close election. We assumed that whomever the Democrats nominated would be a formidable opponent and that there would be times when we were behind and the election would be close, because that's the nature of where the country was.

We also saw that the race in the 2003 primary to be the most anti-Bush candidate had a negative effect on the Democratic party. I don't think that either John Edwards or John Kerry were helped by voting against the $87 billion for our troops, having voted to send the troops to battle. I think that was partially a result of that 2003 primary.

The entire "follow Dean" effort you saw—in terms of rhetoric, in terms of tone, in terms of issues—was not positive. If you stop and think who recently has gotten elected as Democrats—Jimmy Carter, Bill Clinton—they have not run the traditional, hard left Democrat model. They, from the beginning, said, we're different kinds of Democrats. I think 2003 undermined the ability of candidates to credibly say, without having flip-flops they could turn back to, I'm a different kind of Democrat.

JUDY WOODRUFF: You just heard Ken say the vote not to fund the troops was not helpful to the Democrats. Bob?

BOB SHRUM: Mary Beth [Cahill] said earlier—and I think it's the profound reality of all of this for John Kerry—whether it was politically smart or not, his first concern was the troops. He thought the policy was in very bad shape. He thought someone had to stand up and try to push the policy in a different direction. We spent a lot of time talking with him about that vote. He understood the political problems of the vote and what the long-term political problems were because he did have his eye on the general election. But it was a vote that he thought he needed to make.

JUDY WOODRUFF: You had an inkling of the problem that Ken is describing?

BOB SHRUM: Sure. The President tried to say, for example, in July and August, that Senator Kerry agreed that we should have invaded Iraq and that he supported the war. His position all along had been, and still is, that it was right to vote for the resolution. It was right, as Steve Murphy suggested, to give the President the power to go to the UN to build an international coalition, to do a whole set of things. But, as Senator Kerry very clearly said as the fall campaign began, if you had known there were no weapons of mass destruction, you would not have gone into Iraq.

KEN MEHLMAN: Here's the challenge. Two weeks before Kerry made the vote, he was on *Face the Nation* and said, it would be irresponsible to vote against the $87 billion. That was the challenge. While he did say that in the fall, a month before, at the Grand Canyon, he said, I would still have voted to authorize the war in Iraq even if I had known then that there were no weapons of mass destruction.

So my point is that, regardless of the merits, which we don't need to get into, I think the effect of 2003 was not helpful.

BOB SHRUM: At some level, I agree with that. Although, I think it ultimately helped John Kerry that 2003 was the "go after Bush" year and that in 2004 the voters decided they were going to look at someone that they thought might get elected president and could get elected president.

But let's be clear about what Kerry said on *Face the Nation*. He was saying, we obviously have to support the troops, we also have to change the policy, we have to pay for this, and we have to make the president accountable for what he does. When none of that happened on the $87 billion, he did vote against it.

KEN MEHLMAN: [CBS's] Bob Schieffer explicitly said to him, if you don't get it funded the way you want and paid for the way you want, how would you vote? Kerry said it would be irresponsible to vote that way.

BOB SHRUM: No. He also said we need accountability and accountability is a sine qua non of what we have to do in order to make this policy right.

This is a guy, for better or for worse, who fought in a war, who came back, and who was criticized by some of the 527s,[18] who of course weren't related to you, for criticizing the Vietnam War and for taking it on in a very strong way. He believed that there was a need for accountability and a need to hold the President responsible. Now, was it an easy vote? Did it dog us in the general election? Sure. But that's what he actually believed.

JUDY WOODRUFF: A question on Dean. It was widely reported, in *Newsweek* in particular, that you all were salivating at the idea that Dean might be your opponent. Is this the case?

KEN MEHLMAN: Howard Dean would have been an easier opponent than John Kerry. He certainly would have been an easier opponent by the time 2004 rolled around. If you asked me in September of 2003, when Dean was just beginning to catch fire after the summer, I would have told you Dean would have been a tougher opponent than John Kerry. The reason is that Howard Dean tapped into a genuine populous impulse that was out there. He was an outsider. He had an interesting record and an interesting potential appeal to people. Because John Kerry had a twenty-year record and because he is less familiar in his touch with people than some politicians are, I thought that Dean potentially could have been a tougher candidate.

The problem was what happened in the fall and the winter of 2003 and 2004. Dean somewhat fell in love with his own rhetoric. You also saw his response to capturing Saddam Hussein, saying America's not safer. There was a kind of going off the tracks a little bit. By the time Dean was in Iowa, we were looking at the prospect as a good thing. I think he would have been an easier opponent than Senator Kerry.

JUDY WOODRUFF: Do you remember a turning point then when you changed your mind?

KEN MEHLMAN: There was a whole series of things. Certainly the capture of Saddam Hussein led to several other things that happened. Ultimately, what appeared to happen was the pressure came on and he didn't do particularly well standing up to a lot of the heat and the pressure.

One of the things I'm a big believer in when it comes to campaigns is

---

18. A 527 is a tax-exempt, non-profit political organization formed under section 527 of the Internal Revenue Code. With the passage of the 2002 Bipartisan Campaign Reform Act, limitations were placed on traditional forms of campaign fundraising and spending. As a result, the 2004 election saw a dramatic increase in the use of 527s as a key component of electoral strategy.

planning and the extent to which you plan and think stuff out. You're much more likely to be able to deal with tough situations if you plan than if you wing it, because winging it entirely depends upon a gut instinct that sometimes is right and sometimes is wrong.

JUDY WOODRUFF: So again, at that point, you were taking Dean seriously?

KEN MEHLMAN: There came a point late fall of 2003 and toward 2004 when I think Dean became less formidable.

JUDY WOODRUFF: At that point, you knew it was down to either one?

KEN MEHLMAN: I thought it could have been Dean or Kerry. I also thought it could have been Gephardt. And we thought it could have been Edwards. All four were serious possibilities. It was a genuinely open field.

The fact that Michael Whouley was out in Iowa was very impressive to me.[19] He's extremely effective. I know who he is. Others know who he is. I was the guy that did Iowa in 2000 for the President. Fundamentally, that comes down to a very hard-eyed, very serious, very focused effort to count hard votes. People that have done it before, and people that don't believe in hope as a strategy, are going to be the most effective people, and that's Whouley. You heard all the talk about this organization being better or that organization being better. My experience in 2000 was the best organization is the one that is the least overly optimistic, the most realistic about things and that approaches it in the most methodical way possible, which obviously meant that Kerry was someone we took very seriously.

Look, Senator Kerry had a fabulous period going into the caucus. When Jim Rassman did that event, that was a huge event, and the combination of momentum, plus that they had built this thing so solidly, was very impressive.[20]

JUDY WOODRUFF: I want to close out with one question and maybe this broadens out into something else. John McCain?

KEN MEHLMAN: Yes.

JUDY WOODRUFF: You answered very quickly. Were you worried in 2002 and 2003 that this thorn-in-your-side might be more than that?

---

19. Michael Whouley is a Massachusetts political strategist who served as a senior advisor to the Kerry campaign in 2004.
20. On January 17, 2004, the Kerry campaign staged a widely publicized event with former Green Beret Jim Rassman, who credited Senator Kerry with having saved his life in Vietnam.

KEN MEHLMAN: We did not think John McCain was going to run for president or run on a ticket for president with John Kerry or anyone else. We were very pleased that John McCain was very supportive of the President. The fact is that John McCain in some ways, at key points in this campaign, acted almost as an honest arbiter, from a press perspective, of who was right and who was wrong on certain issues. That was something that he personally gave himself and the press gave him a little bit.

John McCain signed up to be the President's campaign chairman in Arizona back in the middle of 2003. We talked to John McCain about campaigning for us in New Hampshire in the middle of 2003. He went up to New Hampshire for us the day of the New Hampshire primary. Certainly by the middle of 2003, the end of 2003, we knew what he was going to do. We also knew that, because of how he had positioned himself and the media had positioned him, he had a credibility with the press that was very important.

JUDY WOODRUFF: Was there anybody else on the horizon—Republican, anybody?

KEN MEHLMAN: There was a rumor for a while that the Alabama judge, Judge Moore, might run. It was a rumor. It was nothing more than that and I didn't think that was a serious possibility.

In terms of a primary, you had a president that had a higher level of support than Ronald Reagan did in 1984 among Republicans. That was one of the strongest things we went in with. We knew it would be close. You're talking about a Republican base, the biggest base that's ever been in modern times just in terms of self-identified Republicans, and a higher level of support among those Republicans, over 90 percent consistently. So all this talk about restiveness among the base, I always said there was restiveness among some of the conservatives in Washington who had direct mail firms to meet their goals each month! But around the country, you didn't find that.

JUDY WOODRUFF: Very last question. Was there ever a point leading up to January 1, 2004, or the first caucuses in Iowa when you thought the President could lose reelection?

KEN MEHLMAN: This is a very early period. I always thought the President would win reelection. I always thought he would win because the nature of the challenges the country faced meant the public was going to look for someone who they thought was a strong leader who would take on what needed to be taken on.

JUDY WOODRUFF: Even with all the upheaval in 2003, the reaction to the war?

KEN MEHLMAN: There was some upheaval. The worst time, if you look at the numbers, was probably the spring of 2004. But, at the end of the day, there was an incredible floor that we had constantly. If you looked at it, whether it was during Abu Ghraib[21] or other times, there was a floor that we had in our support that was very useful. I always thought it would be tough. I always thought we could lose. I never thought we would lose.

JUDY WOODRUFF: So you never went to bed thinking—

KEN MEHLMAN: We're going to lose? No.

JUDY WOODRUFF: Maybe?

KEN MEHLMAN: Anybody that tells you that they're in a competitive presidential campaign and didn't think at some point they could lose is not telling you the truth, or they're foolish. Of course you worried about it. Again, the reason we ran around the country campaigning was because we thought it could be that close. At the end, I always thought he would win, but I always thought it would be close and tough. And, a three-point race is one that anybody could lose.

JUDY WOODRUFF: Before we close down, is there any question you'd like to ask any of the Democratic candidates about why they didn't do something they should have done or why they did do something they shouldn't have?

KEN MEHLMAN: I was curious about what Steve Murphy said about the fundraising base and the ability that Congressman Gephardt seemed not to be able to have to raise that. From your folks in labor who have the ability to generate some resources, was there discouragement to running? I was surprised by the tepidness of their response to someone who had done so much for them over the years. That surprised me.

STEVE MURPHY: There wasn't any overt discouragement. If one were to be discerning about the signals that were being sent, they were quite discouraging.

JUDY WOODRUFF: Why?

STEVE MURPHY: There was this perception that Dick Gephardt couldn't win and what was defining Democrats in this cycle completely was beating

---

21. In the spring of 2004, it was revealed that there was widespread abuse of prisoners by U.S. soldiers at the Abu Ghraib prison in Iraq.

George Bush. We did our first focus groups in January 2003. The first question the moderator asked was, what do you want to see in a Democratic candidate? The moderator could not finish asking the question before somebody said, "Beat Bush." Dick didn't have the image of a winner.

KEN MEHLMAN: Two other quick questions. First, one for the Kerry campaign. Was there a single thing that convinced you all, because I thought it was incredibly bold that you did it, to abandon New Hampshire for the time and go to Iowa? In other words, was there a tipping point on that? How did that decision get made?

MARY BETH CAHILL: Money really defined this race, as I've said before, in a lot of ways, and we had a very finite amount of money available to us. It was essentially the amount of Kerry's mortgage, the mortgage that he took out on his house, which was $6.4 million. We had to figure out how we were going to use that both in Iowa and New Hampshire.

Now there was, as most people here know, the American Research Group poll daily in New Hampshire which, to some degree, mirrored our own polling showing that Kerry's personal numbers were extremely high in New Hampshire on leadership, on being smart, on caring about people like me. All of that was great. But that was when Wesley Clark was going up like a rocket and he had that field more or less all to himself. We were in much better shape in Iowa, and we did not have the sort of hangover from the Boston media, which was disappointed that we weren't doing better at that point in time than we were.

Looking at what was available to us—quite good horse-race numbers in Iowa—we thought that the Dean organization out there was not what it was cracked up to be. We had pretty good day-to-day evidence of that from what we had going on. It just seemed like, as Bob Shrum said once, if you have one road, take it. We looked at all of this and decided that getting a strong finish in Iowa was the only way that we were going to get where we thought we needed to be in New Hampshire.

KEN MEHLMAN: One other question for Joe. When things happened on the campaign trail, like the comment about America not being safer, did Governor Dean realize he had done things that were not helpful, and did someone make him realize it?

JOE TRIPPI: Yes. Thanks for asking that one.

KEN MEHLMAN: No one was on the plane saying—

JOE TRIPPI: Oh, no, that might happen. But, he didn't necessarily think he had said anything. My favorite one—I can't do it. No, I can't.

JUDY WOODRUFF: It's off-the-record.

JOE TRIPPI: My favorite story is when Dean said that he had a hole in his résumé on foreign policy and defense. The first call I got telling me that he had said that was Jody Wilgoren of the *New York Times*. Her question was, "Joe, your guy just said he has a hole in his résumé on foreign policy and defense, you're his campaign manager, I'm just asking you one question, does your guy have a hole in his résumé?" You got in this position with him all the time. If I say, no, I don't know what he was saying when he said that, we're in trouble. And if I say, yes, he's got a hole in his résumé, I'm in trouble. There was no way to get out.

KEN MEHLMAN: Afterwards, did anyone sit down as a team and say, that wasn't helpful, how do we avoid that?

JOE TRIPPI: Part of what made Dean such an attractive candidate to so many people was how blunt he was and how he did say what he believed, or what came into his head, at that moment. That's what sustained us for most of 2003. Then, all of a sudden in 2004, it was different. In 2003, Dean said, "If Bill Clinton can be the first black president, I want to be the first gay president." He said that in December of 2002 or something. But when he said it, no one was watching or the reporters thought, ahh, he's not going anywhere anyway, he's an asterisk, why jump on him?

He was saying things like that and now, all of a sudden, we're the front-runner for the nomination and he's saying very similar things and the lights are on and now it matters. Everybody thinks, oh my God, what happened to him? Look at what's going on every other day. I just think it was a change of the klieg lights on him. That's just who he is. There's a courage there, but there's also—

I think our populist message—the one we were using when we were soaring—would have been very damaging—a very tough and strong message. The problem would have been you take, "If he can be the first black president, I want to be the first gay president," and you take, "I have a hole in my résumé on foreign policy and defense," seeing what you guys did to Kerry, to a guy who had a great record, served his country, etcetera, just those two clips alone probably would have killed the party in the general.

In the end, I think the right thing happened. Us crashing when we crashed was probably the best thing that could have happened to the Democratic Party.

JUDY WOODRUFF: You think Dean should not have been the nominee?

JOE TRIPPI: I think we would have lost forty-nine states. Not because of things he was going to say. There was absolutely no way that the Bush campaign would not have been able to go through that record, find these quotes, and destroy us with them. There were just too many of them out there. Even if we had intervened, Ken, and from that day forward we changed him, there were too many.

The caucus tapes in Iowa are another example of that.[22] I realized at one point, even if we stop today, the Canadian tapes are coming and there's not a whole lot I can do about it. That meant it was a struggle the whole way. But, again, I think that's what also made him so wonderful to so many people. That attracted them.

JUDY WOODRUFF: I think Ken is just sitting here jealous that he didn't have that kind of undisciplined candidate. (Laughter.) Terrific kickoff from all these campaign managers. Let's give them all a hand. (Applause.)

Editors' Note: Due to a scheduling conflict, John Edwards' campaign manager joined the conference on the second day.

• JOHN EDWARDS •

JUDY WOODRUFF: What we did last night was we had eleven of the twelve campaigns represented, and we went through the decision to get in, pretty much chronologically, and the one hole that was left in our deliberations was what happened early in January of 2003 when John Edwards, who had already been spending time in Iowa and New Hampshire, announced that he was a candidate. What was behind the rationale? He had only been in the Senate for a couple of years. What in the world made him think that he had a shot at the White House?

NICK BALDICK: For those of you who lived in the Manchester or Des Moines media markets or have spent quality time there, I think it would go back to his life story and his message. Based on his background and the message that came from it, John thought that he could make a convincing case to be president and that he had the values and leadership to do so.

---

22. In the weeks leading up to the Iowa caucuses, tapes of Governor Dean's frequent appearances on a Canadian public affairs program were widely circulated. The tapes, which encompassed ninety guest appearances by Governor Dean between 1996 and 2002, included disparaging references he made about the caucus system, including: "If you look at the caucuses system, they are dominated by the special interests in both parties . . . [and] the special interests don't represent the centrist tendencies of the American people. They represent the extremes. And then you get a president who is beholden to either one extreme or the other, and where the average person is in the middle."

John Edwards' campaign manager Nick Baldick explains why Edwards thought
he had a chance of winning the presidency.

JUDY WOODRUFF: But there had been 9/11. The country was very focused on security and on the War on Terror. There had been Afghanistan.[23] Senator Edwards had very little in the way of credentials in that area. How much pause did that give you inside?

NICK BALDICK: Historically speaking, if Senator Edwards, with his six years as a member of the Intelligence Committee, had been elected president, he would have had more foreign policy experience than any president since Nixon except for Bush senior. More importantly, while the voters are looking for a certain level of credibility on foreign policy issues, and it is more important since 9/11, they are not looking for a résumé. They are looking for character and leadership. I don't know how much you guys talked about it last night, but we would argue that we came within a couple thousand votes, or a couple of days in Iowa, of winning the nomination, so I'm not so sure the voters cared about résumé either.

JUDY WOODRUFF: You're going to get into that this morning, but just to close the circle here, how much did you talk about it on the inside, as he was making the decision to run? Was it just a given from the beginning before 9/11?

---

23. In the aftermath of the September 11 terrorist attacks, the United States launched a series of strikes against Afghanistan which led to the fall of the Taliban regime.

NICK BALDICK: My mother always told me not to worry about things you can't fix. He couldn't run out and do more than be on the Intelligence Committee, so it's not really worth worrying about it too much, right?

JUDY WOODRUFF: When the campaign first got under way, who were you most worried about among the others?

NICK BALDICK: Senator Kerry obviously was the frontrunner when we filed. Actually, he had already filed, if I remember correctly, when we filed. I think he was seen by most of the people in this room and by conventional wisdom as the frontrunner. When we started, since we were at one percent name recognition, we weren't really worried about anybody else. (Laughter.)

One of the questions that usually gets asked at these panels is, "Who is your base?" I was prepared to come and say we didn't have a base at one percent. We weren't really worried about other people—we had a plan. I think a lot of the reporters in the room heard our plan. We thought that we needed to spend 2002 doing some serious policy speeches—we did four. We thought we had to have a very good first quarter to show we were credible. We did that—we raised 7.4 million dollars. Then we thought that with John's innate abilities to communicate with voters, if we could get him into Iowa and New Hampshire and spend a lot of time there, we could make up ground and finish either fifth or fourth—we kept on changing it because people kept on dropping out of Iowa. (Laughter.) We thought if we finished credibly, considering where we came from, we would get to New Hampshire and try to finish at the top among the non-New England candidates, and then win South Carolina. At the beginning, we thought it would be Senator Kerry, and then somewhere in the summer, we thought it would be Governor Dean, so there would be a candidate from New England against us. Then in the states that followed—Virginia, Tennessee, Wisconsin—we would take our chances one-on-one. It didn't quite work out that way. I think we are really happy about what happened for us in the primaries, considering we did better than expected in Iowa.

JUDY WOODRUFF: That's a good point to segue.

The Democratic Primaries and Convention

2

> "We did our first focus groups in January 2003. The first question the moderator asked was, what do you want to see in a Democratic candidate? The moderator could not finish asking the question before somebody said, 'Beat Bush.'"
>
> —Gephardt Campaign Manager Steve Murphy

> "I actually think there were two primary campaigns. There was the 2003 campaign, which Howard Dean won, which was who dislikes Bush the most or who can express, most fervently, opposition to Bush. Then, there was the 2004 campaign, which was, who do I think might beat Bush and who do I think should be president."
>
> —Kerry-Edwards Media Consultant Bob Shrum

PHIL SHARP: We are very pleased to have everybody with us again this morning. Let me now introduce folks that are very well-known to everyone— the political director of ABC News, Mark Halperin, who also, by the way, was a student at Harvard and on the Student Advisory Committee of the Institute of Politics and the chief political correspondent for the *New York Times*, Adam Nagourney. For the next two hours, they are going to moderate the session, taking us through the Democratic primaries into and through the Democratic Convention.

MARK HALPERIN: The campaign is over, all right? There is one guy who won and there are other people who lost. The tendency at these things is to say the better candidate always wins or it was a 9/11 election and there was no way the President could lose. This is fun—we all like to come to this. It's interesting but it's also important. This is one of the few chances we have to talk about what happened. This is about campaign managers. The premise, as I understand it, is what happens in campaigns matters and how they run matters. You all were involved in making decisions.

Joe [Trippi] had a candidate who seemed like he was going to be the nominee and wasn't. There has been a lot written about that. Mary Beth [Cahill] and Bob [Shrum] had a candidate who a lot of Democrats think, if he had run a better campaign, would be president-elect right now. We are not trying to create gossip, although some people in the room I think will be happy if we do. We are not trying to create news as much as we are trying to leave a record about the decisions that were made. We ask you to not give speeches, to try not to justify errors that you think you made or others in the campaign made, but rather to talk about the process, including your interactions with the candidate.

It's a strange off-the-record situation—off-the-record for now, but we are trying to leave, for people to study, a record of what happened in this campaign at the level of the decisionmakers within the campaign. Not everybody is here. John Kerry's first campaign manager is not here. Other key people are not here, and obviously the people at this table need to try to represent their own point of view as well as those of the people who are not here.

We've got an ambition here to run through seven sections of this cycle—from the time John Kerry became the frontrunner, in the minds of people who create such things, all the way through the convention. Adam will start with the period in February of 2003 when John Kerry was at least perceived as the frontrunner.

• KERRY: THE PRESUMED FRONTRUNNER •

ADAM NAGOURNEY: When Kerry hired Bob Shrum, people began perceiving him as the frontrunner. Mark Mellman, since you were with the cam-

Early Morning, Day 2—Campaign managers and reporters get together to discuss the Democratic primary strategies.

paign then, what was the thinking behind that? Did people think about the risks involved in presenting him as the frontrunner so early on? Complacency? Arrogance?

MARK MELLMAN: There was a debate about whether to embrace the frontrunner label. On the one side, some folks argued that the real indicia of frontrunnership were not there. Traditionally, frontrunner means you are ahead. John Kerry was ahead in only one state in the country. It happened to be an important state, New Hampshire, but it was only one state in the country. A second indicator is whether you have raised a tremendous amount of money. The potential was there but, at that point, he had not raised more money than anybody else. The third indicator seems to be some kind of clear base or firewall to fall back on. That wasn't there either. So there was not honestly a real traditional indicator of frontrunnership that John Kerry owned. What he did own was a very clear sense that people had that he could be president and that was something that followed him.

ADAM NAGOURNEY: That he would win, right?

MARK MELLMAN: No, that he could be president. That was something that followed him throughout the campaign—really through the general election. But that was the only thing that really could have led to the label of frontrunner. People were worried that if you embrace the label and you don't

ABC's Mark Halperin, the New York Times' *Adam Nagourney, and CNN's Jeff Greenfield listen to answers from the Democratic candidates' staffs.*

have the underlying indicia, at some point, you are going to suffer a huge fall and it's going to look very bad.

ADAM NAGOURNEY: A worry that proved to be correct, right?

MARK MELLMAN: A worry that proved to be correct.

ADAM NAGOURNEY: Was it the *Wall Street Journal* who was pushing that?

MARK MELLMAN: Let me just give you the intellectual part. We can get into personalities if you want but I heard from Halperin you weren't interested in gossip— (Laughter.)

MARK HALPERIN: We have to cater to certain people in the room though.

MARK MELLMAN: I see, okay. Not you, of course, Mark. (Laughter.) The other side of the argument was that there are things that John Kerry can get—money, endorsements, political support—that would not be available to him were he not to claim, or the campaign not to claim, the frontrunner title. So, at the end of the day, the campaign did claim that title. It claimed that title and, frankly, it got a lot out of it that later became important to us. A lot of people came on board as endorsers and a lot of fundraisers came on board raising money because John Kerry was perceived as the frontrunner early on, even though it was hard to say he truly was the frontrunner.

ADAM NAGOURNEY: How did you pull that off do you think? How did you do that? How did you get people to start thinking of him as the frontrunner?

MARK MELLMAN: I think you guys wrote it. I think there are a couple of facts. One, he was ahead in New Hampshire. The second thing, and I think this was pushed very hard with folks and there was a real response to it, was that he was seen as the one person who obviously could be president, had the résumé to be president, had the presence to be president, had the bearing, the intelligence, the ability, the whole package to be president of the United States. I think there was a general consensus that he brought those qualities to bear in the campaign and others were missing at least some aspect of the ultimate package.

ADAM NAGOURNEY: I think here is where we first began seeing what some Democrats would say was complacency or a sign of a coasting campaign

*John Kerry's pollster Mark Mellman weighs the pros and cons
of running as the "frontrunner."*

by Kerry which you saw, I would argue, frequently during the campaign. In other words, vote for me because I'm a Vietnam veteran, vote for me because I can win. Do you think that this idea of presenting him as a frontrunner early on—as the strongest person in the field—helped create that kind of template that came back to maybe haunt you guys a couple of times throughout the campaign?

MARK MELLMAN: You know, honestly, I don't think so. I don't think there is any point at which the campaign was coasting. It certainly didn't feel internally like it was coasting at any point. I think there was a problem that I, and you, picked up on, which is when you say you are the frontrunner, certain things are supposed to happen and, if they don't happen, people start to say you are not the frontrunner. That's exactly what happened. Certain things were supposed to obviously happen which didn't because, the truth is, John Kerry didn't have all of the indicia that one should have to be properly labeled a frontrunner. It was a tactical decision. It was a tactical decision that, at the end of the day, probably paid off in the net, but there is no question it caused some problems along the way.

MARK HALPERIN: We'll maybe close off this period by asking Bob two questions that I think are things that come up in presidential politics all the time and I know a lot of people who worked for President Clinton and President Bush saw. During this period, did you think about how to focus on having a general election message and a general election strategy or did you not have that luxury, in your view? Did you simply have to figure out how to win the nomination? And, to the extent it's the former, what were the hallmarks of that?

BOB SHRUM: Senator Kerry was always focused on the general election. As we have reason to know, if you get the nomination and you don't win, if it were for the honor of the thing, you might just as soon skip it, and so he really was focused on that. For example, in the formation of his tax policy,[1] we knew the Bush people would come at us and say that he wanted to raise taxes on everybody. So we had a very different tax position than Congressman Gephardt or Governor Dean, who were both going to repeal the entire Bush tax cut.[2] So, yes, he was focused on that.

• KERRY'S VIETNAM WAR RECORD •

MARK HALPERIN: The other question which I'm going to return to throughout this period is, what had been done specifically related to the candidate's war record and antiwar record on Vietnam to have all the facts? Obviously, not enough was done. I think that's pretty clear, even by the time it became an issue in the general election. But what was done during this period to say to the candidate, you need to be forthcoming about what you did, what you said, where the records are, who we should talk to?

BOB SHRUM: Actually, I disagree with you on that because the arguments that arose later, especially about his war record, related primarily to stuff that was in the public record or to false charges that were made by people who had served in Vietnam at the same time. You knew that that was going to happen because it had happened in 1996 in Kerry's senate campaign. We had gone through it then and dealt with it. One obviously knew that his testimony from when he came back was going to be brought up in the election.[3]

MARK HALPERIN: I'm choosing an extreme example, but can you say today what the candidate's position was on whether he had ever been in Cambodia?

1. The Kerry tax plan proposed to roll back tax cuts for those families making more than $200,000 while preserving the cuts for those outside the top income brackets and adding new benefits such as a college tuition tax credit.
2. In the summer of 2003, Congress passed an amended version of President Bush's tax plan, which cut taxes by $318 billion over ten years.
3. In 1971, John Kerry testified before the Senate Foreign Relations Committee after his return from service in the Vietnam War and offered a harsh condemnation of the war.

BOB SHRUM: Yes, he was in Cambodia. The date that he had recollected originally was the wrong date.

MARK HALPERIN: Would you say that, even at this period, you had done all the research that needed to be done?

BOB SHRUM: No, we did not. We obviously did not know at that point that he had recollected the wrong date for being in Cambodia.

MARK HALPERIN: I'm talking about the general question of his war record and antiwar record. Would you say that, during that period, again, looking at the practice of how to run a presidential campaign, that everything that could have been done and should have been done to know about his war record and antiwar record had been done and that a system to respond to press inquiries had been set up?

BOB SHRUM: I would say that the campaign was well equipped to deal with attacks on what he said when he came back and did not anticipate the form that the Swift Boat attacks[4] would take. Frankly, it didn't occur to people that there would be questions raised about whether or not, for example, he had earned his medals, which he clearly had and which there was a stack of official Navy documentation to support, which we did have.

MARK MELLMAN: We are getting ahead of the game here, in terms of the time period, but it's very hard to prepare for things that are completely made up. It's easy to prepare for things that are sort of half-truths even but when they are wholly made up, it's very hard to prepare. For example, one of the accusations I remember well was that the initials at the bottom of the after-action report, which were KCR or something, were John Kerry's initials and that he had written this after-action report.[5] Well, it's absurd on its face. Why would somebody looking at that say, gee, we should prepare for the charge that those initials, KCR, are actually JFK? It's absurd. No, you can't prepare for things that are completely made up. So, in the context of the war record, there were so many things that were completely made up that it really was impossible to prepare for them.

---

4. In August 2004, Swift Boat Veterans for Truth, a 527, aired a variety of advertisements claiming Senator Kerry had lied about his war record.

5. An after-action report, filed after a battle in 1969, was among the documented sources of Senator Kerry's valor in combat. Some of his critics asserted that he was responsible for writing the report.

• THE DEAN PHENOMENON •

ADAM NAGOURNEY: Actually, let's hold off on that for later. Dean comes along in June and comes out with a fundraising report[6] that all of a sudden blew you guys away and, later, made Dean the flavor of the month. Mary Beth, at what point did you begin worrying about Dean, and at what point did Kerry begin worrying about Dean? Was it because of the money? How serious of a threat did you see him?

MARY BETH CAHILL: When I came along, everybody was worried about Dean. Dean had been on the cover of all the major news magazines. He was leading the coverage. He was new and interesting. The campaign was different—it was based in Burlington. It was sort of out-of-reach and the pictures that you saw of the people supporting Dean were just different from anybody else in the Democratic primary. He was raising money, he was getting fabulous press attention, and he was getting all kinds of institutional endorsements that everybody else wanted. He was really at a high point then. Kerry was worried about it. We were all worried about it.

ADAM NAGOURNEY: Your predecessor, [Jim] Jordan, and I think Chris Lehane—he was still around then—were pushing, as I recall, to go after Dean.[7] I guess you were resisting, is that correct?

BOB SHRUM: Let me say something about the question you asked a moment ago. We were at a meeting with Senator Kerry in early July.

ADAM NAGOURNEY: This would be right after the fundraising report came out?

BOB SHRUM: Yes, when the fundraising report came out and it was very clear that Dean was real. Senator Kerry had worried all along about the power of the Internet and kept pushing the campaign to get its Internet operation up to speed. When the report came out, we were sitting there and I said, look, he is going to raise enough money and go out of the system and we are going to have to get ready to go out of the system—he is going to raise $10 million in the next quarter.[8]

---

6. Governor Dean raised $7.5 million between April and June of 2003, significantly more than the other candidates for the Democratic nomination. Senator Kerry placed second with approximately $6 million.
7. Chris Lehane served as Senator Kerry's communications director from the early days of the campaign until his resignation on September 15, 2003.
8. The public financing system entitles presidential candidates to public funds to support their campaigns. To qualify, candidates must agree to adhere to a spending cap. In the 2004 primary season, that cap was $45 million.

*Mary Beth Cahill and Bob Shrum listen to Joe Trippi
talk about the Dean campaign.*

Dean's campaign was a phenomenon that had taken off so there was no sense of not worrying about Howard Dean. In fact, I would say that John Kerry probably started worrying about Howard Dean before most of you started seeing what the Dean phenomenon was.

ADAM NAGOURNEY: And he was more worried, as I recall, about Dean than Edwards or Kucinich or Sharpton or any of the other candidates?

BOB SHRUM: At a very early point, as Joe [Trippi] said last night, nobody was worried about Howard Dean. But if you looked at his fundraising, which in the first quarter was ignored, it was not huge but it was substantial, and you could see that it was coming from the grassroots. Then, when you got the numbers for the second quarter, you saw how much money he had raised and you saw the potential, which I thought was huge, for him to go and raise money out of the system. You knew you were going to have to deal with that.

ADAM NAGOURNEY: So why not try to take him down then?

BOB SHRUM: I believed then, and I believe now, whatever other mistakes I made in the campaign, I don't think this was a mistake. I believe it would have been a terrible mistake for John Kerry to run television ads attacking

Howard Dean. I think it would have done him great damage. There was an internal campaign discussion about this which Mary Beth and the candidate resolved by saying, no, we are not doing it.

ADAM NAGOURNEY: [Chris] Lehane was still with the Kerry campaign? He popped around so many candidate's campaigns.[9]

BOB SHRUM: He left in September, but he actually left before that discussion completely came to a head, although he had helped introduce that discussion. It's sort of elementary politics—in a multi-candidate field, if you go out and you attack somebody, and they attack you back, and you're having a fight, and there is an attractive alternative—

ADAM NAGOURNEY: Then Gephardt would move up. We'll definitely get to that.

BOB SHRUM: I think there is a very good chance that if we had done that—I said this in a meeting—I said, do you want to make John Edwards the Democratic nominee for president? At that point, Edwards was at about one or two percent.

I thought what the country needed, what Iowa needed, what New Hampshire needed, was to get to know John Kerry. The question was who can be president and who should be president? I think Mark [Mellman]'s addition to that is very important and, if that became the question, we thought it was possible to position John Kerry as the answer.

MARK HALPERIN: Did you agree with the notion that attacking Dean at that point was a bad idea?

MARK MELLMAN: On TV, absolutely. I think there was some discussion about TV that was not all that serious, in my recollection, and I may have a slightly different recollection of this. But I think there was a question and differences of opinion among the candidates on how much to go after Dean in speeches. There was a discussion about that. The truth is there were some times when Kerry did go after Dean, there were some times he didn't.

BOB SHRUM: For example, in one of the early 2004 Iowa debates, Governor Dean had said something like he didn't want to prejudge the guilt of

9. After resigning from the Kerry campaign, Chris Lehane served on the presidential campaign of General Wesley Clark as his press secretary from October 2003 until Clark's withdrawal from the race in February 2004.

Osama bin Laden and wasn't sure he deserved the death penalty. Each candidate was given thirty seconds to ask the other candidate a question. John Kerry's question was simply to repeat that quote and say, what in the world were you thinking? Because the truth is, there is no good answer to that question. Whatever way you answer it, you'll have a problem.

Voters were much more tolerant of that kind of exchange than they were of the kind of television exchange. Maybe Mark [Mellman] wasn't there that day, but we had a very vigorous meeting about this and about whether we should do this on television. One of the reasons not to do it, by the way, aside from the fact that structurally I thought it was a bad idea and Mary Beth decided it was a bad idea and John Kerry decided it was a bad idea, was that the negative arguments against Howard Dean were testing at 28 percent. It was ridiculous.

ADAM NAGOURNEY: You mean there was no strong argument to use it?

BOB SHRUM: There was none. I agree with Joe [Trippi]. In some ways, Howard Dean made the best arguments that were made against Howard Dean.

ADAM NAGOURNEY: How involved was Kerry, at this point, in saying, let's not go after Dean?

BOB SHRUM: Totally.

MARY BETH CAHILL: It was a conversation that he was very much a part of.

MARK HALPERIN: We want to move to the rise part of Dean-rise and Kerry-fall. Although we are talking about the period where Dean was rising, we want to look under the rock of that to see how much you all were thinking about consolidating the fundraising gains and the free press or media attention you got. How much thought was given to thinking, here is a guy who fancies himself a conservative, a centrist on a lot of issues, but his supporters are largely on the left right now in this process—not exclusively, but largely? Was there any thought given to sitting down, having, if you'll pardon the expression, an "adult" meeting, saying, what is our general election message and let's start doing that now and trying to broaden Howard Dean's appeal? I'm talking June through December.

JOE TRIPPI: We never got to that point. Like Nick [Baldick] was talking about earlier, when we started out, we weren't worried about anybody because we were an asterisk. We had a couple of long-term goals in the campaign from the very beginning. When we were 432 people in January, we decided that we were going to raise $200 million—that whomever the nominee was had to be able to do that to beat Bush. So the audacity of what we were planning when there were seven staff people and 98 grand in the bank, I look back on it now—what were we thinking?

What we were really focused on was building the grassroots campaign that could fund a competitive campaign with Bush. We believed that with Dean's record of balancing twelve straight budgets, lowering the income tax twice, raising the minimum wage to seven bucks, and his health care record as governor, we would be able to present it later on in the campaign, whether it had to be in the primary or the general, but present that. In fact, our bio and stuff in Iowa was all on those kinds of things. But to have that meeting, no, we never thought we were the frontrunner or had to worry about that stuff until, we just never got there, that's the best way to say it.

MARK HALPERIN: Much has been written about your relationship with the candidate and the fact that this was an untraditional campaign in a lot of ways—maybe even more chaotic and personality-driven than a normal campaign—so that underlays a lot of these questions. Dean does an announcement speech where he talks about reform and health care.[10] It was an interesting speech, it was a pretty good speech, but, again, those never were the big themes that he talked about. Obviously, the war interceded to an extent and you couldn't take that completely off the table. But why wasn't there a greater effort to try to make his message broader, including the themes he talked about in his announcement speech in Vermont?

JOE TRIPPI: You know the truest thing that was said about the campaign—I think it was in [*U.S. News and World Report* political editor] Roger Simon's piece—was Kate O'Connor,[11] saying, I kept trying to tell those guys they couldn't manage Howard Dean. He would be the guy in that announcement speech but then he would revert back to the war stuff. We were trying to get him to do the announcement speech stuff as our core message. You saw this, to some extent, with Kerry, where you have two really decent messages and you're not quite sure which one is going to work and the candidate tends to slip into one and slip out of one. At least this is what was going on with Howard. I would love to hear what the Kerry folks would say about it.

---

10. Governor Dean formally announced his candidacy for president in Burlington, Vermont, on June 23, 2003.

11. Kate O'Connor first served with Howard Dean as his personal aide when Dean was the lieutenant governor of Vermont. She remained with him for more than a decade, eventually joining him on the presidential campaign trail as a senior campaign strategist and one of Governor Dean's closest personal confidants.

People forget that Howard Dean had never run for office before—he became governor when the governor died.[12] He actually did all these great things for the people of Vermont, which meant Bozo the Clown ran against him every time. He was told, just don't honk the nose of the guy with the pointy red hair and the clown face in the middle of the campaign and you're going to win. His first contested race for anything was for president of the United States of America. There were freshmen members of Congress who had one more tough campaign under their belts than Howard Dean. So a lot of this was a guy who is very talented, learning and making mistakes along the way—freshmen, rookie mistakes that unfortunately happened in a campaign for president. On the message, that was part of it, because if you look at the announcement speech, it was really well thought out. Your question about did we really have adult conversation and think out the message—that was the one that was thought out.

ADAM NAGOURNEY: Joe, was he involved in that? I remember that speech. It was remarkable because it was so different from everything else he was saying, and then, bam, it was gone.

JOE TRIPPI: Right.

ADAM NAGOURNEY: Was he involved with that or was that you guys telling him what to say?

JOE TRIPPI: He was involved in it, but the only thing I can go back to is his DNC speech. He gave the DNC speech twice—once at the DNC and once at the California State Convention.[13] It would not matter if you broke his arm in four places, he was never giving that speech again and he never did give that speech again.

MARK HALPERIN: If I can disagree, he gave the thematics of that speech again.

JOE TRIPPI: Yeah, I mean that's true, but—

MARK HALPERIN: But you never heard that. It was a very interesting sort of Ross Perot–influenced speech. It suggested moving to a general election. Then, we never heard it again.

---

12. Howard Dean was lieutenant governor and was appointed governor of Vermont following the death of Republican Governor Richard Snelling in August 1991.
13. Governor Dean spoke to the Democratic National Committee's winter meeting on February 21, 2003, and to the California State Democratic Convention on March 15, 2003.

JOE TRIPPI: Yes, the announcement speech was our move to the general election.

MARK HALPERIN: Did anyone ever go to him and say, why don't we give that speech again?

JOE TRIPPI: Yes, over and over.

MARK HALPERIN: And why wouldn't he?

JOE TRIPPI: In fact, the next time you'll see us do it was in Boston in the "Tea is in the Harbor" speech in September of 2003.[14] We had rewritten another version of the announcement speech with him and said, now let's move to this. Here is what happened. There were a lot of people who thought that message was disastrous and that we should not do it and they would work on him continuously not to give it.

MARK HALPERIN: People in the campaign?

JOE TRIPPI: Yes.

MARK HALPERIN: Like who?

JOE TRIPPI: Kate O'Connor. I don't want to get into that stuff. They're not here to defend themselves. My point is that the most telling moment for me was the Boston "Tea is in the Harbor" speech, where I was begging him to give the speech, begging him, I mean on my knees. I think it was a six-page speech. I remember him calling me up, moments before he went on stage, to tell me that he had decided he was going to give maybe a page and a half of it and then he was going to go back to his stump, and then getting the call from the staff that said he did the first three paragraphs. We had already handed this thing out to the press and he had agreed, two days earlier, to do it, and now he went out there, did three paragraphs and went to his stump. It was just impossible to get him to move there.

MARK HALPERIN: I want to ask you one more question about this and then talk to Steve Murphy about Congressman Gephardt. It's a concept that's going to invoke people who aren't here, including Kate O'Connor, who you mentioned, who was oftentimes the senior traveling aide to Governor Dean. It's an issue that came up for Senator Kerry as well. This concept of putting an "adult" on the plane. You spend all this time raising money,

---

14. Howard Dean gave a speech at Copley Square in Boston on September 23, 2003.

planning a schedule, advertising, meeting with constituency groups, and dealing with the Hill. Yet, so much of the free media, which everyone seems to agree drives what happens, is generated by what happens with the candidate on the plane. Was there ever a move to put someone with more presidential campaign experience on the plane? And then, Mary Beth, if you could talk after Joe does. Did your candidates resist having an "adult" on the plane until it was too late?

JOE TRIPPI: Did we? Yes, about every other two weeks and they would be dead within five days.

MARK HALPERIN: You mean someone would go out or someone would be proposed?

JOE TRIPPI: Someone would go out there and suddenly he would be dead. (Laughter.)

MARK HALPERIN: Describe this rigor mortis process. How did they die? (Laughter.)

JOE TRIPPI: It kind of worked like this—if you put a really smart eighteen-to twenty-nine-year-old out there, which wasn't an adult but just to try to give it some discipline, they would immediately become someone's assistant or be canned. If you put anybody like Mark Mellman out there, with a brain, they would come back after three days and say, no way in hell am I going to stay out there because I will be killed. So they were smart enough to figure it out. It was basically the private domain of the person who was currently in that position, and if anybody looked like they were a threat, they were dead. I became a threat at some point, too.

MARK HALPERIN: For people who are thinking about running campaigns in 2008, would you agree that it is an important thing to have someone with presidential campaign experience on the plane, whether the candidate is experienced and has run before or not?

JOE TRIPPI: Yes, definitely. That's the most important job out there. The problem you have is that it's got to be somebody the candidate trusts, obviously, and feels comfortable with. You just can't throw anybody into that position. They are literally the person that is next to the body the whole time. That was a real problem in the campaign because you have a governor who has been with a certain group of people for twelve, fifteen years, who trusts them more than he trusted the mercenary guys, or whatever I was supposed to be. That's a clash that happens in a lot of campaigns.

MARK HALPERIN: Mary Beth, just briefly. Eventually, John Sasso, who fits the description Joe described, went out.[15] There were other people out with him, but no one at that level of stature and experience. Why not?

MARY BETH CAHILL: I think it's easy to overstate the desire of people to spend months and months and months on the road with a presidential candidate. (Laughter.) The people that you want to accompany the candidate, and who the candidate knows and trusts, say, I'll go out every once in a while but I'm not going to go, no. Now we had people, like David Morehouse who was on the plane with Al Gore in 2000 and traveled with Kerry, I think, from late January on. Bob [Shrum] went out off and on. John Martilla went out.[16] We tried to work in a person who Kerry would pay attention to and would want to have with him, and people who would stay, who would be a constant presence, and I think that is a harder thing than most people give credit to.

ADAM NAGOURNEY: I want to go back a little bit. Tad, when the Dean campaign was playing around with their reform message, what did you guys in the Kerry campaign think about it? Do you think it would have been a potent message if Dean had stuck to the original campaign announcement speech?

TAD DEVINE: Yes. I think Howard Dean's candidacy was remarkable and, in many ways, it was a harbinger that we took advantage of, particularly in the pioneering use of the Internet. We raised, I think, $80 million on the Internet in the primary campaign and another $40 million in the general election. That's $120 million, principally in small dollar donations. That can be the beginning of the reform of American politics. I credit Governor Dean's campaign for showing the way and I credit Senator Kerry for talking about it before, really, the time Governor Dean was doing it.

Dean's reform message was very powerful, but I think, in everything that I saw when I started getting more involved a bit later in the campaign as we came into Iowa and New Hampshire, that the voters were very serious about nominating someone in the process who had the capacity to be the president of the United States in the aftermath of the events of September 11, 2001. That was the reality of the nominating process.

---

15. John Sasso managed Governor Michael Dukakis's presidential campaign in 1988 and served as the Democratic National Committee's general election manager in 2004 before becoming the senior campaign staffer aboard Senator Kerry's plane and one of the campaign's leading strategists.
16. John Martilla is a Boston political strategist who served as an advisor to the Kerry campaign.

ADAM NAGOURNEY: Did you guys adjust what you were saying in response to what Dean was saying at this point?

TAD DEVINE: Tactically, we dealt with the reality of Governor Dean. But we made strategic decisions, particularly with regard to Iowa and New Hampshire. We devoted resources to Iowa and recognized the impact that it would have on New Hampshire. I've always believed, in a process like this where you have a competitive Iowa—not like 1992, but a real competitive Iowa—that Iowa and New Hampshire have a symbiotic relationship and that what happens in Iowa will very much affect the outcome of New Hampshire.

John Kerry, in many ways, demonstrated his strength in standing as a national candidate in Iowa and was able to, therefore, succeed in New Hampshire. In many ways, like Mike Dukakis did in 1988, Kerry reassured voters in New Hampshire of his national standing by getting winnowed into the top tier of candidates in Iowa.

So it wasn't so much a reaction to Dean as an understanding of the dynamic that favored John Kerry and John Kerry's ability to enter that dynamic in such a forceful and positive way.

MARY BETH CAHILL: Sounds good.

ADAM NAGOURNEY: We'll get to that. (Laughter.)

• GEPHARDT AND LABOR •

MARK HALPERIN: Steve Murphy, last night you said a big problem was that Congressman Gephardt didn't have a hard dollar fundraising base. You did, as you pointed out, have a successful announcement.[17] You got a lot of attention for your health care plan, even though I don't think it ever got taken to the next level after the first wave of publicity.[18] What do you think were the missed opportunities, if any? Were there things you could have done in 2003 from June through the end of the year that you think would have, had you taken a different course, given the congressman a better position for Iowa?

STEVE MURPHY: I think it was a high-wire act throughout the entire campaign. The big decision that we had to make in that period was whether to take on Howard Dean—the same decision the Kerry campaign and others

---

17. Congressman Dick Gephardt officially announced his candidacy for president in St. Louis, Missouri, on February 19, 2003.
18. Congressman Gephardt proposed a health care plan that asked employers to provide health insurance for their workers and offered tax credits to cover much of the cost.

had to make. Our situation was a little bit different in that, in order to stay in the game financially, or to get in the game because we were doing this with slightly less than $4 million in the second quarter and the third quarter, in order to have a shot at the AFL-CIO endorsement, an early endorsement which we desperately needed, we needed not only to eventually win, and obviously Gephardt wasn't going anywhere if he couldn't win in Iowa, but we needed to be perceived as the winners in Iowa through that late summer, early fall, later fall period.

Howard Dean had taken the lead in Iowa, so we did the research in May, June, and July, and we had an internal debate in August about whether to begin to take on Howard Dean. Dick was resistant to doing it.

MARK HALPERIN: Because?

STEVE MURPHY: Because, number one, he'd been around long enough to understand the dynamic that Bob [Shrum] was talking about—that if you get into a fight, the voters are going to start moving to another alternative. Number two, he knew and liked Howard Dean. Howard Dean was a supporter of his in 1988 and he was one of the first people to recognize that Howard Dean had some real potential in this race. He was kind of bemused by his candidacy at first but, at the same time, recognized its potential. And thirdly, it's just not his nature. He's an optimistic, positive guy. He doesn't like to go around attacking Democrats.

ADAM NAGOURNEY: Literally, you had three weeks or a month there, what changed that?

STEVE MURPHY: The reality of what was going on in Iowa.

ADAM NAGOURNEY: In other words, he realized he had no chance of winning the presidency and started going after Dean? Was there a conversation like that?

STEVE MURPHY: He realized that he had no chance to win the presidency if we couldn't raise more money in the third quarter—if we couldn't get labor off the dime and get an AFL-CIO endorsement. We realized that. Finally though, we did the research and we had an internal debate. Bill Carrick, Hank Morris, Ed Riley, and Joyce Aboussie were against doing it.[19]

---

19. Bill Carrick managed Congressman Gephardt's 1988 presidential campaign and served as a senior media consultant to Gephardt during the Democratic primaries. Hank Morris, a partner in Carrick's consulting firm, and Ed Riley, a Democratic pollster, also advised the campaign. Joyce Aboussie was the campaign's vice-chair.

Those of us within the campaign—myself, Steve Elmendorf, David Plouffe, Karen Hancox, and Erik Smith—those of us who were in contact with voters every day—wanted to.[20] If not panicked, we felt like we were slipping. What tipped the balance was when we showed the research to Dick [Gephardt] on Medicare. Dick was offended when he saw what Howard Dean had said about the Republican efforts to cut Medicare.[21]

MARK HALPERIN: How painful were the conversations with labor, as it became increasingly clear that you weren't going to be able to get a two-thirds vote for their endorsement?

STEVE MURPHY: The conversations with labor were conflicted all the way throughout. They were always painful because Dick [Gephardt] had an expectation. We had a hope that we would have strong labor support out of the box. It was always a struggle to get even what we had. It's not fair to say that organized labor should simply line up with Dick Gephardt, but it was fair for him to believe, to expect, that the AFL-CIO would support him if we ran a strong race. It was always a conversation with folks that said they were leaning towards Dick, but the unspoken was that you've got to show us that you're going to win—you've got to show us that you can win.

ADAM NAGOURNEY: My sense was that Congressman Gephardt almost felt that after all he had done for labor in Congress over the years, to some extent, they owed him?

STEVE MURPHY: No.

ADAM NAGOURNEY: I don't mean that in a bad way.

STEVE MURPHY: No. I don't think Dick felt that they owed him. Dick felt like they should recognize that he was their guy, that he was their voice, that he was the one candidate that was speaking to the issues of their concern.

---

20. Steve Elmendorf was Congressman Gephardt's chief-of-staff when he was House Minority Leader, a role in which he continued during the campaign. David Plouffe, a partner at Axelrod & Associates, was one of the campaign's senior political advisors. Karen Hancox, a veteran of the Clinton administration, served as deputy campaign manager beginning in April 2003. Erik Smith, formerly the communications director in the House Minority Leader's office, was the campaign's communications director.

21. Congressman Gephardt attacked Governor Dean for supporting Republican efforts to cut Medicare in 1995. He quoted Governor Dean as having referred to Medicare as "one of the worst things that ever happened."

ADAM NAGOURNEY: But they realized, and he must realize that they realized, that he was a problematic candidate—he was going to have trouble winning, right?

STEVE MURPHY: Yes, but Dick was always optimistic, up until the October [AFL-CIO endorsement] meeting, that we were going to get an AFL-CIO endorsement. He was having a variety of conversations—some of them with people who were public, overt supporters and some of whom were privately saying we're with you, Dick. Right up until October, whenever it was, 12th, 13th, he was expecting to get the endorsement.

• THE EARLY GAME: IOWA AND NEW HAMPSHIRE •

ADAM NAGOURNEY: Nick, the same question to you. Were there different paths to take in 2003 that would have better positioned you to enter January? Obviously, you entered stronger than a lot of people thought, but do you see missed opportunities for you all in the year before?

NICK BALDICK: Not many, but I would say there were two things I think we made mistakes on—and we don't like admitting mistakes. The first is a minor one. Probably most people didn't recognize it, but we wasted some money buying Oklahoma television at one point. It was an effort to try to knock numbers up in the polls and to try to raise money in the third quarter.

Steve Murphy, Charles Halloran, and Tad Devine (left to right)
discuss the early Democratic primaries.

Some of the same concerns Steve [Murphy] had. It was wasted money that we could have used in December.

Our major problem was we were broke. In December, we had no money. We had 100 points on New Hampshire television and 400 points in Iowa.[22] Joe [Trippi]'s candidate's numbers were slipping on about December 4th in our IDs and John [Kerry]'s numbers were going up, but we had no money to go on television to take advantage of it. Zero. We didn't pay our staff in December. Not a single member of Edwards for President got paid in the entire month of December because we were waiting for a match check on January 2.[23] So that Oklahoma money could have been useful.

The second thing we could have done better with was the Internet. I don't think anyone could have done the great job that the Dean campaign did. I think his position on the war helped. But Elizabeth Edwards, who is a true blogger for anyone who ever goes out on those blogs, is a true Internet person who understands the Internet probably better than anybody on our campaign, except for our Internet director, and that was a close call at times. She really wanted us to do more on the Internet. I'm not sure how much of a financial difference it would have made. We would never have had a Dean-like presence. We raised millions, but I think we could have raised more.

The other factor for us was when Dean went out of the public financing system. We all knew Dean was going to go out of the system. We didn't think Kerry would go out of the system because when Dean was slipping, we didn't think Kerry would have the money to take advantage of it. The loan killed us.[24]

ADAM NAGOURNEY: I thought you guys anticipated Teresa.

NICK BALDICK: Well, that's not the Teresa factor. From what I understand, Senator Kerry took out a mortgage on his house.

ADAM NAGOURNEY: I apologize for that. Right.

NICK BALDICK: That was actually a lot riskier move than I think people give him credit for. Let's be honest here. If Dean had kept going up or if we had won Iowa, Kerry doesn't get the matching check and he owes somebody

---

22. Gross Rating Points refers to the aggregate number of ratings points accumulated in a given advertising schedule.

23. Federal matching funds are a component of public financing of presidential elections which allows the government to partially subsidize a presidential campaign if the candidate agrees to adhere to a spending cap during the primary season.

24. In December 2003, Senator Kerry loaned his primary campaign $6.4 million, which he financed by mortgaging his family home on Beacon Hill.

six point something million dollars. That's not a simple little decision. At least, I'm not going to make that decision for somebody. We didn't have that opportunity and we didn't have the cash in December.

ADAM NAGOURNEY: Coming into January, did you guys in the Lieberman campaign really think that in such a partisan charged environment with so much anger from 2000, Lieberman could really win primaries by positioning himself as the most moderate candidate in the field? What was the thinking there?

BRIAN HARDWICK: We always thought there was an opportunity for us in New Hampshire because of what McCain had been able to do with Independents in New Hampshire in 2000. We felt like we could make a strong play for those. We knew that, with two neighboring candidates in Dean and Kerry, a strong third place was really what you needed to get out of New Hampshire, and that was all predicated on Gephardt or Dean, frankly, winning in Iowa. The Iowa result changed a lot of that so by January, we were shifting.

Joe Lieberman moved to New Hampshire—physically moved there—he and Hadassa rented an apartment. We thought that we had a unique opportunity to connect with the voters of New Hampshire with Joe's best one-on-one campaigning skills. We put all our eggs in that basket but we also reserved money[25] for February 3. We thought that if we could get a strong third place out of New Hampshire, which was still not a far off possibility given the polls and the connection that we were getting in New Hampshire, that on February 3, we would go to a series of states that would favor a more moderate candidate and a centrist.

MARK HALPERIN: Senator Lieberman was one of the most aggressive in going after Governor Dean.

BRIAN HARDWICK: Right.

MARK HALPERIN: How did you all make the calculation to do that? How much did you spend on opposition research, as opposed to just using what was in the papers?

BRIAN HARDWICK: A lot of it was driven by the news of the day. A lot of it was the statements that Governor Dean would make from time to time.

---

25. The Arizona Presidential Preference Primary, Delaware Democratic Presidential Primary, Missouri Presidential Primary, New Mexico Democratic Caucus, North Dakota Caucuses, Oklahoma Presidential Primary, and the South Carolina Democratic Presidential Preference Primary all took place on February 3, 2004.

We also felt that as Dean started to rise in August in a big way, people would be looking for an alternative to Dean—maybe even somebody who was perceived to be so different than Dean that they would take a look at Lieberman, given where he was on the issues. Wes Clark getting in the race took up some of that real estate for us.[26] We felt like we were starting to position ourselves in that place and distinguish ourselves.

The conversation we got in with Dean and the decision in the debates to go after Dean was really more about reminding people and defining where Senator Lieberman was in this big field, where it was hard to distinguish yourself.

MARK HALPERIN: Joe, eventually, in this period, everybody was attacking your candidate after their initial reluctance. Should history record that Dean's loss was due to any of the particular attacks by any of the particular candidates or was it the cumulative effect and your candidate's mistakes?

JOE TRIPPI: It's obviously both those things.

MARK HALPERIN: Do you recall either particular days or particular lines of attack seeming particularly effective?

JOE TRIPPI: During the Rock the Vote debate, you had Sharpton and Edwards giving a devastating attack. I can't remember all of the different sundry players who hit us on the Confederate flag thing, but it's a typical moment.[27] There was probably a much better way of saying it than using the Confederate flag so that's us providing fodder. And everybody obviously had a big motive to take us down. That's what this is about. Too many times I think we provided the bullets—many times we didn't.

The Club for Growth was running an ad in Iowa, for hundreds of thousands of dollars, calling us a bunch of sushi eating freaks or something.[28]

---

26. General Wesley Clark entered the presidential race on September 17, 2003.

27. At the February 2003 meeting of the Democratic National Committee and again in a November interview with the *Des Moines Register*, Governor Dean invoked the Confederate flag to make a point about Democratic outreach. He asserted, "White folks in the South who drive pickup trucks with Confederate flag decals on the back ought to be voting with us, and not [Republicans], because their kids don't have health insurance either, and their kids need better schools, too."

28. In the weeks before the Iowa Caucuses, the Club for Growth, a conservative 527 organization, aired an ad that depicted a man and a woman exiting a barber-shop. The two were questioned about Governor Dean's alleged plan to raise taxes. The man began: "What do I think? Well, I think Howard Dean should take his tax-hiking, government-expanding, latte-drinking, sushi-eating, Volvo-driving, *New York Times*-reading," and the woman concluded, "body-piercing, Hollywood-loving, left-wing freak show back to Vermont where it belongs."

There was another 527 that David Jones put together to run attacks that said we were pro-gun.[29] I don't remember all of them because there were so many coming during this period. I think this was the first time this had happened to an antiestablishment candidate that had emerged.

ADAM NAGOURNEY: Had you vetted Dean? In other words, were you aware of some of this stuff? For example, were you aware of the cable TV shows in Vermont?

JOE TRIPPI: Yes. But there is no way to explain the Dean campaign to anybody. It was not a normal campaign. (Laughter.)

ADAM NAGOURNEY: We realize that. (Laughter.)

JOE TRIPPI: We did opposition research.

ADAM NAGOURNEY: On yourselves?

JOE TRIPPI: Right. And then the governor believed that, if no one saw it— For example, the Canadian tape thing. We had all the Canadian tapes. Kate [O'Connor] screened them and then put them back on the shelf.

ADAM NAGOURNEY: Did Kate see the Iowa thing?

JOE TRIPPI: We'll never know because that tape never ended up back on the shelf.

ADAM NAGOURNEY: Back up, back up. Why is that? Did she keep it and take it home?

JOE TRIPPI: I'm not getting into that. It was just not there anymore, okay? (Laughter.)

ADAM NAGOURNEY: I'm sorry. It was there originally and then it was gone?

JOE TRIPPI: Yes. There are about 116 boxes of stuff that we never got to look at. When the final [research] report came back, it got locked in a safe

---

29. In December 2003, David Jones, a former aide to Congressman Gephardt, and Robert Gibbs, a former spokesperson for Senator Kerry's campaign, through "Americans for Jobs, Healthcare and Progressive Values," a 527, ran advertisements aimed at derailing Governor Dean's campaign in Iowa, New Hampshire, and South Carolina.

and I was not allowed to look at it. So when [reporters] got the caucus tape, you all ask, how the hell did you guys not know that the caucus tape was out there? I had no clue the caucus tape was out there.

MARK HALPERIN: Who had access to the safe?

JOE TRIPPI: Not me and not the opposition research team. I mean this was the way this thing ran.

MARK HALPERIN: Who would you refer us to on that? (Laughter.)

JOE TRIPPI: What was going on during this period was that we had decided, for a lot of different reasons, that we were going to do it differently. We were going to do this Internet thing and we were delighted that the other campaigns were saying things like, it's like scenes out of *Star Wars,* and just ignoring it. On the Net, we were in a totally different world. On the Net, we were the first mover, and every day that no one tried to do anything to get in it meant it was another day we were getting closer to having that $200 million that we thought we could get to.

We were executing a bunch of stuff that was totally different, but we were also executing the old politics really well. For example, look at who had more to do with stopping labor's endorsement of Gephardt and blocking some of the bigger unions, or getting anybody to think that AFSCME and SEIU would endorse the same guy, and how we wired that kind of stuff. It was actually pretty amazing that a supposedly decentralized Internet campaign could actually pull off stuff like that, too.

On the bigger questions of discipline on message, I think Howard Dean had to go through this to learn that lesson. I don't mean that in a bad way. I go back to the fact that we had a guy who hadn't really run before and had to learn these lessons on the campaign trail.

MARK HALPERIN: Tommy Thompson, you said last night that Senator Graham didn't raise as much in Florida as you thought he would be able to and that money, for so many campaigns, was the big issue. One of the things that the Bush campaign, I believe, looked at and thought about Senator Graham was that for a guy who had a lot of experience and was seen as kind of a member of the establishment and a centrist, he made a lot of wild accusations and used pretty inflammatory rhetoric about the President. Was that part of a strategy? Was that in the candidate's heart?

TOMMY THOMPSON: That goes back to his initial sort of gut reaction to why he wanted to run. He was incensed at the direction he thought the country was going in Iraq and he had something he wanted to say about it. I think there was just a genuine fear in him and he wanted to speak out.

MARK HALPERIN: Did people in the campaign say, that's fine if that's in your heart, but let's broaden out and talk about Social Security, health care, other issues?

TOMMY THOMPSON: One thing about Senator Graham—he has such a depth of knowledge and institutional knowledge that you really didn't script him much. He had a lot to say. We would talk to him about how to phrase it more than tell him to specifically say this or say that.

MARK HALPERIN: I want to go to the period now where Mary Beth Cahill and Stephanie Cutter and others came into the campaign. You talked last night about how you transitioned, but I want to ask you some specific things about what you found when you came in. Were you surprised at all at, or interested in changing, the role that Mrs. Heinz Kerry was playing in the campaign?

MARY BETH CAHILL: When I first came, she was largely in Iowa and New Hampshire. She really was not in Washington or our discussions very much. She was very helpful, and she was on the road a lot.

Patricia Ireland makes a point while Tommy Thompson listens.

MARK HALPERIN: So that wasn't a piece that you changed at all?

MARY BETH CAHILL: It wasn't.

MARK HALPERIN: I'll ask you the question that Bob [Shrum] talked about earlier. Did you say, as you came in, what do we know about the candidate's background about things that are likely to come up, particularly his Vietnam and antiwar record?

MARY BETH CAHILL: I did. I asked Mike Gherke, our research director, for the book on Kerry. It was one of the first things that I asked for and it was pretty thoroughly done. Some of the allegations—I really agree with what Bob said—that were made against Kerry, we couldn't be prepared for. There is no way to rebut something that absolutely isn't true. But we had his record pretty clearly.

ADAM NAGOURNEY: I never got a sense that we really came up with an answer to the testimony, which seemed very devastating. How does Kerry explain what he said when he came back from Vietnam and testified?

MARY BETH CAHILL: He talked a lot about that period in his life and that was always in our advertising. It was in our first bio ad because it's a very big part of who he is and who Democrats know him to be. It's something that he was extremely proud of. It was part of his approach to the situation in Iraq. He really felt strongly that having served, and having felt the effect of a mistaken policy in Vietnam, that it was just as much a badge of honor to come back and protest the war in as public a way as possible and to try to stop it so that the same thing that happened to him and his crewmates didn't happen to other people. It's something that he referred to pretty often. As I said, it was in our advertising. There was the question of how much are you going to talk about this in the past and how much are you going to address the real desire of the voters to talk about the future. So he talked about his period of protest and he talked about what that had meant to him, but we also talked to him about health care and the economy.

MARK HALPERIN: Stephanie Cutter, what was your first day at work on the campaign? What month was it?

STEPHANIE CUTTER: It was November. It was just a couple days after Mary Beth came on.

MARK HALPERIN: You came into a campaign which had been, as we've discussed, reluctant to systematically make the message of the day an anti–

Howard Dean message and yet you created an operation that put out a big, hefty book about Howard Dean's record and had the candidate talking regularly about him. What was the logic behind doing that? How did you convince those who had been reluctant to make an anti-Dean argument the daily message to change? Did the candidate himself participate in that?

STEPHANIE CUTTER: I actually didn't find any reluctance. It was just a matter of work. We came in and found that there was an appetite in the campaign to start pointing out things on Howard Dean that were contradictory to what Howard Dean was saying—a lot of things about the war that people didn't know about and his record as governor. In terms of opposition research, we were very well prepared on Howard Dean. We had ample research on his record—what he did as governor, things that he had said on the campaign when nobody was noticing. Every day, we started putting out a "Dean Daily Report."

ADAM NAGOURNEY: There was no resistance to that? There obviously was a switch, at some point, between the change in regime of let's ignore Dean to let's start going after him in a systematic way.

STEPHANIE CUTTER: If there was resistance, I didn't feel it.

BOB SHRUM: There are two different arguments here. One argument is whether or not the heart of our television campaign, or a big piece of our television campaign, should have been to go after Dean. In my view, that would have been a bad decision and would have been devastating to the campaign. The second question was when, and on what terms, did you engage Dean? There was no resistance to doing it in the debates. There was no resistance to doing it in a serious way. Senator Kerry gave a speech in New Hampshire, toward the end of December—the "Two Roads" speech—that said the party basically faces a choice of going down one of two roads.[30] That was not badly received by voters at all.

Stephanie did a terrific job of putting this all together so that we had a plan, week by week, that moved this ahead. The one thing I was absolutely convinced of was that just going out there with a hatchet in your hand which, frankly, we had done a couple of times, sort of spontaneously in the summer or in the first debate in South Carolina in May,[31] was actually hurtful. You had to do this the right way.

---

30. Senator Kerry delivered his "Two Roads" speech in Manchester on December 27, 2003.

31. The nine Democratic candidates appeared in a televised debate in Columbia, South Carolina, on May 5, 2003.

JOE TRIPPI: That's what I was going to say. I actually think the South Carolina debate, and the week going up to that, poured gasoline on us. I don't know that we wouldn't have gotten where we were going to go any-way—just a little slower. This was a stage where people really still didn't know who the hell Dean was and we were percolating on the Net. But, all of a sudden, the Kerry campaign—Chris Lehane—for some, to me, inexplicable reason, for about a week, seemed to get Dean fever or something and started attacking us every day and I would answer back. There was one day where we had five press release exchanges.

The press corps started calling the debate in Columbia the "collision in Columbia." All the reports were there was going to be a big Dean-Kerry col-lision in Columbia and, suddenly, we were getting huge pay dirt. People were signing up like crazy. We got a lot more notice than we would have gotten. We probably would have been dead in the weeds for another month or so, but it helped create us. What we found out was when one candidate came after us, it helped us.

So there was a problem. If you're the Gephardt campaign and you come after us on your own, it kind of fueled us. But if Kerry came after us too—it was when everybody got to the point at the same time where, hell, we've always wanted to do this, let's go do it—then you had a collective thing where it was all being reinforced and counter-reinforced and it started to cause a lot of damage.

STEPHANIE CUTTER: Can I just add to that? Part of the Dean strategy was not just about the candidate attacking Dean. It was also changing the way the media looked at Dean. When we came in, we felt like the media hadn't really started to pick apart who Dean was—what his record was. So, in addition to using the candidate in a selective and strategic way, we had to work under the radar screen to make sure that all the information on Dean was getting out there. If Dean did a health care event, we would make sure that everybody covering that health care event knew exactly what Dean had done as governor. That hadn't been done before.

MARK MELLMAN: Just to follow up on what Joe and Stephanie said because I think it's absolutely right. Someone said last night that the core of Dean's message was anti-Bush. I think it was much more than that. And I think the reason it helped Dean when Democrats attacked him was because Democrats were angry at what they perceived—a wrong perception in my view—to be a capitulationist, accommodationist Democratic Party and Dem-ocratic leadership. We saw this very clearly in the stuff we did for various Democratic Party entities. Donors—small donors—had an overwhelming sense that the party had been too accommodationist, too capitulationist.

What Governor Dean was really doing, I think, was directly—and, in many cases, frankly inaccurately—arguing against the Democratic Party.

I heard Dean's speech at the California State Convention where he started off saying, I'm tired of Democrats who vote 80 percent of the time with George Bush. I was trying to figure out who those Democrats were, frankly, because I don't think even Senator Zell Miller voted with President Bush 80 percent of the time.[32] The point is that it was an attack on the Democratic Party and the Democratic leadership, and it was very well received by Democrats.

When individual Democratic candidates went after Dean, it reinforced, to some people, the sense that, yes, this was an accommodationist party. Dean is the guy that's really standing up to Bush and against the party leadership who is being too capitulationist, and here they are arguing that he should be quiet and stay still. That did help him. It reinforced his appeal.

BOB SHRUM: There is one thing I think that's really critical in all of this, in terms of what worked against Dean, and I don't know what Joe [Trippi] thinks about this. For John Kerry, the attack on Dean or the critique of Dean, which was never, as I said, done in television ads, had to dovetail with a positive argument that was being made for John Kerry. The umbrella had to be, is this guy ready to be president? The heart of the critique was not a random selection of things that Howard Dean had done over time or said yesterday. It was how they all fit into a pattern that should allow voters, or should induce voters, to raise in their minds the question of, should this guy be our nominee? Should this guy be president?

ADAM NAGOURNEY: Josh, can I ask you a quick question? In retrospect, should General Clark have been part of this whole process in Iowa at this point?

JOSH GOTTHEIMER: In retrospect, sure, because we probably would have had more of a shot. But, at the time, based on what we saw of our strategy, we had no other choice except to focus on New Hampshire. We were never going to make a good run in Iowa, so we thought, based on the strategy, that we should really shore up New Hampshire.

ADAM NAGOURNEY: Was Clark involved? I was told that Clark was not involved in that decision, is that correct?

---

32. Democratic Senator Zell Miller of Georgia endorsed President Bush in the 2004 election.

JOSH GOTTHEIMER: Totally untrue.

ADAM NAGOURNEY: So he was?

JOSH GOTTHEIMER: We had a meeting in December and he was involved. We presented all the choices—here are the dollars you have, here are the unions you have, here is what's going on in Iowa, here is the presence that the other candidates have and we don't have any presence. We really thought you needed people on the ground and had to get in earlier. We thought that if Dean did well in Iowa, we would be okay.

We were also attacking Dean underground earlier on and above ground in January. So we were hurting ourselves, if you think about it, now that I look back at this conversation, because we were hurting Dean. We were trying to slow Dean down, but at the same time that was hurting our own chances in Iowa.

ADAM NAGOURNEY: Would you or Brian advise, assuming the calendar doesn't change, which I think is a big assumption, Democratic candidates in 2008 to skip Iowa?[33]

BRIAN HARDWICK: If you ask it in a generic sense like that, it's difficult to answer not knowing which candidates are in the field. When I joined the campaign in August, this debate was very much part of a strategic decision by the Lieberman campaign. This debate went on and on and on and, frankly, probably should have been decided earlier, given the resources and the candidate's time that we spent in Iowa. If we were going to do it, we should have done it much earlier. So, if a candidate decides that it's to their strategic advantage not to play in Iowa because of the mix of candidates, because they think they can somehow run the kind of campaign that John McCain did in New Hampshire, and if the opportunity with Independents in New Hampshire is a real opportunity, then it would be better advised to make that determination earlier so you don't spend the candidate's time or resources in Iowa.

JOSH GOTTHEIMER: I would just like to say that I think no candidate should ever skip Iowa again. (Laughter.)

MARK HALPERIN: The period from December to January, where Governor Dean really made a lot of mistakes—some of which have been mentioned—and then what happened on the ground in Iowa has been incredibly

---

33. In recent years, an effort has been mounted to revise the order of the early caucuses and primaries so that a greater number of states can play a significant role in the nominating process.

well covered. If you haven't read Roger Simon's piece [in *U.S. News and World Report*] on that, I recommend it to you. It's pretty comprehensive and pretty accurate. Joe, you'll be happy to hear, we're not going to get into detail about Governor Dean yelling at that elderly man or all the other things he did.[34] But, before we leave Iowa, I just want to ask Charles a question. Dennis Kucinich put a lot of investment on the ground there. There seemed to be a constituency for his message. Last night, you talked about how Governor Dean took up a lot of space. Was there more you could have done in Iowa? Could the congressman have been a factor in Iowa if he had done different things there—maybe even worked Iowa harder than other places?

CHARLES LENCHNER: He split his time between Iowa and New Hampshire. I think he could have done better if he had made a decision to stick to Iowa.

Another problem we had is that, in many ways, the people most experienced in how to run campaigns and do politics were not the ones making decisions on the ground in Iowa. We had some of those people, but a lot of our support came from people with an activist background whose form of politics was more in the street than doing electoral stuff.

Finally, by that time, there had been this decisionmaking process among the voters that they wanted to choose someone who the pundits thought was electable. They wanted someone who would win. They were not necessarily asking themselves, which candidate represents my passions? Which candidate is speaking in my voice? At least half of the Iowa voters were against the war and 90 percent of the delegates at the Democratic National Convention were against the war. But they voted for people, overwhelmingly, who did not harp on that message. You had this real disconnect which, I think, is just part of a larger issue in American politics.

MARK HALPERIN: Patricia Ireland, what can you tell us, that has not been reported, about how Carol Moseley Braun's decision to endorse Dean came about?[35]

PATRICIA IRELAND: I can tell you that a number of things that were reported were not accurate. One of the first things I ever heard Joe Trippi say in Iowa was that it was an illusion that he was in charge of the campaign. Having heard his discussion this morning, I understand that a little better.

---

34. On January 11, 2004, when challenged by an elderly Iowan at a televised forum, Governor Dean lost his temper and said, "You sit down. You've had your say and now I'm going to have my say."

35. Carol Moseley Braun dropped out of the presidential race and endorsed Governor Dean on January 15, 2004.

(Laughter.) It was with Joe Trippi that we had discussions, sitting in the Fort Des Moines Hotel, because there is just nothing else to do there. (Laughter.) Those discussions hinged on the ambassador's chemistry with Dean, as well as the politics. What happened is, after Joe and I reached some agreement in connection with the principals, it got bounced back to Burlington to implement. Someone in Burlington, who shall remain nameless—

MARK HALPERIN: Was this someone who had access to the safe? (Laughter.)

PATRICIA IRELAND: Probably. Someone started telling the press stories about Ambassador Moseley Braun. It went from $20,000 to $50,000 a month that the Dean campaign was going to pay her, which was a total and absolute fantasy—not just because the month after we made that deal, Joe Trippi was gone from the campaign, and three weeks after that the campaign folded, but it was never part of the discussion. It really wasn't. You have a different recollection?

JOE TRIPPI: No. What I was going to say is that one of the things that people don't realize is that when Carol [Moseley Braun] had run for Senate for the first time against [Senator Alan] Dixon—at a moment when no one in Washington was helpful trying to go against an incumbent senator—I was one of the people in town who took her around and tried to introduce her. So we had a long-standing relationship that went back to before she had ever run. I think that had something to do with the endorsement. Plus, she had amazing chemistry with Howard [Dean] and I think that just made it happen.

PATRICIA IRELAND: I came into the campaign in November. It began with Andy Pringle as the campaign manager and it was set up in a way that imagined there was going to be a whole lot more money than there was. If Bob Graham could not pick up sufficient money for a campaign of the nature that you needed, it was clear that Ambassador Moseley Braun was not going to. So, at that point, my goal was to increase the funding and increase the media visibility, which we did. That was what we hoped to bring to the eventual nominee—this constituency. I never thought we were going to win, but I did think we could mobilize and organize and bring to the ultimate nominee, which is what we had hoped to bring to Howard Dean, a constituency that was excited.

MARK HALPERIN: Charles, you talked last night about your role in the campaign with Reverend Sharpton, keeping him within certain boundaries. He was treated with incredible respect in the debates and other multi-candidate events. There was some criticism, but not very much, from people on the right saying all the candidates should be going after Reverend Sharpton for his past statements and actions. How surprised was Reverend Sharpton that he was being treated commensurate with people who had been elected to public office, in most cases, and who had, if you'll pardon the euphemism, more of a mainstream political career?

CHARLES HALLORAN: Before I describe how gracious everyone was, let me say, in the interest of full disclosure, that the twenty grand a month came out of the Sharpton campaign. (Laughter.) I had dinner with Jay Carson from the Dean campaign[36] the night before and Reverend Sharpton was curious about this endorsement. (Laughter.) So I had dinner with Carson to float a number by him, just to see if there was any truth to what Reverend Sharpton thought—Sharpton is a suspicious man by nature. Carson dropped a piece of pizza he was eating when I floated the twenty grand figure and I knew we had something there. Whatever the deal was for travel and whatever, it shook them up. Two days later they were issuing a release that there was some type of travel being paid for. So, in the interest of disclosure, that was our shot across the bow.

[DNC] Chairman Terry McAuliffe and all the other candidates were extremely gracious to Reverend Sharpton. That was one of the things that was key in keeping him on his message of growing the party base and inclusion. I think it played well for everybody.

MARK HALPERIN: The period after Iowa—

BOB SHRUM: Mark, are you going to move on from Iowa? Because I would like to say one thing about Iowa.

MARK HALPERIN: Sure, please do.

BOB SHRUM: I'm sure that all of us made mistakes of various kinds that impacted our campaigns, either in the primaries or in the general. I think the press' misreading of Iowa which, with the exception of the *Des Moines Register*, up until the day before the caucuses, tremendously magnified the impact of Senator Kerry's victory and of Senator Edwards coming in second.

MARK HALPERIN: By making them surprises?

BOB SHRUM: I was on the campaign bus for most of December, January, February, and the first three weeks of March. As we campaigned in Iowa in

---

36. Jay Carson served as the national spokesperson for Governor Dean's campaign.

those last two weeks, you could see it on the ground, and we could see it in Mark [Mellman]'s data and in the last *Des Moines Register* poll. But when the Fox guy handed me the entry poll[37] and I gave it to John Kerry, the small press corps that we had with us was stunned. I think the coverage tended to give us a tremendous boost.

There was this story in one major national newspaper, I think two days before the Iowa caucuses, saying that in the end, the organization is all that really matters and it's a fight for first between Dean and Gephardt and a fight for third between Kerry and Edwards. We didn't think that was true.

NICK BALDICK: I've got to disagree on one thing. I think Bob is right about the fact that Senator Kerry and Senator Edwards came out of nowhere. It was a shock to some national reporters. But the story out of Iowa, instead of being Kerry-Edwards, was Dean's scream.[38] We came within a couple thousand votes of winning Iowa and got buried in the ninth paragraph. For four days in New Hampshire, we talked about the scream. Kerry campaign's numbers are going up six points a day and the press is talking about the scream. I would argue that our surprise second got buried. Roger [Simon] writes this piece and he sits down with me to talk about Iowa and the first five questions were about Howard Dean. We finished second in Iowa and the first five questions that reporters ask us are about a guy who finished third.

MARK HALPERIN: I want to come back to that exact issue, but Joe, do you want to say something before we move on?

JOE TRIPPI: I think the Edwards campaign, if you're honest about it, was probably executed better than any and had the worst luck of any. Wes Clark got in and stepped on their announcement. Unlike John Kerry, they didn't have a $6.4 million check to write and then they get beat by a few thousand votes in Iowa. I'm not arguing that the $6.4 million had anything to do with destroying Dean or Gephardt, but I think it had something to do with the three or four points that stopped Edwards from winning Iowa. I don't mean to step on the decision to do the $6.4 million—I think it was a courageous decision. It told me that this guy could be president. To do that was an amazing thing—we didn't think it was easy. The final capper on this thing is that while it was more miraculous that Edwards got the 32 percent, or whatever it was, and the Kerry campaign got the 38 percent, they had to listen to Howard Dean's scream for a week and no one paid any attention to the Edwards campaign. That just destroyed them.

---

37. Entry polls reflect voters' candidate preferences as they enter the Iowa caucuses.
38. After finishing a disappointing third in the Iowa caucuses, Governor Dean delivered a fiery speech to his supporters that included a widely replayed, energetic howl.

MARK HALPERIN: I think it's pretty well accepted that the win in Iowa was amongst the most decisive we've ever seen in one single win propelling the nomination so much.

JOE TRIPPI: The other thing I would say though is that when the caucus tape came out, we fell ten points in one night. When you're at 40 percent and you fall to 30 percent, that's a quarter of your support that just went out the window. That happened. If you have 37,000 Dean supporters who are identified by your organization, somewhere in that pile, a quarter of them are gone—we're down to 23,000 or 24,000. I went through this in the 1984 Mondale campaign where all our ones disappeared in a state ten days out and we still had to pull them because that's all we had at that point.

On the Friday before the Iowa caucuses, our polling had Kerry at 36 percent and Dean at 18 percent. This thing was going away fast and the Edwards campaign didn't have a great organization on the ground because of the resources. There were at least two decent organizations on the ground—the Gephardt campaign and the Dean campaign. The Kerry campaign by far had the best organization. But we're now knocking on thousands and thousands of doors that are no longer for us. Gephardt's supporters were doing the same thing. Those people were already active anyway and many of them were probably already going to go to the caucuses. That's how the Edwards campaign happened.

CHARLES LENCHNER: One more thing. A lot of Kucinich's voters went to caucuses where they weren't going to get a delegate and they switched their vote to the Edwards camp.[39] That had a significant impact and we always felt really good about that because of how Edwards behaved as a campaigner. It was something that generated a lot of positive feelings.

ADAM NAGOURNEY: Bob, do you think that Edwards could have won if there had been just a couple more days in Iowa?

BOB SHRUM: I think Edwards was helped tremendously by the deal with Kucinich. I believe that the answer to that is inherently unknowable, but the *Des Moines Register* endorsement had a big impact.[40] Day after day after day,

---

39. Under the Iowa caucus system, if a given candidate's supporters do not meet the necessary numerical threshold to secure him or her a delegate from a particular precinct, those individuals have the option of throwing their support behind another candidate. In the days before the Iowa caucus, Senator Edwards and Congressman Kucinich struck an agreement whereby any Kucinich supporters who did not meet the necessary threshold would switch over to Edwards.
40. The *Des Moines Register* endorsed Senator Edwards on January 11, 2004.

as John Kerry campaigned, our crowds were getting bigger and bigger and bigger and more and more responsive. In some ways, I think Senator Edwards' other problem—aside from the scream—was that the structure of the race was such that once Kerry won Iowa, the soap opera question was, could Dean come back in New Hampshire? So the race was going to be covered from that perspective.

MARK HALPERIN: So we've got a pretty decisive victory in Iowa. Coming out of Iowa, it was a question of whether Clark and Edwards, the only two major candidates staying in the race, could somehow take Senator Kerry out. Nick, this is a classic example of where there was a big free media story going on. Did you all, at the time, recognize that the missed opportunity to capitalize on Iowa was slipping away? Could you have done anything to get Senator Edwards more credit—more attention—for having done so well in Iowa?

NICK BALDICK: It was tough to beat the scream story. The first two days it ran on the news—on cable—for sixteen hours a day. I don't know if there were things we could have done. We tried to take Edwards out of New Hampshire for a day or two because we were afraid that the story was going to become Dean trying to come back in New Hampshire, instead of us finishing second. That didn't work.

The national press corps spent six months writing the "Howard Dean out of nowhere Internet story," and you spent a month-and-a-half writing about the fall of the Dean campaign. You couldn't resist yourselves.

JOE TRIPPI: There is one thing that I think is important for people to understand. Part of our strategy was to drive everybody else into the ground financially. Our strategy was, from the very beginning, that we were out there to get $200 million and we believed that anybody who didn't opt out of the public financing system had no chance of beating Bush. When Kerry opted out, I was actually happy because I was trying to urge other campaigns to do the same thing.

The counterbalance to that was that our whole strategy was to run every single one of the other campaigns into the dirt financially. I think one of the things that happened was we actually had accomplished that—including Kerry. So, by the time we "scream" and they take second, they are broke, waiting for matching funds. If Kerry didn't write the $6.4 million check, I don't know if the whole strategy would have worked or not, given the mistakes we made.

It's important for people to understand that was a critical piece of our strategy—to run everybody else into the ground financially. We had accomplished that which meant that anybody who was still alive against Kerry, who had money, was now in trouble because they had no resources to go on.

MARY BETH CAHILL: Can I say one thing about this though? I always thought that Edwards was much more interested in South Carolina, and so when we went to New Hampshire, the Edwards campaign went in and out of New Hampshire and went to South Carolina. I thought that was where they were going to really make their stand and they were going to blow us away. I thought that the Edwards campaign was really distracted, in terms of the race in New Hampshire.

MARK HALPERIN: Nick, telescoping all the way through to Senator Edwards getting out of the race, were there different decisions you could have made, from Iowa onward, that would have given you a better chance to take Senator Kerry down? Were there other places to win?

NICK BALDICK: I think, overall, after Iowa, if there were other decisions that we could have made, we could have slowed down Senator Kerry, but I don't think anyone could have stopped him. I think the only thing that we could have done differently is we shouldn't have gone to Missouri. There were so many delegates there, it was tough not to get the third we knew we would get. Any time there was a waste of time.

As it turned out, we lost Oklahoma by 1,100 votes. If we had gotten those 1,100 votes, maybe Clark gets out the next day, maybe he is not around for Virginia and Tennessee, and maybe those races are very different. I don't know—there are a lot of "what ifs." As far as the calendar goes, we are not sure where it will be in the future. But the difference between a one week, one primary race in Wisconsin and a one week, five state primary after February 3 was immense for us because we could plop John Edwards in a state and he was just great—we had a great message resonating.[41] I think Senator Kerry was sick during that week in Wisconsin. I think he had the flu or something because he was not his normal self.

MARK MELLMAN: If I could just underline something Nick said. I'm not a person known for my sunny optimism as a general matter, but I think it was very clear—to all of us—that once John Kerry won in Iowa, it was almost inevitable that he was going to win New Hampshire. The reality is he was

---

41. The Michigan Democratic Presidential Caucuses and Washington Presidential Caucuses were held on February 7, 2004; the Maine Democratic caucuses were held on February 8, 2004; and the Tennessee and Virginia Presidential Primaries were held on February 10, 2004.

playing at home. John Kerry was known there. He was popular there. There is no question he had been eclipsed by Governor Dean who had established a unique relationship with the Democrats of New Hampshire. But, once that spell was broken, the natural, almost inevitable person to fill that hole was John Kerry. Once he won both Iowa and New Hampshire, the only question was, is it going to take us months to win this nomination or is it going to take us a short time? From my point of view, the nomination was effectively decided in Iowa and was actually decided in New Hampshire. Everything after that was just filling out the calendar—the formalities.

MARY BETH CAHILL: I wish he had told me that at the time. (Laughter.)

BOB SHRUM: The other advantage we had in all this was that John Kerry could run a national campaign. He could compete in every state. Senator Edwards had to cherry pick his places. It would have never occurred to us to skip Missouri or, for example, Oklahoma, which we were not likely to win. We made a major effort in Oklahoma and came in third, but not very far behind General Clark who came in first. By competing everywhere, after having won Iowa and New Hampshire, there was tremendous pressure on everybody else to come up with some really breakthrough performances. Otherwise, the whole process was just going to move on to its inevitable conclusion.

NICK BALDICK: And you could compete everywhere because you had money.

BOB SHRUM: Right.

NICK BALDICK: And in increasing amounts at that point.

• KERRY: THE PRESUMPTIVE NOMINEE •

ADAM NAGOURNEY: Let's move to the spring, after Kerry effectively had the nomination. A lot of Democrats I've spoken to think that if you were to pinpoint moments in the Kerry campaign that ended up being a problem at the end, spring was it. I know there were a lot of stories written about this. Coming into the spring, the Bush people immediately telegraphed what they were going to do. I believe the Bush campaign had an ad on the air the day after Kerry won the nomination. You gave on-the-record interviews saying you were going to go after him on "flip-flopping." This was even before the "I voted for the $87 billion before I voted against it."[42]

Talking to Democrats and looking at what you were doing, it looked as if you guys were just, for a while, ceding the stage, letting the Republicans have their time, letting them do the attacks. Mark, in retrospect, was that a mistake? Was there a debate in the campaign about what to do? I know Democrats outside were becoming increasingly agitated.

MARK MELLMAN: I don't think anybody in the campaign felt like we were ceding any stage to anybody. Others, particularly Mary Beth, can speak more fully to this. The reality is we had no money at that point. We needed to raise a lot of money. That takes a lot of time and effort and energy. Tremendous amounts of time, effort, and energy were expended by the campaign to put together the resources that enabled us to compete, starting in March or April, when we got on the air with ads.

ADAM NAGOURNEY: The polls showed you guys ahead at that point, as I recall, right?

MARK MELLMAN: Yes.

ADAM NAGOURNEY: Were you dealing with complacency on the part of the candidate?

MARK MELLMAN: I don't think so at all. I think there was a very clear sense that there was a job to do. Obviously, we had to do the press and do the other things we were doing. I think we did pretty well or very well during that period. But, there also was a priority on raising money. I think it's completely wrong to suggest that what happened in the spring was dispositive. The reality is that this race was very close all the way through. Sometimes we were a couple points ahead in the spring and sometimes we were a couple points behind. The truth is that was the case the whole way through. I don't think it's at all accurate to suggest that the spring was dispositive. They got a message out but—

---

42. In the spring of 2004, Senator Kerry attempted to explain his vote against a supplemental spending bill for the conflict in Iraq by saying, "I actually voted for the $87 billion before I voted against it." Senator Kerry supported an earlier, Democratic version of the bill before voting against the final spending plan on the Senate floor. However, President Bush's campaign seized on the awkward declaration, using it as part of a series of efforts targeted at portraying Senator Kerry as a "flip-flopper" who would say anything to get elected.

*Mary Beth Cahill and Bob Shrum listen to questions about
John Kerry's primary strategy.*

ADAM NAGOURNEY: Matthew, maybe dispositive is too strong of a word, but did you think that what happened in the spring turned out to be effective? Did it influence what happened in the fall?

MATTHEW DOWD: We understood the financial situation they were in. That's why we did what we did. We thought it was going to last a couple weeks longer, but the prison scandal surfaced, which we couldn't do anything about, and then it occupied the front pages and news for a month.

People missed—and I think people are still missing—what we were trying to do in the spring. It was the beginning of a definitional period for John Kerry for the general election, and we wanted to impact his credibility to make an argument against us. That was the main point of what we were doing in the spring, so that his ability to affect our numbers would be reduced because, in my mind, for an incumbent president—especially this president— what our approval was and what our numbers were were more important than anything else. So, if we can cause voters to say, John Kerry is attacking the President on X—whatever it is, Iraq, the economy, health care, whatever—if they have a question in their mind that what they are hearing is true, it is a benefit to us. It has a much bigger effect on his ability to effect our numbers over the course of the long haul. That was the main purpose of what we were trying to do in the spring. We did it in different ways. We talked about him on taxes. We talked about him on defense. But all of those, we thought, were going to be attacks. In the course of that discussion, he would "flip-flop"—he would do something—the voters would get a sense that this guy didn't have a core set of principles. So, over the next six months, he would have a harder time dropping our numbers by what he said or did. That was the main reason why we did it and I think we were effective at it.

MARK HALPERIN: Mark Mellman, I may have gone to Harvard, but I'm not sure I know what dispositive means in this case. Do you not think that what Matthew said laid the predicate for what they did the rest of the year, making it very hard for your candidate to make an effective, negative argument against the President? Do you not think that was a period during which more could have been done to try to keep them from defining John Kerry?

MARK MELLMAN: I think there are two fundamental asymmetries here. One is an asymmetry in money, which the campaign moved to address and did so in almost miraculous fashion. I certainly had no anticipation that the campaign was going to be able to address the financial asymmetry in the way we did.

The second asymmetry is one of information. The President is the best known figure in the country by far. Every droplet of additional information that people get about President Bush constitutes an infinitesimally small proportion of what they know about him.

Every new piece of information they get about John Kerry constitutes 50 percent—25 percent at the least—of what they know about John Kerry. So, yes, if you spend $80 million saying anything, people are going to repeat that back. The truth is they could have started a new religion for $80 million, if they wanted to. You spend $80 million and some people are going to repeat it back. So, did they lay a foundation in that period? There is no question that they did, on "flip-flopping." Is there something we could have done to prevent that, given the resources that we had? I'm not sure we can prevent people from repeating back something where $80 million is spent saying it. I'm not sure that it could have been different.

TAD DEVINE: Can I stick to this for a minute? Because I have the perspective of 2000 and what happened in that campaign, and then what happened in 2004. In 2000, then-Governor Bush clearly won the spring of the contest and I think he won it decisively. He infused meaning into the words compassion and conservatism. He took positions on issues which were bold, and I think it helped him ultimately win a very close race for president. I believe, in the spring of 2004, something else happened. They had four years. I give them a lot of credit because I think they were very disciplined about it and developed a strategy in the course of those four years to take on a Democratic opponent. Really, we had four weeks. That's the reality of what happened. The four weeks were the four weeks from the middle of March to the middle of April of 2004. In those four weeks, there had been positioning, as Bob

[Shrum] pointed out before, whether it was on issues like the middle class tax cut, on Senator Kerry's position on adding 40,000 active duty troops, or on reiteration of his record with respect to issues like welfare reform.

Those four weeks covered the time that we effectively seized the nomination. We made the transition from the Iowa and New Hampshire wins to the broader base, multi-candidate, multi-state strategy, secured the nomination, and engaged in our general election messaging. At the end of April, we began broadcasting television advertising, which struck for the first time about when John Kerry said, "I'm John Kerry and I approved this message because together we can build a stronger America." That's what we talked about until Election Day. In those four weeks, we talked for the first time in the way that you need to, in a disciplined way, with real research, focus groups, individual state polls, national polling, and the depth of research that you need to construct a real message on a national stage. Then, we went to that message.

So I don't view the spring of 2004 as a period where we lost ground. In 2000, I think we lost considerable ground and fell well behind. I think it was a period of advance for us when we made great gains with voters. Mark [Mellman] talked about the asymmetry. We made up for that asymmetry in terms of resources and the answer that we provided, in terms of these attacks, was the story of John Kerry's lifetime of service and strength. That was our answer and we provided it on a very big stage.

MARK HALPERIN: A decision that was made by the campaign, and was discussed openly by Bob [Shrum] and Tad [Devine] and others, was that the country is not in the mood for negative commercials, that this is a period when the President's ads were going to backfire, that you all didn't need to do that, and, in fact, that it would be counterproductive and the President would eventually pay a price. You said that consistently and publicly throughout. Did that turn out to be right?

BOB SHRUM: What would you have expected me to say? (Laughter.)

MARK HALPERIN: I would have expected you to run negative ads.

BOB SHRUM: Tad just said something very, very important. I heard you, at the beginning, lay down the Halperin ground rule, which I'm now going to violate. I think the Bush campaign wisely understood that this was, in some fundamental sense, a 9/11 election. That's how they began and it's how they ended. The notion that you could dump a lot of negative information on George Bush and change a lot of people's minds about George Bush was completely wrong. I would argue that even the notion that you could dump a lot of negative information on us and change a lot of people's minds was fundamentally wrong.

This was an election where each candidate was going to get 46 or 47 percent of the vote, period. You were fighting over, A, turning out your base or changing the composition of the electorate, which the Bush campaign did a very good job of, and, B, you were trying to reach people who were in the middle and who were undecided. I always thought it was intriguing to think about the people who would get up every morning and say, I don't know whether I'm for Bush or for Kerry, because the choice to most people seemed pretty stark.

We had no money to speak of. It would have been completely preposterous for us to dribble out little, negative attacks on the President or to play entirely on the President's playing field. Letting him define the race and then letting us just keep returning the serve would have served us very badly. One reason we were in pretty reasonable shape going into the convention was because we resisted that. We raised the money and we went out and told John Kerry's story and told people what he wanted to do as president.

ADAM NAGOURNEY: Let me ask Steve Murphy to bring the outside perspective here. Do you agree? Did the Bush people succeed in laying a predicate that hurt Kerry in the fall? I don't mean to put you on the spot, because you might work with these guys again, but could they have done something in the spring to push back on the "flip-flop," leave aside the Kerry quote about I was for and against it, or to lay out a theme or lay out a message to say no? There was a lot of concern in Democratic circles during that period that, maybe for money or for whatever reason, they just weren't doing that much.

STEVE MURPHY: I think Bob [Shrum] is correct. There was very little that the Kerry campaign could have done, that the Democrats could have done, that we ever were able to do, to hurt George W. Bush. And I agree with Matt [Dowd] that Bush's job approval numbers—the right track/wrong track numbers—were determinative in terms of the final vote.

The attacks on Kerry worked. I think they helped. They drove up his negative numbers and they were an impediment to the Kerry campaign being able to communicate their message of strength. So, at least in a tactical sense, at that time, they were harmful.

I don't think the Kerry campaign had a lot of options. I think they did the right thing in transitioning from the nomination process to the general election, to figure out their message and aggressively communicate it. But, yes, I think we were slowed down a little bit by that.

ADAM NAGOURNEY: Did you ever hear the Kerry campaign come up with an answer to the "flip-flop" charge which these guys made clear from the beginning was going to be a central part of the Bush campaign?

MARY BETH CAHILL: We thought that John Kerry's story and John Kerry's approach to issues was the answer. Ads that would have said, John Kerry is not a "flip-flopper" in response would not have exactly served us well. We thought that giving people an eye into the man, his approach to running for president and what he wanted to do when he was there was the answer to that.

To put some facts into what we've just been discussing, after March 18th, I think the Bush campaign had $114 million cash-on-hand and we had $2.3 million. So the disparity was pretty enormous and that was the first thing that we had to address.

MATTHEW DOWD: Could I just say one thing on resource allocation? We were outspent by $26 million in the spring if you add in all the 527 money that was spent. So this wasn't like we were sitting here with $80 million defining the race. We were outspent. When you take the Kerry campaign's money before June 1 and the 527 money that was spent against us, we were outspent by $26 million. It's just a question of what was being said and how it was being said.

I think Tad [Devine] is right. We had three-and-a-half years to plan work on this and they had three-and-a-half weeks, or whatever the period of time was. But it wasn't a resource question. It was not a resource question because there was a lot of money getting spent out there by Democratic groups to either define us or define John Kerry. Now, is the question, was the money spent wrongly? I think that's a different question. The money was there.

BOB SHRUM: The money constraint obviously applied to us. We didn't control the 527s. The 527 experience illustrates, at least when you have an incumbent president and people have very strong views about him, that with the exception of the prescription drug stuff that one of the 527s did, I don't think that they had a large impact on Bush by running negative ads on him.

I also think there is one other factor, that I've talked about in other contexts, that needs to be thought about here. One of the unintended consequences of McCain-Feingold[43] is that voters take much more seriously an ad where the candidate appears and says, "I'm John Kerry and I approved this message" or "I'm George Bush and I approve this message," and take less seriously ads that come from other places.

---

43. The McCain-Feingold reforms, known as the Bipartisan Campaign Reform Act of 2002, were signed into law on March 27, 2002. The legislation sought to control campaign fundraising and expenditures. Among its stipulations was a regulation that required candidates to include verbal approval as part of any paid media message broadcast by their campaigns.

We were in a situation where—you and I talked about this and we obviously still disagree—we had to make a very serious decision. The decision was, would we take the resources that were coming in the door each week and play on the President's ball field or would we allow those resources to grow to the point where we could make a large enough buy to seriously introduce John Kerry? We made the second decision and I would make that decision again today.

MARY BETH CAHILL: Yes, but the thing is, we were on the air that entire time.

BOB SHRUM: And a huge buy, right.

CHARLES HALLORAN: Let me just say one thing. It might have not made a huge difference, but one of the problems with the short schedule is that it's hard to ramp up a serious surrogate operation. Mary Beth knew to hire Maura Keefe as quickly as possible.[44] But there were thirty days where no one was defending John Kerry in a systematic way. Who would have thought you would set up a surrogate operation in April? It's usually in August. That's something that people need to pay attention to next time and be ready to have their troops out there. It eventually came together and we had hundreds of good surrogates.

ADAM NAGOURNEY: Mary Beth, was there concern in the campaign at all that what Bush was doing was having an impact during this critical period?

MARY BETH CAHILL: If someone is unloading millions of dollars in negative advertising on you, it's always a concern. (Laughter.)

ADAM NAGOURNEY: This goes back to what Bob said a second ago. The whole public stance of the campaign was that no one cares, it's negative stuff, it's the President just dropping garbage.

MARY BETH CAHILL: But I think that, for us, we had a plan of how we were going to get into this game. We realized we were behind the eight ball here in terms of timing. Despite what it looked like to Nick [Baldick], we did not have a lot of money. Wednesday morning every week, we said, how much do we need this week? Where are we going to get it? Going from that to being able to run an enormous advertising campaign and have a much, much

---

44. In 2004, Maura Keefe served as a senior advisor to the Democratic National Committee and was responsible for the design and maintenance of the Committee's surrogate operation.

larger staff and organization took us some time. We had to be confident, we had to unite the party, we had to give people the sense that we knew where we were going to go. That was also one of our aims. What should we have said—yes, this is hurting us?

BOB SHRUM: Well, quoting your quote, if I had given you a quote saying, boy, I am really worried about this, that would have done us a lot of good. (Laughter.) I mean, come on.

CHARLES LENCHNER: While I understand it's the common wisdom to go to the center for the swing voters, other people like George Laycoff or Adam Stern have talked about a strategy of appealing more strongly to the base—of reinforcing the set of ideas that strongly distinguish Democrats and Republicans—and not necessarily going towards the middle. That was an alternative that was out there. Other groups wanted to pursue that. They were being told, in the name of unity, not to do it and to stay on message. I think that that cost votes and lost enthusiasm for the Kerry campaign later on when, for example, at the convention or during the platform process, people were being told to support things that they weren't enthusiastic about or didn't believe in. That needs to be said.

• THE VEEP SELECTION •

MARK HALPERIN: As it is invariably always the case, we now have about eight minutes to do the selection of the vice president, the roll out of the vice president, and the convention, so everybody is going to engage in zen-like focus and say only really smart things and historically fascinating things.
    Mary Beth, let me just start with the—

MARY BETH CAHILL: First, I'll put my light bulb on. (Laughter.)

MARK HALPERIN: The vice presidential selection process. I don't want to overstate the level of disorganization of the campaign, as all campaigns are, but the debate preparation, the selection process of the vice president and the convention planning all seemed to be pretty well done, very well organized, no leaks where the candidate didn't want leaks, sensible outputs in all three cases. Why is that? What characterized those processes separate from the day-to-day operation of the campaign that made them stand out that way?

MARY BETH CAHILL: They were all really small. They were all a very small number of people and a group of people that were hand-picked for the task and who understood, from the beginning, in each case, that their charge

Nick Baldick and Steve Murphy (left to right) discuss the vice presidential selection process.

from Kerry and the campaign was that this was supposed to be quiet. The people that were picked were outstanding. Jim Johnson did an outstanding job on the search for the vice president.[45] It was much more wide ranging than was ever written about and there were a lot more meetings than were ever written about.

MARK HALPERIN: Do you want to submit that list for the record? (Laughter.)

MARY BETH CAHILL: Very little of that made it into the press and that was because of the quality of the people involved in it and the commitment to that process.

ADAM NAGOURNEY: Were there candidates who were not aware of it, Mary Beth?

MARY BETH CAHILL: Yes. There was a much wider list.

ADAM NAGOURNEY: Serious candidates that we could talk about here?

MARY BETH CAHILL: No, because I believe this is eventually on-the-record.

---

45. Jim Johnson headed up Senator Kerry's vice presidential search team. Johnson had previously served in a variety of public and private capacities including chairman and CEO of Fannie Mae, managing director in corporate finance at Lehman Brothers, and campaign manager for Vice President Mondale.

The same is very much true of the debate prep process. Everybody wants to be involved in debate prep and people can add into a process like this. But we were very much informed by what happened with Gore, and what a sideshow that was. We were not going to let that happen. And so, early on, I gave Senator Kerry a concept of what this ought to look like and, despite huge pressure from people who wanted to be part of that, it never got any bigger.

ADAM NAGOURNEY: Stephanie, you were involved in the rollout for both the vice president and the convention planning, and the technical competence of both was rated quite highly by your peers and by the press. You could argue that because, as Bob [Shrum] said, it was 48-48 and there wasn't any room to grow that perhaps you could have been even more successful and nothing would have happened. For somebody doing those two tasks in 2008 for either party, what lessons did you learn about it can look successful but you don't see an indication in the polls that it has a positive effect on the candidacy?

STEPHANIE CUTTER: I have to start by disagreeing. It did have a pretty big effect. Let's start with the V.P. roll out. The way that we were able to generate news coverage and manipulate it in a way that we thought was helpful to us was hugely advantageous to us. Going back to the period from the spring into June and July, it was hard for us to get national attention in a way that would have a big impact. We were mostly focusing on regional coverage. We saw the V.P. roll out as the first big opportunity to generate national news coverage in a way that would continue to fill out Kerry's biography, put excitement behind the campaign, and introduce the new team for the new America, which is what we were calling it.

What I would tell people in 2008 is exactly what Mary Beth said—the smaller the group working on something like that, the better. We were able to keep it in a tight confine and keep it from leaking out to the press. That had a huge impact on what type of coverage it received.

The same holds true for the convention. A lot of people are saying a lot of things about the convention after the fact—a lot of revisionist history—but that was a very successful convention for us. We controlled the message very well on a day-to-day basis. If you go back and look at it, we laid out a very effective plan for the future and filled out Kerry's biography. We were very happy with it.

MARK HALPERIN: Positive clips in both cases—national, regional, and local—but can you point to evidence that it had an enduring effect on your chances of winning the election?

MARY BETH CAHILL: Can I say something about this? I think the race kept going back to essentially even—nobody ever got a balance and kept a balance during the course of this. You could have a blip up and a blip down, but this was essentially an even race throughout most of the year.

ADAM NAGOURNEY: Do you think Bush's convention served him better than your convention served you?

MARY BETH CAHILL: As I said last night, and really my biggest truism from this whole year, the five weeks between the Democratic and Republican conventions was the biggest problem that we faced, unquestionably. The fact that they were able to sit back and look at our convention and look at what we did. I think they read the same positive clips that we were reading and they made a different plan on what they were going to do with that intervening period of time and with their convention, as a result.

MARK MELLMAN: This is for posterity—as a pollster, I would just say beware of the polls in interpreting this or any future election. The reality is you could take any two polls at any two points in time in this campaign and tell any story about any event that you want. You could look at polls before and after the Democratic Convention and say that John Kerry got an eight point bounce. You could look at polls before and after the Democratic Convention and say there was a five point negative bounce for John Kerry. You could look at polls before and after the Republican Convention and say George Bush got a six point positive bounce. You could look at polls before and after the Republican Convention and say George Bush got a negative four bounce. So, when we talk about what evidence we have, we have evidence to tell any story you want. (Laughter.)

UNIDENTIFIED: It speaks well of the polling business. (Laughter.)

MARK MELLMAN: It does. As I said, I'm a pollster—beware of these polls. But I think the reality is that all of the evidence, at the time, suggested the convention, as well as the vice presidential selection, did have a very positive impact on both our vote standing and on people's image of John Kerry.

MARK HALPERIN: Nick, going back to the vice presidential selection, Senator Edwards, through his public actions and through what's been reported, clearly made an effort to be selected.[46] What can you tell us that has not been reported or discussed about how well organized that effort was?

NICK BALDICK: The Senator, after getting soundly beaten on March 2 and then dropping out on March 3, and after taking a small break and resting,

---

46. Senator Kerry officially chose Senator Edwards as his running mate on July 6, 2004.

turned over and whatever Mary Beth wanted, we did. To be honest, we needed to get rid of George Bush. People made a big deal out of us going to Ohio and all these places that we traveled to every weekend. Every one of those requests were out of the Kerry surrogate shop. It wasn't like we said, we'd like to go here—they asked.

MARK HALPERIN: But you can't deny that Senator Edwards discussed with you and other associates his desire to be picked and the best things to do to be picked, right?

NICK BALDICK: Senator Edwards thought he could add to the ticket, but that wasn't the reason we were traveling.

MARK HALPERIN: Right but, again, leaving aside the travel, the red herring that you've now brought up twice—(laughter)—what efforts did Senator Edwards make in discussions with you and other political advisors to try to be picked?

NICK BALDICK: Besides going out there and demonstrating that you can excite the base and that people like you, which I think Edwards did in the primaries and then continued to do, and that you could raise money, there wasn't much else you can do. The press corps tends to make a big deal of nothing and the inside process of this. Jim Johnson, Mary Beth, and Senator Kerry ran the most disciplined V.P. selection process, as far as leaks, I remember in my short time in campaigns. Anyone who said it was a lobbying effort, with people calling or any of that—

BOB SHRUM: I think if that had occurred, it would actually have hurt Senator Edwards' chances of being picked.

ADAM NAGOURNEY: You guys didn't sense that was going on then?

NICK BALDICK: No.

MARY BETH CAHILL: I don't think it was directed by the Edwards people, but there was a pretty significant group of Edwards' supporters who felt they should demonstrate to us their desire to have Edwards on the ticket. I spent a fair amount of time meeting with people from around the country who were Edwards' supporters.

ADAM NAGOURNEY: You don't think the Edwards family had anything to do with helping to push that along?

BOB SHRUM: I can tell you it didn't.

• BOSTON: THE DEMOCRATIC CONVENTION •

ADAM NAGOURNEY: Can I ask you a convention question that's mystified me? Whose idea was it to put Michael Moore in a box with Jimmy Carter at the convention? You guys knew this happened, right?

MARY BETH CAHILL: This is the first I've heard of it.

ADAM NAGOURNEY: Oh, okay, it was on TV. Stephanie?

STEPHANIE CUTTER: I didn't know it at the time. I learned about it pretty quickly. (Laughter.) We had a pretty big debate about whether to credential him as a member of the press. Only because he was credentialed for the Republican Convention did we credential him. But never in our wildest imagination would we picture him in a box with Jimmy Carter.

ADAM NAGOURNEY: Did you figure out how it happened? Because you guys really scripted that convention.

BOB SHRUM: I assume President Carter invited him.

STEPHANIE CUTTER: Or Michael had a way of getting himself around, too.

TAD DEVINE: I heard it was Dowd's idea. (Laughter.)

CHARLES LENCHNER: I just wanted to say one small thing about what led up to the convention and the platform process. I remember there was an occasion on the platform committee, which I know isn't very significant, where the Kerry people were saying we must not call the Iraqi War a mistake. Later on, when he did say that going to war in Iraq was a mistake, it brought out the fact that by not having a message incorporated into such a large portion of his base, he made himself weaker on the one hand but didn't strengthen himself on the other. To have so many of his supporters in the antiwar camp thinking of Kerry not only as a "flip-flopper" but as someone who enforced a counterproductive discipline on the base was an issue that certainly isn't getting much attention here but, in the circles I travel in, was very significant.

MARK HALPERIN: Let me just ask one more question to Bob and Mary Beth and Stephanie. There has been criticism of the convention in various quarters, particularly the question of whether you should have been more negative about President Bush. I know you all were positive about the convention coming out of it. If you could have replanned the convention, knowing how it was received and how it was perceived, would you change anything or would you run the same convention you did?

BOB SHRUM: I don't know what Mary Beth would say. I would run fundamentally the same convention. Our biggest problem, and I go back to what Mary Beth said last night, was that we had to run a thirteen-week general election and they had to run an eight-week general election. The biggest problem we had coming out of the convention was that we were not able to convey, in the way that I would like to have conveyed—through buying television coverage in the battleground states—John Kerry's plans for America. That would have been the logical next building block on top of the convention.

One person in our party who made that comment—and it's been picked up by a number of people—called me as the convention ended and said, that was wonderful, that was spectacular, that was exactly what we needed. The truth of the matter is that John Kerry spent a large bulk of his acceptance speech talking about his plans for America and about major domestic issues. Anybody who takes the point of view that we would somehow or other have been stronger had we not addressed, in a serious way, the issue of national security and whether he could be commander in chief seems to me to be completely wrong.

MARK HALPERIN: You two agree, I bet.

MARY BETH CAHILL: Actually, I would go in a little different direction. People really knew all the negatives on President Bush. Everything that we tested, they already knew, and they kind of accepted it. There were definitely some—like President Carter, President Clinton, and Senator Kennedy—who talked about Bush's policies in a pretty negative fashion in their speeches. But a convention in which the leaders of our party and major elected officials have a negative personal discussion about President Bush would not have been to John Kerry's benefit.

STEPHANIE CUTTER: I agree with Mary Beth that we tried to put on what we perceived as a forward looking, positive convention. But the reality was there were people standing up there—like Al Sharpton—who were giving pretty tough critiques of the President. Jimmy Carter gave a very tough critique. Al Gore gave a very tough critique. So the reality of it was a convention that was looking to the future but basing it on the policies of the present. In addition to that, if you look at John Kerry's speech—I went back last night and read the speech—it's a page and a half on his military experience and everything else is about his plans for the future or how his upbringing and lifetime of strength and service shaped his plans for the future. It was very forward looking, laying out plans. All this criticism only came after the Republican Convention. In comparison, they were very different. We didn't have—and I'm not saying this was ineffective because it was effective—Arnold Schwarzenegger standing up there calling Republicans "girlie men."[47] That had an impact, but it was just a different way to go.

So, in retrospect, I don't think we would change anything. Maybe in terms of being so public that it was going to be a positive convention—setting an expectations game—but, other than that, no.

ADAM NAGOURNEY: Joe, what do you think of how they handled their convention?

JOE TRIPPI: I think this whole discussion is a little warped because I agree totally with what Bob [Shrum] and Mark [Mellman] and everybody is saying that people knew everything they needed to know about Bush.

The Kerry campaign didn't have resources. If you start filling that $80 million vacuum, or even if you are outspent, the money is going to work more to fill out a blank slate on Kerry than it is for the other way around—it's just a fact of life. You could have $200 million on our side floating around in 527s. A lot of the stuff that we were talking about actually didn't matter. It was a great convention. But, in the end, this thing gets down to who could expand the electorate beyond the current pile of voters? When you get down to it, if you stay in a non-expanded electorate, John Kerry wins, if the Republicans don't expand the electorate the way they expanded it. In the end, they did a better job of doing that. They got 50 million votes in 2000 and got 60 million in 2004. Somewhere they expanded the electorate beyond the 2000 election. Even here, it gets down to who had four years to do that versus somebody who fights for the nomination, gets it, but gets it in March, broke.

I know a bunch of people were out there trying to do that, but Democrats didn't have a four-year, disciplined plan. There wasn't that kind of discipline.

MARK HALPERIN: A much different perspective than the one Ken Mehlman said last night—that it's harder to run as an incumbent than it is as a challenger—so that's a good segue to break. Thank you all.

---

47. In his speech to the Republican National Convention on September 1, 2004, California Governor Arnold Schwarzenegger challenged critics not to be "economic girlie men."

The Republican ``Primary'' Strategy and Convention

3

"The 2000 campaign convinced us of a lot of different things, but one of the most important things was that we needed a plan to try to expand the electorate and particularly expand our part of the electorate. There was a four-year plan to accomplish that which included lots of different things."

—Bush-Cheney Campaign Manager Ken Mehlman

"At a technical level and as a political operation, I think they ran a very good campaign."

—Kerry-Edwards Media Consultant Bob Shrum

PHIL SHARP: Now we are going to turn to a discussion of the Republican primary strategy and convention. We are very pleased to have moderating this session the political columnist for *U.S. News and World Report* and special correspondent for NBC News, Gloria Borger, and John Harwood, the national political editor of the *Wall Street Journal*. We'll turn it over to them to proceed.

GLORIA BORGER: We want to divide this into six main areas. The first thing we want to talk about is the time before John Kerry emerged as the nominee, to try and get a sense of what the Bush-Cheney campaign was thinking. I'll turn it over to John for that.

• PREPARING FOR 2004 •

JOHN HARWOOD: I wanted to start at the outset of the year. The Democrats had a full-blown primary process—you didn't have a primary and were seen as somehow waiting. But, of course, you have discussed how you spent several years, ever since the President was elected, planning for this campaign. I wonder if you could just take a couple of minutes to talk about that planning process. What kind of research was done? How voluminous a plan was prepared? What had you concluded by the time the calendar turned to January 2004 that you needed to do that wasn't obvious on its face from what we saw?

KEN MEHLMAN: Let me divide it into three areas—one is the structure of the campaign we wanted to run, second is the broad message, based on the structure, and then third, something that Joe [Trippi] and Mary Beth [Cahill] eluded to, was expanding the electorate. The 2000 campaign convinced us of a lot of different things, but one of the most important things was that we needed a plan to try to expand the electorate and particularly expand our part of the electorate. There was a four-year plan to accomplish that which included lots of different things. Fundamentally, it included two big things. One, to use the 2001 and the 2002 elections to test out all kinds of different political tactics and make sure we were being most effective in 2004.

JOHN HARWOOD: A lot of that was turnout stuff?

KEN MEHLMAN: It was turnout, it was television advertising, it was where we bought, how we bought, it was all those things. It was the effectiveness of voter contact and the different programs to do that. But secondly, just as important, was a way of communicating to key audiences that would expand the electorate. For instance, there was a key effort made on how to improve our performance among Latino Americans. How do we improve our

Late Morning, Day 2—Campaign managers and reporters discuss the Republican "primary" strategy.

U.S. News and World Report's *Gloria Borger* and the Wall Street Journal's *John Harwood probe President Bush's campaign staff about how decisions were made.*

performance in the suburbs with women? How do we improve our perform-ance with African Americans? How do we expand, among believers, participa-tion in the political process? For every single state, we thought about developing a plan to accomplish this. That was something that we spent, frankly, a four-year period doing.

JOHN HARWOOD: Did you in fact have fifty state notebooks?

KEN MEHLMAN: There aren't fifty states there, obviously.

JOHN HARWOOD: Twenty?

KEN MEHLMAN: Yes, effectively, and that informed everything we did. That's the third of the three prongs and a little bit of the second of the three prongs.

The first of the three prongs, in terms of research, Matthew [Dowd] went to the previous presidents' libraries—the Bush Library, the Baker Center, the Ford Library, the Reagan Library in Simi Valley—and got a lot of that research. Matthew talked about a lot of what he found, but the general con-clusion of everything we had was two things. One, the reason I said it's harder to run a reelect than it is to run an original election campaign is because in an original election campaign, you are your own entity, and in a reelect, as I said last night, you're a little bit of a colony—you are a colony that's necessary for the survival of the mother country, but you obviously serve the White House. The result of that is if a good organization requires clear lines of authorities—knowing who is in charge, who is doing what, who is making decisions—when you are not just a campaign for you but are working on behalf of the White House, that's much harder to do.

JOHN HARWOOD: How much money would you say you spent during that three-year period in preparing the plans that you are describing, through the Republican National Committee or whatever political entities were spending?

MATTHEW DOWD: Before we do that, there are a couple of points that happened early—in December of 2000 and in January or February of 2001. Through a lot of research and by looking at previous elections, there were two charts I did that drove our thinking, to a large degree, for the next three years. One was a chart that said what Bob [Shrum] said which was, basically, if you look at it, over the last twenty years, and look at 2000, 92 to 93 percent of the electorate was decided. When you figure out that there are not 20 percent swing voters, there are not 15 percent swing voters, there are 7 percent swing voters, that drives your thinking about how you are going to approach 2004, meaning that motivation becomes as important as persuasion. In every previous presidential election that I recall, persuasion was always where people spent most of their money. We made that decision early on in 2001.

The other chart that we did was a chart that was, how do we move from 48 percent to 51 percent? Who are the people in that? Who are the 3 percent that will move us to a 51 percent presidency? It consisted of driving extra turnout among Republicans—adding people. But, to a large degree, two-thirds of those people in that 3 percent were women that we thought we had to get. A part of that was Latinos, as Ken [Mehlman] mentioned. Those two charts—that motivation becomes as important, in some cases more important, than persuasion and the fact that we have to get 3 percent and a big part of that is women and Latinos—drove a lot of the decisions we made. It drove what we were going to do about turnout, how we were going to test it, the "72-Hour Task Force."[1] All of that kind of stuff culminated in the 2004 race, which we had obviously identified in the early parts of 2001.

• THE CAMPAIGN VERSUS THE WHITE HOUSE •

GLORIA BORGER: Well, Ken, I want to get back to the colony point for a moment and then we'll branch this out to the campaign. The notion that

---

1. The "72-Hour Task Force" was an effort by the Republican Party to turn out sympathetic voters by means of a targeted series of phone calls, mailings, and electronic communications in the three days leading up to Election Day.

you are a subsidiary, essentially, of the White House, and you are trying to broaden your base. Talk about how this affected policy decisions at the White House in terms of issues like Medicare, prescription drugs, etcetera, etcetera. Where is the wall, if there is a wall?

KEN MEHLMAN: The wall was really important. Looking back at the history, what inevitably happens in these campaigns is you've got a bunch of people at the White House thinking they know how to run a campaign and trying to micromanage the campaign and a bunch of people at the campaign obsessing over White House policy decisions. We were very, very, very clear that if you came to work on the campaign, while obviously people's input was important, you were not to get in the middle of policy decisions. And, if you came to work at the White House, Andy Card and Karl Rove made it very clear you were not to worry about the campaign.[2]

GLORIA BORGER: Are you saying that you play the hand you are dealt?

KEN MEHLMAN: More importantly, I'm saying that the danger is if everybody is doing five things, they are not doing two things very well. If people at the White House are worrying about the campaign, they are not doing a very good job laying out policy. If people at the campaign are obsessing over the White House, they are not doing a very good job of putting together an ad strategy, helping define our opponent, helping put together a plan for ourselves, turning out the vote, or doing voter registration. So I actually think of it differently than that. I think it's important to being effective. We set up a structure very early that said, here is who makes decisions at the campaign, here is who makes decisions at the White House, here is the process for spending money, here is the process for hiring and firing, here are the people that are involved in those decisions.

GLORIA BORGER: There is an overlap. Let's say Karl Rove, for example.

KEN MEHLMAN: Absolutely. Look, Karl [Rove], Dan Bartlett, myself, Matthew [Dowd], Nicole [Devenish]—obviously any decision that we are talking about involving communication, we all needed to be involved in.[3] But if you set up a process by which people can communicate, can have input, can quickly come to decisions, then you have an effective process. People aren't appealing things, people aren't going outside the process, and people are focusing on the things in which they have responsibility and control over.

---

2. Following President Bush's election in 2000, Andrew Card served as White House chief of staff.

3. In 2004, Dan Bartlett served as the White House communications director.

*President Bush's campaign team—Ken Mehlman, Mattthew Dowd,
and Nicole Devenish (left to right).*

What we tried to build at the campaign, and they also did at the White House, was this small group—the "Breakfast Club" we've talked about—that does these things.[4] Then, beyond the group, you have concentric circles in both places of other people that need to be involved in all of our decisions that are made. By doing that, you make sure you have all the input and people have an investment in the process. You have an effective system of making decisions, but you don't have a lot of people trying to get in each other's lanes, reducing your effectiveness at doing what you are supposed to do. Ultimately, the true danger in politics, I believe, is when decisions are made based on internal politics, not external politics.

JOHN HARWOOD: Could I just close the loop on that? On the pre-2004 preparation, could you give us an idea of how much was spent on the entire effort?

KEN MEHLMAN: Here is the challenge. We spent $50 million in 2002 on victory-type programs.

---

4. The "Breakfast Club" was a small group of President Bush's closest political advisors who met at Karl Rove's home on weekends throughout the election cycle to measure the campaign's progress and devise political strategies.

JOHN HARWOOD: Fifty? 5-0?

KEN MEHLMAN: 5-0. But those were things that helped elect Senator Norm Coleman and they helped elect Senator Jim Talent and they helped elect Senator John Thune—well, they didn't help elect John until two years later. Ultimately, what we were doing when we spent that money was using it as a way of testing our tactics—testing and researching.

GLORIA BORGER: What didn't work? What did you test that failed?

KEN MEHLMAN: The thing that I got out of this process that was most important was that we now live in a world where the old ways of communicating—the traditional buying ads on three channels, doing some robo calls, and doing some paid mail as a voter contact program—is insufficient. What we learned and what we concluded was that we needed, from a paid media perspective, a plan that was very multifaceted—that reached people not just on the networks but increasingly on cable, increasingly on radio, increasingly in different venues—and that our mail and our phones needed to be supplemented by a huge volunteer effort. The thing we got out of it was that the contact that is both personal and from a credible source is most effective. That informed where you bought television, where you earned media, where you booked people, how you built your ground organization, and how you reached new voters.

• EARLY 2004 •

JOHN HARWOOD: Let's go to the state of play that we found at the beginning of 2004. I remember you indicated early on the conclusion that Matthew [Dowd] just mentioned. Motivation was much more important in this election than it had been in some in the past. I remember a conversation with Matthew, maybe it was in late 2003, where I said, what would most concern you, as we move through 2004? And Matthew's answer was, if our support among Republicans drops below 90 percent. That ended up not happening.

As the year began, how did you assess two things—one, the Democrats' ability to remain cohesive and motivate their base, and, secondly, what was the greatest single threat that you guys perceived to the unity of your base, that didn't ultimately materialize? There were things out there related to Iraq, the deficit, the economy, social issues. What most concerned you, from the standpoint of keeping above 90 percent?

KEN MEHLMAN: Let me just say two things. One, I think we all thought that, as Mary Beth [Cahill] said, the election would be fundamentally a relatively dead-even election. The reason we thought that is, again, remember, we went through three presidential elections where no one got 50 percent of the vote—1992, 1996, and 2000. You have a whole series of House races where you have a reduction in ticket splitting. These aren't just aberrations. There is a pattern here and that is both parties, increasingly, are more ideologically coherent, which means there is less ticket splitting.

One of the interesting phenomena we are seeing, and that this is reflective of, is the fact that the parties mean more than they used to mean. They mean more about where you stand on the issues, which is why we knew we would face an opponent, no matter who the Democrats nominated, who would be able to mobilize and be able to count on 48, 47 percent of the electorate because 47, 48 percent of the electorate has come to agree with their world view on issues.

JOHN HARWOOD: What was the softest spot in your base?

KEN MEHLMAN: The issue I worried about was spending and fiscal conservatism. The fact that we were so strong on taxes made it not to be a huge issue. But I think that that was an area where you potentially could have had an issue. Now given who we ran against—

JOHN HARWOOD: Was the gay marriage amendment that the President endorsed in February not an indication that values were, or that social issues were, where you were most concerned?

KEN MEHLMAN: No.

JOHN HARWOOD: No?

KEN MEHLMAN: It wasn't like we were out there saying, let's endorse an amendment—let's look for a way to talk about this issue. The President endorsed it, reluctantly, after there were, in San Francisco and in Cambridge, Massachusetts, and other places, elected officials who were ignoring laws of the states based on a decision by the Supreme Court in Massachusetts.[5] That's why he did it.

MATTHEW DOWD: Let me just say one thing on that. If you think about what we were worried about—motivating soft Republicans to turn out that

---

5. In February 2004, the Massachusetts Supreme Court found a ban on gay marriage to be unconstitutional. That same month, San Francisco Mayor Gavin Newsom issued an order allowing the licensing of same-sex marriage in that city, a move that prompted a number of other cities to permit same-sex marriage licenses.

might not have turned out before—the gay marriage amendment was not something that was going to do that. This might be something that would be supported by a part of the base that was probably going to turn out anyway. The soft Republicans that live in the Philadelphia suburbs or the Cleveland suburbs or the Cincinnati suburbs or the Milwaukee suburbs—this was not something that was going to turn them out.

JOHN HARWOOD: Do you agree with Ken that it was fiscal issues?

MATTHEW DOWD: I was worried about that. If soft Republicans or Republicans got disappointed—if the President didn't perform as well at something, he didn't give a good speech, the first debate, which we'll get to at some point—then their level of support would drop some. It wasn't specifically issue-driven. They were disappointed on the budget deficit—Ken is exactly right—from an issue perspective. But it was disappointment in performance less so than an issue that people were worried about.

• THE DEMOCRATIC OPPONENTS •

GLORIA BORGER: Last night, you spoke a little about watching the Democratic primaries unfold before your very eyes. We heard Ken [Mehlman] say that he thought Gephardt might have been the toughest opponent at some point—

MATTHEW DOWD: Lieberman.

GLORIA BORGER: Lieberman would have been your toughest opponent? Why?

KEN MEHLMAN: I think he would have. We had words of disagreement on this.

GLORIA BORGER: All right. Let's talk about that, very quickly.

KEN MEHLMAN: We had a big discussion about this in the campaign. I think Gephardt would have been a tough opponent. Anybody would have been a tough opponent, as I said. I think Dean would have been less tough. By the time he was nominated, I think there would have been an opportunity, despite the coherence of their base, to run a kind of Nixon-McGovern campaign against a Dean. Basically, the guy is not ready for the job because of what happened late in the primaries.

But I think that Gephardt and Lieberman would have been the two toughest—probably Lieberman a little bit tougher. Ultimately, Lieberman would have appealed very strongly to Catholic voters. His personal faith, his grounding, his ability to talk about values in a way that both appeals to people that are center, and even sometimes center-right, and also appeals to people on the left. He had strong national security credentials. The weakness with Lieberman was whether people were going to see him as a strong leader. I don't think Lieberman appears that well on the stump. I don't think he wears well. I think he appears tired and not as much of a strong leader.

GLORIA BORGER: Terry, in the internal discussions in the campaign, who was your toughest opponent?

TERRY NELSON: For a while, actually, I worried about Dean. The concern I always had about Dean was that if he were successful in the primary, he would turn the corner on fiscal conservatism. He would talk a lot about it and that would have an impact with centrist voters and with some moderate Republicans. But you can make a case for a lot of the candidates. Throughout the course of the primaries, people were up and down. There were always discussions about who would be better.

GLORIA BORGER: Matt, who was yours?

MATTHEW DOWD: You have to think about it in timing because we had these discussions throughout and, at different times, different people would surface. Terry is right—Dean was a concern. But, come December, we said, I hope to God Dean stays in there—I hope he survives and the blood doesn't go out—because he basically was going to be unelectable at that point. It would be close but he would be unelectable. I was most worried about Edwards—that was who was my fear all along. I always thought Gephardt was old, tired, people weren't going to vote for him. They would think that's just the past. I never thought Lieberman had a chance in the Democratic primary with his stand on Iraq. He was never going to be the anti-Bush candidate, so I thought he could never win that part of it. In May, and I've said this before, I thought John Kerry was one of the people that I thought were possible to win. Of Dean, Edwards, Kerry, and Gephardt, Kerry was the best one for us to run against. First, his demeanor doesn't warm people up. Second, he has a twenty-year record in the Senate that we thought we could pick apart, deal with, and which would occupy a lot of time.

I was most worried about Edwards. If you see some of the things we did in the end of the process—in January—of who we attacked and when, you'll get a sense that we were, even though Ken is not saying it now, worried about Edwards. I was very worried about a guy that can win North Carolina, that is an attractive candidate, that knows how to appeal to Republicans and knows how to appeal to Independents. He didn't have a lot of history behind him and there was this false assumption that somehow he was not qualified to be president. The funny thing about this is as soon as you get the nomination, voters think you are qualified to be president. If you get the nomination of a major party, it automatically qualifies you to be president. It says, of course he could be qualified—he is the nominee of the Democratic Party or the nominee of the Republican Party. I never thought that was a big weakness on his part.

GLORIA BORGER: Okay, Nicole, where were you in the Democratic primaries? Who was your candidate?

NICOLE DEVENISH: I distinctly remember a reporter who called Edwards "The Natural," and I thought, oh God, if he wins, we're in trouble. Just from a press perspective, he was someone that when we started forming some messages around some of the primary candidates, a lot of them didn't apply to him.

GLORIA BORGER: Such as what?

NICOLE DEVENISH: Such as lack of convictions, "flip-flopping," reckless—

MATTHEW DOWD: Nutty.

NICOLE DEVENISH: Nutty. A lot of the messages that we crafted in preparation for whomever emerged would not have applied to him. The press was quite taken by him in the Democratic primaries. More than one reporter had referred to him as "The Natural" and, as a press person, that always makes you nervous.

JOHN HARWOOD: A related question that gets to something Matthew hinted at in terms of things you guys were doing at the time and who you were attacking. We saw in 2002 a path-breaking tactic by Gray Davis in the California Governor's race where, during the Republican primary, he went in and used money to advertise against the candidate he most feared running against. Were there any circumstances under which you were prepared to advertise against an emerging Democratic candidate who you thought might get the nomination and you could do something about it?

MATTHEW DOWD: The difference is whomever we attacked was going to be embolden in Democratic primary voter's minds. If we go out and attack Howard Dean, what we are doing is helping Howard Dean. You'll see, during this process, who we attacked, who Ken might have attacked, or who others in the campaign or surrogates might have attacked, was to embolden that person. So we started attacking John Kerry a lot in the end of January because we were very worried about John Edwards and we knew that if we focused on John Kerry, Democratic primary voters would sort of coalesce. It wasn't like we could tag somebody. Whomever we attacked was going to be helped.

JOHN HARWOOD: So it was in reverse?

NICOLE DEVENISH: We refused to respond to the Edwards attacks. The Edwards press corps would call and say, we don't understand why you won't give a comment. We sent every caller over to the RNC. We refused to ever engage in an Edwards attack. There is not a single quote from any of us.

GLORIA BORGER: Are you all saying that if Edwards had been the nominee, he would have had a much better chance of beating George W. Bush? Is that what you're saying?

MATTHEW DOWD: At the time, that's what we thought. My own perspective on this is that the highest point of Edwards' candidacy was in the Democratic primaries. I think, over time, he wore on people. His convention speech, from all the research we saw and everything in it, wasn't received very well by voters. So, at the time—during the Democratic primaries—that's what we thought, but by the time we got to Election Day, I don't know if that was any longer applicable. During the primary process, we saw how attractive he was.

GLORIA BORGER: Let's move on to the point where John Kerry actually becomes the presumptive nominee—not the definitive nominee but the presumptive nominee. In the February 16 CBS poll, Kerry is ahead of Bush 48-43. You started an ad in March talking about 9/11 families and that creates an awful amount of controversy.[6]

MATTHEW DOWD: Shucks.

GLORIA BORGER: Do you want to talk about that 9/11 ad for a moment and why you decided to do that at that particular point?

---

6. In March 2004, the Bush campaign released three campaign commercials that depicted images of the September 11 terrorist attacks and prompted an uproar from family members of 9/11 victims who claimed that the President was exploiting their loved ones' suffering for political gain.

KEN MEHLMAN: We always thought this election was fundamentally an election about leadership and an election about the challenges the country faces, and what's bigger than the War on Terror? September 11 is central to that whole debate. The fact that our opponents immediately attacked it and there was a lot more focus on the ad and the President's leadership after 9/11 wasn't necessarily a bad thing. All of the research we did indicated that people liked when we talked about 9/11, as long as it was done in an appropriate way, because they viewed it as central to what our country had been through. They viewed it as central to what we had to deal with going forward. They thought it was entirely appropriate.

They also, as we talked about it, viewed it as an example of the President being a strong leader. So, if you added those two things together—people thought it was relevant, they wanted to hear about it, and they, as a result, viewed the President's leadership post-9/11 as being positive, then having a big debate involving post-9/11 leadership wasn't a bad thing for us.

JOHN HARWOOD: You felt that no aspect of that controversy—the images in the ad or anything—were detrimental to the President at all?

MATTHEW DOWD: We had a lot of time and we did a lot of research based upon using certain images. Those images were chosen fairly carefully because we knew what it would elicit. We benefited by the fact that so many people in the press corps thought this was a huge controversy. There was actually a discussion. Some people got a little queasy and said, are we doing the right thing? We got seven to eight million dollars worth of free run on this. The fact that George Bush's highest point of his presidency is related to 9/11 and we got ads with 9/11 in it, and everybody is talking about it—we couldn't have asked for better.

GLORIA BORGER: So no downside?

MATTHEW DOWD: There was no downside.

• THE 87 BILLION DOLLAR QUESTION •

GLORIA BORGER: That was in March. March 17 is the, now famous, "I actually did vote for the $87 billion before I voted against it." There are press reports, as you all know, in *Newsweek* that talk about the fact that this was a set up. I want to know the truth about what really happened with "I voted for the $87 billion before I voted against it." I don't know who is best qualified to answer this question.

KEN MEHLMAN: It was a Sunday afternoon, as I recall, and we heard that Senator Kerry was going to West Virginia to talk about support for the troops.

NICOLE DEVENISH: No, veterans' health care.

KEN MEHLMAN: Veterans' health care.

MATTHEW DOWD: And he might bring up body armor.

KEN MEHLMAN: He had brought up body armor before.

MATTHEW DOWD: Yes, but he was going to be before a veterans' group.

KEN MEHLMAN: So we thought if he brought it up before and he is talking about support for the troops, that issue might come up again, so let's try to cut this ad. I think he went on a Tuesday.

MATTHEW DOWD: Yes, he went on a Tuesday because we had to send it out by Monday night.

KEN MEHLMAN: Right. So we found this out and put this ad together quickly.

NICOLE DEVENISH: Put out flyers, too.

KEN MEHLMAN: One of the things that we did whenever we could—we tried to locally go in and do ads a lot—was Terry [Nelson] would have his folks with flyers doing the same thing, or sometimes newspaper ads doing the same thing, so that you really would create some earned media. We put the ad up. Kerry got there that day, it was all over the television, and he made his famous statement.

MATTHEW DOWD: And then we recut the ad. We got the statement. Everybody in the campaign realized this is a perfect thing to clarify.

GLORIA BORGER: Was it your heckler? That's the question.

MATTHEW DOWD: No.

KEN MEHLMAN: No, it wasn't. Remember, the heckler spoke. He wasn't our heckler, but he asked the question in a different form. It was later on when that question was asked. There was the Pennsylvania guy that brought it up.

MATTHEW DOWD: Kerry brought it up himself in response to the ad. He said, they're running an ad saying that I voted against this but let me tell you the truth, this is the deal. Then, he said that statement. We realize it's a great nine-second clip which we immediately, that day, put in another ad and send right back out.

NICOLE DEVENISH: There was controversy with this one, too, because we had used C-SPAN footage. It was running everywhere. There was also controversy about us using footage from the floor of the Senate.

MATTHEW DOWD: This became a funny thing.

NICOLE DEVENISH: It became an oxymoron—"ad controversy." It's TV running a message that works over and over. But this is the second time it had happened.

KEN MEHLMAN: Because you are not supposed to use roll call votes from the floor. So we thought that, from now on, we were going to have all of our ads have controversy. We were going to do another "rats" ad—rats two—but we decided not to.[7] (Laughter.)

NICOLE DEVENISH: No, we weren't.

• CRITIQUING THE KERRY CAMPAIGN •

JOHN HARWOOD: This incident underscores the point that you guys made, and were driving, before Kerry said that, which was that you thought he had a problem both connecting and with "flip-flops" with the long record. That goes to the candidate.

   After Kerry emerged from the primary period, how did you assess, from a distance, the effectiveness of their campaign operation? That is the Kerry campaign operation, decisionmaking, fundraising, communications, their political operation. How well did you think they were doing and did you see problems there that were benefiting you?

KEN MEHLMAN: They ran a great primary race.

JOHN HARWOOD: I'm talking about in the post-primary period.

KEN MEHLMAN: They raised a tremendous amount of money. I thought that there was a month period where we were more nimble, more quick, and

---

7. In 2000, a television advertisement placed by the Republican National Committee quickly flashed the word "Rats" in reference to Vice President Gore's prescription drug plan. Critics asserted that the word's rapid appearance and disappearance was an attempt at subliminal advertising.

more able to rapidly respond to things than they were. That's partly what they identified—your supply lines take a while to follow up and we experienced that in 2000, which informed our thinking. One of the reasons we thought March was such an important time to do a lot of television advertising, to do a lot of earned media things, to try to do the things like the West Virginia thing was, having been there in 2000, that's a tough period for a campaign. It's a dangerous period because you are growing quickly and the ability to make decisions quickly can be hard. We thought that was a period of vulnerability for them and we tried to use it to be very aggressive in driving the message and in defining Senator Kerry. The other thing was he had support that was a mile wide and very thin, very shallow, because of the fact that people didn't really know who he was. All they knew is he won each week. So they knew he was a winner and they had seen him on television every Tuesday night. We thought the combination of the natural way that campaigns are—right when they win the nomination and have to expand big time—with someone who is not very well-defined presented a very good opportunity.

JOHN HARWOOD: As you were watching them operate, given the assets and the liabilities that they had, were you sitting there seeing fifteen things—had you switched places and you were running their campaign—that you would have done differently? If so, what were they?

KEN MEHLMAN: You're never in their shoes, so you don't know. One of the things that I did think was that, for a while, they seemed to take the bait a lot. If we brought up an issue, they would respond to it.

GLORIA BORGER: Such as?

KEN MEHLMAN: Such as the $87 billion.

NICOLE DEVENISH: Such as, some questions the commander in chief has to answer with a yes or no—knowing now what you know, would you have voted the same? We really didn't think he would answer that question.

KEN MEHLMAN: In fact, there was even a debate on that.

NICOLE DEVENISH: We had a huge internal debate about that. If he said no, that would be bad for us, we would have a real difference, he would have seized a position.

MATTHEW DOWD: We all play the hand we're dealt. We knew they were lacking resources in that post-primary phase. It's a big reason why we were going to spend $40 million in March. One, because, as Ken said, he was a mile wide and an inch deep, but also because we knew they couldn't respond.

NICOLE DEVENISH: They were just staffing up. We had had a communications and a rapid response operation in place. We had forty people, waiting to see who emerged, who had studied his record. There are advantages in the communications shop to having all this time to set up a response apparatus—to get to know the press covering the Democratic candidates. We were ready to go and we really did spring into action.

MATTHEW DOWD: The thing that I think should have been done differently, and they probably had no control over this because 527s are independent— (Laughter.)

JOHN HARWOOD: The record will reflect he rolled his eyes.

GLORIA BORGER: We'll get to that.

MATTHEW DOWD: I thought the 527s on their side would have benefited Kerry more by putting ads up on Kerry, defining Kerry rather than putting these bullshit ads up, excuse me, on us. All these ads calling Bush a liar—voters weren't going to believe it, they weren't going to change. All of these negative ads on the President. As people have mentioned, they would have been much better having $50 million spent by the 527s with ads defining John Kerry.

• A ROUGH SPRING •

GLORIA BORGER: But you had a very rough spring. Somebody before mentioned the prison scandal.

NICOLE DEVENISH: All the books, Dick Clarke.[8]

GLORIA BORGER: Okay, so you had John Kerry winning every Tuesday night—thumbs up. You had a very bad spring with Abu Ghraib, Dick Clarke, Condi Rice testifying on the Hill,[9] and 9/11 families being angry at you.

---

8. In the spring of 2004, Richard Clarke, the former National Coordinator for Terrorism, released his book, *Against All Enemies: Inside America's War on Terror*, in which he offered a harsh critique of President Bush's counterterrorism policies.

9. On April 8, 2004, National Security Advisor Condoleezza Rice testified publicly before the 9/11 Commission.

Whether or not that was good for you, that's another issue in terms of your advertising. So, Nicole, what did you do proactively here?

NICOLE DEVENISH: We turned our response operation into an offensive. The White House was dealing with being commander in chief and really did control the President's message. We turned the campaign communications operation, really in its entirety, into a response apparatus that was on offense. Do you disagree?

KEN MEHLMAN: Just a little bit, to slightly differ with your analysis. I think we had a very good March and first half of April. I really do.

GLORIA BORGER: Abu Ghraib was April 28. You're right, okay.

KEN MEHLMAN: The beginning of the spring was good. We were on the offensive. We were helping define the race. The second half of the spring was really bad.

There were two challenges that we always have to deal with when we talk about Iraq and it's one of the reasons Senator Kerry was less able to take advantage of it. One, the fact that Kerry's own record was all over the place and complicated on that issue. Secondly, if you look historically, when people reject an incumbent because they are worried about an issue that's out there, they reject the incumbent because they think the challenger has a certain quality that helps deal with the issue they are worried about. In 1980, the public viewed the Iran Hostage Crisis as evidence that Jimmy Carter was a weak leader, which they always thought, and they wanted a strong leader, Ronald Reagan.[10] In 1992, when the famous checkout thing occurred with the former President George Bush, and when people heard economic news they didn't think was good enough, they wanted a guy that was going to focus on the economy.[11] That had always been Clinton's definition.

If people thought Iraq was really messed up and was a tougher battle than before, then they wanted someone who would be a strong leader, which Kerry, at that point, was defined as not being, as compared to the President. That was always the fundamental challenge they faced. He did have a heroic record, he did have national security experience, but he wasn't defined as a

---

10. President Carter's inability to achieve the release of U.S. citizens held hostage in Iran by Islamic revolutionaries contributed to his loss to Ronald Reagan in the 1980 presidential election.

11. During the 1992 election, President George H. W. Bush reportedly reacted with amazement to the technological sophistication of a supermarket checkout scanner, an action that contributed to the perception that he was out of touch with ordinary Americans.

strong a leader as the President was, which made it much harder for them to take advantage of that.

JOHN HARWOOD: Let me ask you one more question about this period before we move to the vice presidential portion of the campaign. As I recall, this was your low point of the year—the combination of Clarke and Abu Ghraib—and I remember conversations with you guys. This is when Bush's ratings, I believe, got to the mid-forties or mid-to-low forties—the lowest they were all year.

MATTHEW DOWD: I tried to set the bar down to forty.

JOHN HARWOOD: But you had earlier set it at forty-five. (Laughter.)

MATTHEW DOWD: I know. I was going to reset it again. (Laughter.)

JOHN HARWOOD: As we got further from Abu Ghraib, Bush's numbers floated back up into the high forties. Had that not happened—had you gotten stuck in the mid-forties—what was plan B? What would we have seen from your campaign that we didn't see to try to cope with that situation?

KEN MEHLMAN: Prayer. (Laughter.) When we looked at those numbers, we lowered expectations further. (Laughter.) You saw a buoyancy to our numbers and a floor that was remarkable. During this period, the Republican support is still staying at 90 percent. So, while it was an unpleasant period and while we certainly were aggressive—if you remember, this is also toward the end of that period when Kerry gave the "heart and soul" comment, which was a gift. In Radio City Music Hall, Kerry said, Whoopi Goldberg and Hollywood are the "heart and soul of America."[12] That was an opportunity for us. It was when he made his comments, I'm actually the conservative running the race, I believe life begins at conception. There were a whole series of things like that that obviously were opportunities to change the debate, and so that's what we tried to do.

NICOLE DEVENISH: What we did, message-wise, is we focused on Kerry. In this bad period, there was nothing, as a campaign, we could do about the prison abuse.

---

12. On July 8, 2004, Whoopi Goldberg and other Hollywood celebrities headlined a Kerry-Edwards fundraiser at Radio City Music Hall in New York. The event included a variety of tawdry references and harsh criticisms of President Bush and was later seized on by the President as an illustration of what he claimed was Senator Kerry's distorted value system.

GLORIA BORGER: Matt, did you have a day when you thought it was over?

MATTHEW DOWD: Over like—?

GLORIA BORGER: Like you weren't going to win.

MATTHEW DOWD: No. I had every day where I was worried about it. We hit our low, it was forty-four or forty-five, which is not good but it's not in the 27 percent range of his father or in Jimmy Carter's 32 percent. But I also thought we were going to have opportunities to fix that a little bit. We always thought our convention was an opportunity to bump our job approval by four or five points. So, even at those low points, which I thought would dissipate after some scandals went away and other things, I didn't think we were going to lose. Obviously, I was very worried. But we couldn't start running positive television spots during Abu Ghraib to help rehabilitate the President's image. Voters would have called B.S. on us. So all we could do was talk about Kerry.

JOHN HARWOOD: Could Bush have possibly won the election if he walked into Election Day at forty-five?

MATTHEW DOWD: I'm glad we didn't have to test that premise.

KEN MEHLMAN: One of the biggest challenges that I'm sure they faced, and we faced, too, is whenever things aren't good, you've got every person in the outside world saying run ads, spend money. There is a hysteria that you have to be confident enough to avoid or else you end up constantly changing strategies.

• THE VEEP SELECTION •

GLORIA BORGER: That's a good segue for us to get to the Democratic veep selection. You were watching your own vice president's numbers go down. Dick Cheney was good for the base but he was a polarizer. On the vice presidential selection process, I'll start with you, Matt, because you were so worried about Edwards during the primaries. Did you think Edwards was the best choice for John Kerry to make?

MATTHEW DOWD: After John McCain, I think he was the best choice for John Kerry to make. My assumption was, how can you not pick John Edwards? He is popular, he is a heck of a campaigner, he is young, he is new generation, he is from North Carolina. To me, he is the natural person to pick and I always thought he would pick him. Once McCain came off the list, or however that happened, I thought Edwards was the next one.

GLORIA BORGER: Well, Ken Mehlman, what did you do to make sure that McCain did not run with John Kerry?

KEN MEHLMAN: Remember, in January, John McCain campaigned for the President in New Hampshire. We had plans for him to do other stuff with the President. They went out on the road again together later on and we cut an ad based on their traveling together. I think the event they did together was about a month before June 7th, before the vice president was chosen, so this was something that we didn't think was a real possibility. The question was, how could we use the buzz about McCain, with our knowledge that McCain was going to be with us, in a way so as to define all their choices being second choices, which is what the ad did.

GLORIA BORGER: How did you make sure McCain wasn't going to be with them? That's my question. Was it Karl [Rove] who went to McCain?

MATTHEW DOWD: McCain is easily controlled and we went to him and then— (Laughter.)

GLORIA BORGER: This is delicate. How did it happen?

KEN MEHLMAN: You know, a million dollars and a plane. No, I'm kidding. (Laughter.) The fact is he wasn't going to do it. This was something that he didn't want to do.

JOHN HARWOOD: He said it would have weakened it.

KEN MEHLMAN: Exactly. This was his decision. As Matthew says, John McCain is not somebody that you could control by giving him a good seat at the convention. You just don't do that. He made a decision, and the question is how you managed his decisions.

JOHN HARWOOD: Did you think that they made a mistake in letting the McCain talk get out there as much as it did?

KEN MEHLMAN: Yes, but I don't know that they did that. I think others may have done that.

JOHN HARWOOD: How do you assess how they ran their vice presidential selection process? Would they have been better served by rolling out their veep right adjacent to the convention, rather than doing it a week or two ahead of time and letting some of the buzz dissipate? Would that have made their convention more consequential?

KEN MEHLMAN: I thought they did a very good job. I think what Mary Beth [Cahill] said is absolutely right—they had a limited number of people, there weren't a lot of leaks, it was handled extremely well, it was respectful to the people that were involved in the process. I thought it was extremely well done and I think the timing was good.

JOHN HARWOOD: You do not think their convention would have been more successful, had they done it closer?

KEN MEHLMAN: No. I think the way they did it, which was to have two separate things as an opportunity to define it two separate times, was very smart and very well done.

NICOLE DEVENISH: And with all the interviews that were done, they ran the month.

MATTHEW DOWD: They occupied a few weeks leading into the convention talking about how great John Edwards was, so I think it was done very well.

NICOLE DEVENISH: Yes, it was great.

KEN MEHLMAN: I don't think it was done in any way that caused folks who were not chosen to be viewed as being dissed. That did happen a little bit in 2000 to some people.

GLORIA BORGER: Do you believe that, in the end, John Edwards left a big footprint as a vice presidential nominee?

MATTHEW DOWD: I thought that his high point was in the primary process and, by the time you got to Election Day, his stature was dramatically lower than it was when it started. That's my view. As people watched him give speeches over the course of that time, his stature dropped from the high point it was during the end of the primaries.

KEN MEHLMAN: I agree with that. It reminded me a little bit of Jack Kemp in 1996 where the concept was better than the reality. There were times when it seemed like Edwards didn't really want to get into what the vice presidential nominee's job is. I remember watching the two convention speeches and being struck by the fact that Edwards' speech was less going after the President than Kerry's was. I was surprised by that.

JOHN HARWOOD: One question about your vice presidential process which, of course, wasn't much of a process. I never saw any indication from anybody inside the White House or the campaign that there was serious consideration given to changing the vice presidential candidate. Let me start with Terry. To what degree were you hearing supporters urge you to do something about it, given his numbers? Did that happen at all or was it completely a press fantasy?

TERRY NELSON: It didn't happen. We never heard that from folks out in the states—from the grassroots. There was not a lot of talk about getting rid of the Vice President. There was a lot of enthusiasm for his events. It wasn't a factor.

KEN MEHLMAN: Remember how much he did in 2002 for congressional candidates. Remember how much he did in 2004 raising resources for us. So, among the people around the country, they had seen him in 2002 help elect their congressman or their senator or their governor. He has a tremendous level of support among the grassroots and among donors around the country because there is a personal knowledge and connection with him because he has been so generous with his time on behalf of other candidates.

JOHN HARWOOD: So, to the extent that was in the press, it was either driven entirely by press speculation or by people on the other side?

MATTHEW DOWD: People want a story. They'd love to have a story that we were going to pick somebody new at the convention, as opposed to the same ticket. I'm sure that was a big part of it. People wanted something new. But I'll go back to the original premise on this—the fact that Dick Cheney somehow is polarizing. We had a top of the ticket that either people loved or they didn't like. It wasn't like the vice presidential candidate was going to somehow change the polarization around the President. That was pretty firmly established in people's minds and so I don't think that would have made much difference at all in voters' perceptions. Nobody in the campaign and no supporters were anywhere near it.

• LEARNING LESSONS FROM THE DEMOCRATIC CONVENTION •

GLORIA BORGER: Nicole, we are going to move here to the Democratic Convention. I want to know, first of all, how all of you guys watched it, and

Matthew Dowd and Nicole Devenish share a light moment.

what you were watching it for? I want to find out what ideas you got out of it. Nicole, what were you looking for and what surprised you?

NICOLE DEVENISH: We started preparing our response operation for Boston at the end of June. The RNC had a big role. [RNC Chairman] Ed Gillespie led that with Steve Schmidt, our director of response. We put a lot of time into planning our response operation up there. It really does help when you go second. We learned that the press had some windows in the middle of the day and learned how many opportunities there were for cable packages. We really designed an operation around the needs of the press that would be camped out there for ten days.

Our message that month was priorities and we rolled that out in July. There was some discussion but that was the month that we rolled out ads about opposition to Laci and Conner's Law[13] and partial-birth abortion.[14] Then, we lumped in there, as priorities, tax cuts for families and support for the troops. That was our message that month. Having Rudy [Giuliani] and

13. The Unborn Victims of Violence Act, also known as "Laci and Conner's Law" was signed into law by President Bush on April 1, 2004. The measure made the act of killing or injuring both a woman and her fetus two distinct federal crimes. The legislation was unofficially named for Laci Peterson.
14. A ban on "partial-birth" abortions was signed into law by President Bush on November 5, 2003.

other top-level surrogates up there—available and throwing open the doors to our response operation in Boston—was a bigger success than we could have imagined.[15]

GLORIA BORGER: Matt, what about the general themes of the convention—the John Kerry "reporting for duty?"

MATTHEW DOWD: The funny thing about conventions is they don't matter until the last speech of the last night. Ultimately, they are all great and fun and we all make a lot of plans, but most convention numbers don't move until the nominee's speech—whether it's the President or it's their candidate. There can be a little bit around the vice president. So that's what we were all waiting for—what kind of speech John Kerry would deliver, what he would say. I was actually a little surprised that there wasn't more filled in—in a more formal way—on John Kerry's record in public policy prior to his speech. But again, I don't think that mattered until you get to his speech.

I think there were good parts of Kerry's speech, but I also think there were other parts of it, like the 6 or 7 percent talking about Vietnam. We focus-grouped it that night. We dialed it the night of the convention.[16] I think we did the dial group in Denver in order to get it in time. Voters hated this part. Voters hated the salute thing. They thought it was juvenile. They thought, what is he doing that for?

They were sick of the Vietnam stuff, from what we could tell, and we had sort of known that going into it. They were like, why are we talking about Vietnam? What does that have to do with the cost of health care? What does that have to do with anything I'm facing in my life? When Kerry talked about outsourcing, it tested very well. We thought he would get a small bump out of it. I know I said there was a historical pattern that said he was supposed to get fifteen points out of it! (Laughter.) He didn't meet the historical pattern. But the convention, and primarily his speech, was a much shorter lived bump than we thought it would be. We thought they would go into our convention being up four or five points, but they were even. I think that was a function of his speech not being as long lasting in changing voter attitudes as we thought it would be.

JOHN HARWOOD: Mark and Mary Beth, how did your dials compare to his dials?

---

15. Rudolph Giuliani served as mayor of New York City from 1993 to 2001.

16. A focus group is a tool for evaluating public opinion which brings a group of people together for the purpose of gauging their reactions to a particular event. A dial test is a particular type of focus group, in which participants are equipped with numbered dials and asked to turn the dial to reflect their level of satisfaction at any given moment; this allows observers to break down reactions moment to moment and determine how a particular event is received across different ages, ethnicities, or genders.

MARK MELLMAN: We actually did not test his speech that night. We did have polling on the speech and it was extraordinarily positive. We compared it to the response to the Bush speech and responses to speeches four years ago and it was ten, fifteen, twenty points better than the responses to the other speeches.

JOHN HARWOOD: Does it sound right to you that voters found the salute a big mistake?

MARK MELLMAN: I don't have any particular idea of that. I would say it's hard for me to believe that that was something people carried away or remembered. We never heard about it in any focus group we did. We never heard about it in any polling.

MATTHEW DOWD: The problem is, from what we saw, they didn't really carry anything away from the convention speech. Initially, there was a slight change in whether or not Kerry was a strong leader—he improved that. There was a slight change in how well people trusted him on Iraq. But, within ten days or a week, it was gone. So there was no lasting impact of his speech at the convention.

JOHN HARWOOD: Do all of you agree with Mary Beth that the mere fact of the timing of the conventions was a huge factor in the campaign—that it might have changed the outcome had the timing been reversed? Or did all that wash out once we got to the general?

MATTHEW DOWD: I'll tell you a funny story about that. In 2001, when [DNC Chairman] Terry McAuliffe announced the date of the Democratic Convention—which I think was originally July 15—I sent a memo to Karl [Rove] within a week or two. We thought Terry was trying to force us in a box. Since the Olympics was going to start at the beginning of August, he was going to force us into having our convention quickly after theirs. The Olympics would happen, and then we would have the eight-week campaign. I sent a note to Karl and said, let's hold our convention at the end of August, the beginning of September, and force them into the box where we have five extra weeks of money. We would have the Olympics in between that will step on their bounce. We did have to deal with the fact that you are supposed to have delegates selected at certain times, so we had to change the state law in about twelve states in order to do this. But, in the end—and we knew this was a very important thing—we were able to do it and force Terry to deal with it. Terry ended up changing their convention by a week so; instead of six weeks, we only had four-and-a-half weeks longer. It was very important to have the Olympics in between.

JOHN HARWOOD: Did it potentially change the outcome of the election?

MATTHEW DOWD: I'm not one that says this thing changed the outcome of the election because, in the end, it has a lot to do with the President's job approval on Election Day. It had a big impact.

JOHN HARWOOD: A big impact obviously—just look at thirteen weeks versus nine weeks of money.

MARK MELLMAN: Can I just add to that? Because I think the money piece is a critically important part and the nine weeks versus thirteen. The other point is the actual timing of their convention—in September—abuts the official press start of the campaign on Labor Day. So it not only makes it much closer, with less time for the impact to dissipate, it also affects the coverage.

GLORIA BORGER: Ken, do you want to say something about your overall impression of the Democratic Convention? You certainly liked those Swift Boats.

KEN MEHLMAN: Just to follow up on what both Nicole and Matthew said, let me talk about what we learned in terms of how we executed our convention. The Kerry speech was the culmination of their convention and the danger was, what happens after the culmination? Does it fall? How do you have a bounce coming out?

So what we did is make the President's speech the first time we laid out the future-looking agenda. Then we had an ad campaign behind it. The President did a whole tour where he talked about it, we had books we handed out, and we did all kinds of things to show how serious we were about this. That was one lesson.

Secondly, in our convention, both the speakers before the President and the President himself talked extensively about his record in the last four years to contrast with the fact that the Democrats hadn't talked about their record at all.

Third, we tried to use the month of August to really step on their bounce.

GLORIA BORGER: Let's just talk quickly about the month of August because we've got to get to your convention.

MATTHEW DOWD: One other thing to add on this. Their 9/11 imagery helped us in New York at our convention. There was a huge discussion in the campaign about how we were going to deal with 9/11 in New York at the convention. What are we going to do? We have to be sensitive—how are we going to do it? How political is it going to be? Then the Democrats did the Bic lighter or whatever thing they did—I don't exactly remember—and it was a very well-done, very tastefully done tribute and it was well received.[17] After that, we thought, okay, we have free rein to basically talk about this as much as we want in a way we want because then we can say, listen, the Democrats had their deal, they did their thing. We're in New York—what are you supposed to do, not talk about it? That gave us an opportunity and we became much less worried about what we were going to do related to 9/11 in New York.

JOHN HARWOOD: Did that make it a mistake for them to do what they did?

MATTHEW DOWD: I don't think so. They had to do it. They are the other major party in the country that deals with the most significant event that's happened in the last fifty years. They had to.

KEN MEHLMAN: It gets back to the first question you asked. The public understands the incredible significance of 9/11. You couldn't in 1944 have run a campaign and not talked about Pearl Harbor because that explained where we were. Both campaigns had to figure out a tasteful way to deal with it and, if you hadn't have, you wouldn't have been relevant to the future discussion.

• THE SWIFT BOAT ADS •

GLORIA BORGER: Let's talk about the Swift Boat ads. Ken, we know the President condemned the 527s in general, but why didn't the President come out and condemn the Swift Boat ads?

KEN MEHLMAN: Because the President is not an ad critic and the President doesn't think that it's his job to be out there saying this ad is good, this ad is bad. The President had a principled position on these things which was he opposed all the 527 ads. There are plenty of people who are our friends, who were involved in 527 ads, who didn't appreciate it every time we said that we condemned these 527 ads. But, as I mentioned last night, I thought it was certainly very hypocritical to have Senator Kerry saying that some Vietnam vets have earned the right to free speech and others haven't. The fact

---

17. Democrats staged a memorial to the victims of the 9/11 terrorist attacks on July 26, 2004, the first day of their national convention. Convention goers were given individual electronic lights which they held up in quiet tribute to those who had been killed or injured.

that these guys were following the law, expressing their free speech, we didn't think that we should step on that free speech. We thought that wasn't appropriate.

JOHN HARWOOD: If we accept your campaign's contention that you guys had nothing to do with the Swift Boat ads, like they say they didn't have anything to do with the Democratic 527s, did you nevertheless always expect that somebody would launch an effort like what the Swift Boat Veterans did? And, if that had not happened, how would the campaign have been different?

KEN MEHLMAN: I was actually pleasantly surprised by the effectiveness of Republican-leaning 527s. Republican donors tend to be hierarchical—they give to a candidate and they give to a party. They are much less likely, historically and even this time, to invest in these kind of things for a lot of different reasons. We got outspent by more than $100 million on 527s.

I was very concerned that the strategy we had—to basically say we're not even going to wink-and-nod, we are not going to be in favor of these 527s—would leave us out in the cold. The strategy was based on the President's policy, so we had no choice.

If you look at both the Swift Boat ads and that "Ashley" ad[18] at the end, you saw some extremely effective advertising that actually, even though they spent half as much money, were more memorable and made a case more effectively than the other side's ads did. But it was something that I was very concerned about. I always said that if you said to me, what are you most worried about, the relative disparity on 527s was something I worried about tremendously.

JOHN HARWOOD: You thought the Swift Boat ads were extremely beneficial to your campaign?

KEN MEHLMAN: I don't know if they were beneficial to our campaign. I thought that because John Kerry had so defined himself on his service in Vietnam, his response to one of the Swift Boat ads versus his belief that Wesley Clark ought to be able to speak about the issue was hypocritical. They were well-done ads and, whatever you think of the merits of the ads, the people in

---

18. The Progress for America Voter Fund, a 527, aired the "Ashley" ad in October 2004. It showed President Bush's compassionate treatment of a young woman whose mother had been killed on September 11 and concluded with the woman's father declaring, "What I saw was what I want to see in the heart and in the soul of the man who sits in the highest-elected office in our country."

the ads are incredibly honorable. They served their country incredibly well, just like John Kerry did.

GLORIA BORGER: Joe Trippi wants to ask a question.

• IT'S ALL ABOUT THE MONEY •

JOE TRIPPI: The question that I'm dying to know from both of you is, at any point, was there any discussion in the campaign to opt out of the public funding for the general election?

KEN MEHLMAN: No.

JOE TRIPPI: Was there ever a serious question? Because you would have had to make that decision before you got the nomination.

MATTHEW DOWD: Was it a serious question that came up in discussion? Yes. But the problem is that in order to net the $73 million and then the money you raise, you have to raise $115 to 120 million, and that's just initially. That means you are taking money away from other candidates running for senate. So that's one thing. The other thing is the opportunity costs—you've got to send the Vice President somewhere, you've got to send the President somewhere, you've got to do all that kind of stuff. In the end, for us, we had eight weeks left. It wasn't going to be easy spending $80 million in eight weeks anyway because our time frame was already reduced and because of the cost to raise the money. It was never a serious question.

KEN MEHLMAN: The other thing is, at that time, if you are raising money for the DNC and RNC, you are raising that money in $25,000 increments or $10,000 increments. If you are raising it for yourself, you are raising it in $2,000 increments.[19] So, from that perspective—particularly because, for a lot of our ads, we were able to go 50-50 with the RNC, which the Kerry campaign ultimately did, too—in no way would it have been cost efficient to do.

JOHN HARWOOD: Another question about money before your convention because you were still spending primary money at that point. A lot of

19. During the 2004 election cycle, under the Bipartisan Campaign Reform Act of 2002, individuals could donate a maximum of $2,000 to an individual candidate, $25,000 to a national party committee, and $10,000 to state and local party committees over the course of the election cycle.

Democrats, after the election, were surprised and dismayed to learn that the Kerry campaign had a bunch of money leftover from their primary campaign,[20] aside from the GLAC money that you spend for legal and accounting expenses.[21] What was your thinking about what amount was prudent to have left over, in the event of some post-election controversy? And how could you have used that money, had you had it?

KEN MEHLMAN: We had a wind-down plan. We had left over, initially, in September, for bills, $500,000 and, by the end of the campaign, we had $50,000. From an internal budgeting perspective, if divisions didn't spend their money at the end of each month and, by the time it was the spring, at the end of each week, I took it. The effect was that we didn't have late bills coming in because then they wouldn't be able to pay for it and they would have to come ask for extra resources. So the system was built in a way that encouraged division heads to get their bills in early and paid for that reason.

JOHN HARWOOD: But you felt no reason to have a pot of money sitting around at the end of the process for use later?

KEN MEHLMAN: No. We had some general money that we kept for that purpose. But because I set up that rule in the beginning, nobody kept money.

JOHN HARWOOD: Mary Beth, do you want to speak to this one?

MARY BETH CAHILL: In your last FEC filing, I think you had $2.2 million in your primary account.

KEN MEHLMAN: There are bills that cover all of that.

MARY BETH CAHILL: Okay. So it was the same thing with us. We'll probably end up with about $7 million left. We believed that this was a 50-50 race. We believed we were going to be in a recount. We had four planes standing there on Election Day waiting to take lawyers to various states. We had a huge battery of attorneys and we wanted to be able to fund that. Since the election, Kerry has given $250,000 to the recount in the gubernatorial election in Washington state. We gave $40 million to the DNC during the

20. Senator Kerry had approximately $14 million left over in his presidential primary fund after the 2004 election.
21. The General Election Legal and Accounting Compliance Fund (GLAC) is generally intended for the "closeout costs" of campaigns and could also be used to pay the costs of election recounts.

course of the general election from our primary account because we raised a huge amount of money close to the end and around our convention. The last night of the convention, we raised $5.3 million on the Internet, which was something that was without precedent. We had more money than we thought we would. We gave more money to the DNC than anybody ever has. In the final days, we couldn't buy any more television.

GLORIA BORGER: That's for the general election discussion.

MATTHEW DOWD: The sick thing of all this, about campaign finance reform, is that the total amount of money that was available was ridiculous. The fact that the Kerry campaign ended up with X amount of dollars—what were they going to do, run another 300 points when we all had 3,000 points a week in the last three weeks? It became hard to spend the amount of money that was sitting there.

• NEW YORK: THE REPUBLICAN CONVENTION •

GLORIA BORGER: I'm going to have to move on really quickly to your convention. Let me ask you, Matt, because you were the one so worried going into the convention that you needed to make the President softer, gentler, kinder, cares more about people like me.

MATTHEW DOWD: Shares your values.

GLORIA BORGER: Shares your values. Did it work?

MATTHEW DOWD: Yes. We thought we had a very successful convention for two reasons. The first was the President's speech and, as Ken has talked about, the fact that people were going to finally hear an agenda for the next four years. That was the first thing.

The second thing, which I think people missed, is that the four most popular people in this country were at the Republican Convention, testifying to why the President should stay president. The four most popular people in the country are Laura Bush, Arnold Schwarzenegger, [Senator] John McCain, and Rudy Guiliani. Whether you are a Democrat or a Republican, those are the four most popular people.

GLORIA BORGER: But, except for Laura Bush, they disagree with the President on a lot of issues.

MATTHEW DOWD: It didn't matter because they stood up there at the convention and said, this is the guy at this time that we need for these reasons. That was a huge benefit.

NICOLE DEVENISH: That was a press obsession—that the people at the convention had different positions on certain issues. There was never really a national press story line there.

MATTHEW DOWD: And the Democrats didn't have it. The best they could have was somebody that had a one-to-one fav/unfav at their convention.

KEN MEHLMAN: The fact that they disagreed on some issues was actually a positive thing, not a negative thing. I thought Arnold Schwarzenegger's speech was particularly effective. Here is someone, who the public knows disagrees on some issues, talking about what it means to be a Republican and why, even if you disagree on some issues, you should support the President. I thought that was actually an added benefit. The more the media talked about how they disagreed, and then they said these wonderful things, was good, not bad.

MATTHEW DOWD: One other thing—Zell Miller's speech was a huge plus.[22]

JOHN HARWOOD: That's what I was going to ask you. How did you arrive at the selection of Miller as your keynoter? And how did you critique the effectiveness of his speech?

KEN MEHLMAN: There was a symbolic significance. The guy that in 1992 introduced Bill Clinton in Madison Square Garden would be the keynoter for George W. Bush in 2004 in Madison Square Garden.

GLORIA BORGER: Whose idea was it?

KEN MEHLMAN: I don't remember whose idea it was.

MATTHEW DOWD: Well, I was at the 1992 convention in a different capacity than when I was at this convention. In my Democratic days. (Laugh-

---

22. On September 1, 2004, Senator Zell Miller (D-GA) delivered the keynote address at the Republican National Convention. Senator Miller aggressively challenged Senator Kerry's voting record on issues of national security, proclaiming that "twenty years of votes can tell you much more about a man than twenty weeks of campaign rhetoric." Senator Miller's remarks were criticized by many Democratic observers.

ter.) Zell's speech in 1992 was outstanding. I thought it was the best speech in 1992. He talked about where he came from. His voice was perfect. Since Zell was already with the President, I raised the thought of having him as a major speaker because I thought it would send a signal—a Democratic senator from Georgia. This was the kind of person we needed to testify to the President.

Ken is right. We were in New York. It was the first time Republicans were in New York. The last time Zell gave a big speech was twelve years ago when he nominated Bill Clinton, the new face in the Democratic Party, a moderate. The speech Zell gave was very well received by a lot of voters out there. This idea that people reacted against it, that he was too angry—

JOHN HARWOOD: How did you guys evaluate the critique that he was too hot, too angry?

KEN MEHLMAN: I went on the trip with the President after the convention and everywhere the President went, he would mention Zell Miller and the place would go absolutely nuts in a way that they went with nobody else.

NICOLE DEVENISH: That was the case through Election Day.

KEN MEHLMAN: That weekend, there was all this negative coverage.

JOHN HARWOOD: You saw no fallout with those soft Republicans that you had worried about?

MATTHEW DOWD: No fallout. We saw a big net plus because the average person, let's say, in Green Bay, Wisconsin—and I like to say that because we did research there about this—saw him as a Democratic senator, testifying on behalf of a Republican, at a convention in New York about national security. They don't know all the back and forth—did he vote for this, vote for that? It was a big plus for people.

JOHN HARWOOD: Did the Kerry campaign think it was a big plus for Bush as well?

MARK MELLMAN: Honestly, I thought it was a plus that we tried to make into a minus and—(laughter)—less successfully. For the reasons Matt said. The tone was not a positive. It was not a tone that was well received and we tried to exploit that fact. But the people, at the end of the day, were more interested in the fact that a Democrat had given a speech than they were in the tone of it.

NICOLE DEVENISH: We also had paid and earned messaging leading up to the convention about their party being out of the mainstream. The selection of Zell, and the media we earned off naming him as our keynote, certainly helped further that story line.

KEN MEHLMAN: Zell left the convention and did an event with the mayor of Youngstown, Ohio, the mayor of St. Paul, Minnesota, and the mayor of Miami Beach, Florida—all of whom had endorsed the President, all of whom were Democrats.

NICOLE DEVENISH: You thought Zell was angry! (Laughter.)

GLORIA BORGER: We talked about John Kerry's speech during his convention. We talked a little bit about the President's speech, which was in the theater-in-the-round, in the center of the floor of the convention. He spoke an awful lot about his faith. He admitted to making mistakes, which he had never done before.

MATTHEW DOWD: For all of us who see President Bush on a regular basis, the thing that had been missed a lot in the run up to that was the caring, emotional, connected side of the President. In the aftermath of 9/11, the thing that boosted our numbers the most was not what a lot of people focused on. It was when he almost broke down in the Oval Office. That was a huge thing to voters—that the President cared that much. It's when he saw soldiers and people saw them hug him. The two parts of this were an agenda for the future and, also, the President showing that this war decision was a tough decision, that he cares about the soldiers, he cares about people, that he is affected by these decisions, that these are very tough things, and that he makes mistakes. Those two sides of it were the human side of him that people don't often see and the fact that he had an agenda for the future. I think those things were helpful to us in a close election. This did not change the election by ten points.

NICOLE DEVENISH: I also think he showed humility when he said, "People say I have a swagger. In Texas, that's called walking." I think the most important message—and I think the first time he said it was at the convention—was that you may not always agree with me, but you'll always know where I stand. That became a major theme in the final eight weeks of our messaging.

KEN MEHLMAN: That's exactly right.

JOHN HARWOOD: How exactly did the daughter's remarks get written? And how did you evaluate the effectiveness of them?

NICOLE DEVENISH: Karen Hughes.[23]

KEN MEHLMAN: Karen and Mark McKinnon were the two that worked on them.[24]

MATTHEW DOWD: They didn't go through the process of vetting that a lot of the other speeches went through.

KEN MEHLMAN: It was sincere remarks that they made. They enjoyed it. I think a lot of people who watched it enjoyed it.

JOHN HARWOOD: Did they test well?

KEN MEHLMAN: I don't think we tested the President's daughters' remarks.

MATTHEW DOWD: No, we didn't focus group those specific remarks. There was no need to. (Laughter.)

GLORIA BORGER: We'll leave it on that politic comment.

---

23. Karen Hughes served as George W. Bush's communications director in Texas and as counselor to the President during his first eighteen months in the White House. Hughes left the White House in the summer of 2002 to return to Texas but served as a key advisor to the President during the 2004 campaign.
24. Mark McKinnon, a Texas-based media consultant, served as the head of President Bush's advertising team during the 2004 election.

The General Election

4

"We believed that this was a 50-50 race."

   —Kerry-Edwards Campaign Manager Mary Beth Cahill

"I agree with the concept that it was a close election and the country was closely divided."

   —Bush-Cheney Campaign Manager Ken Mehlman

PHIL SHARP: Ladies and gentlemen, we have now gotten to the general election. We are delighted to have two moderators who serve on the Institute of Politics Senior Advisory Committee. Gwen Ifill is the moderator and managing editor of *Washington Week* and the senior correspondent for the *News Hour with Jim Lehrer,* both on PBS. She is joined by Rick Berke who is associate managing editor of the *New York Times* and who also was a fellow at the Institute of Politics.

RICK BERKE: Thanks to the participants. It's harder for the losing campaign. I appreciate all of you coming and the candor that we are getting from many of you is really helpful.

GWEN IFILL: But not from all of you. We'll fix that. (Laughter.)

RICK BERKE: The one thing that has struck me so far this time, compared to four years ago, is how much friendlier the two sides are. Maybe it was the stalemate, but these two campaigns are much nicer to each other than they were four years ago. Maybe we'll change that. We'll see what happens.

GWEN IFILL: They were still counting votes four years ago at this time.

RICK BERKE: We have three hours. This is the last effort to get, on-the-record, some of the final thoughts and post-mortems on what happened in this campaign, so we have a lot of ground to cover. We are going to go through everything from debates to the first/second lady candidates, the running mates, and Election Day. We have some provocative questions hidden in here so let's get started.

• A VERY CLOSE RACE •

RICK BERKE: Terry McAuliffe said the Republicans ran a brilliant campaign this year. I've heard that from other Democrats. Do you all really think they won because they ran a better campaign?

BOB SHRUM: If you change 50,000 or 60,000 votes in one state, we are sitting here having a different discussion.

RICK BERKE: That's why I asked the question.

BOB SHRUM: In that sense, I disagree with Matthew [Dowd]. Maybe he was always certain the President was going to get reelected. I was hopeful that we were going to win, but I thought it was going to be a very close race so everything mattered.

MATTHEW DOWD: I never said I was certain.

BOB SHRUM: I think confident was the word you used. Everything mattered—everything they did, everything we did, and a series of external events all mattered. If you are asking, at a different level, do I think that they ran a good campaign? In a political sense, they ran a very good campaign. Some of what they said didn't happen to be true. We don't need to rehash old stuff.

Members of the press and scholars observe the two-day conference.

For example, John Kerry never proposed to raise taxes on middle-income people.

GWEN IFILL: Was that the single most misleading thing that was said about your candidate? (Laughter.)

BOB SHRUM: How about the Swift Boat stuff? That was absolutely absurd, as Mark [Mellman] pointed out earlier. Trying to take the after-action report and the fact that "K" was in the initials at the bottom of the report and saying, well, he must have written the report himself, which we now know is absolutely untrue. You could go down a whole list of things. And I'm sure they would say that we said things about Bush that were untrue.

GWEN IFILL: We're going to ask them that, too.

BOB SHRUM: At a technical level and as a political operation, I think they ran a very good campaign. In the spring, when they started out and they started making some gains, they hoped to achieve more than they thought they would. They blame that on Abu Ghraib. I think the country was closely divided and was going to take a long, hard look at both these guys. It was going to make a decision and it was going to be close. I think anybody who

IOP student Adam Katz listens as reporter Gwen Ifill asks the campaign staffs about their general election strategies.

went ahead in this campaign on an assumption that it was going to be any-thing but close, and that not everything mattered, was making a mistake.

TAD DEVINE: I think they ran a very fine campaign. They had a lot of difficult situations to deal with—the reality of an incumbent president and the course of events—which are difficult to navigate.

But I think if the exercise here is to try to learn something from what really happened and to take something away from that, you have to step back from this campaign and look at what happened from a little distance. As I see it, from a little distance, here is what happened.

The state of New Hampshire, which voted for Bush last time, voted for Kerry. Two states which voted for Gore four years ago voted for Bush this time—Iowa and New Mexico. No other state changed. As Bob mentioned, 50,000 net votes in Ohio going in a different direction would have changed the outcome. John Kerry got 500,000 more votes than Al Gore in Ohio. George Bush got 400,000 more votes in Ohio than he did four years ago. So we made up a big part of the difference in Ohio. We just didn't make up enough of the difference.

To say that there was some transitional event in this campaign, in my view, is wrong. I don't think this campaign was about a transition in American poli-tics. Particularly if you look at the margins in the red states, where they did a good job of getting more people out to vote and ran up a lot of the popular vote.

GWEN IFILL: But, Tad, you've all been saying that this election was always a 50-50 race and it ended up the way it began. If that's true, then you never had a chance to win.

TAD DEVINE: No, I think we did have a chance to win. I think it was a tug-of-war on both sides and that, in many ways, we were equally matched. Sometimes we had the advantage and sometimes they did, particularly in the spring. Ken [Mehlman] said before that they did very well in March and the first half of April and I agree with that. In my view, they won March and the first half of April. But I think we began to win in the end of April, May, June, and July. There was a reason we began to win in that period of time. It's because we spent more money than they did from the end of April to the end of July if you look at campaign-to-campaign spending—the 527s are another story. We delivered a message about John Kerry—about his aspira-tions to strengthen the nation, about a domestic agenda that he was con-cerned with, about reassurance on the War on Terror—that was very effective with voters. In the aftermath of our convention, our ability to deliver that message was muted because we accepted public funding and they were still spending money under the primary cap.

If there is one lesson to learn for Democrats, it's to not let that happen again. Do not give an incumbent president an advantage of five weeks of a general election where you have to spend general election money and they spend primary money. That is too big of an advantage to overcome.

GWEN IFILL: Let's bring the Republicans in. I really am curious about your response to what Bob and Tad said and also if you have any sense, now looking back on it with some sleep, how Bush won or Kerry lost?

KEN MEHLMAN: Just a couple of thoughts. First, I agree with the concept that it was a close election and the country was closely divided. I disagree though with the notion that it was just basically 2000 with a couple of states that changed a few thousand votes. The President improved his performance in forty-eight states, got ten million more votes than last time, got more than 50 percent of the vote for the first time—something Bill Clinton never did in the course of his career. We won seats in the House and Senate and it was a huge debate on big issues.

The 2000 campaign was not a big, national debate about what America's strategy for defending itself should be—2004, in part, was. The 2000 campaign was not a big debate over what we do on taxes, on regulation, and on tort reform. The 2004 debate was. There were huge values issues in this debate. Some talk about elections as being "squishy" versus "crunchy" elections. The *Economist* magazine often talks about this—squishy where you try to blunt the differences and crunchy where you try to highlight the differences. The 2004 campaign was a crunchy election. The 2000 campaign was, fundamentally, a much squishier election.

This was a very significant election and the results were very significant in terms of what happened on Election Day. If in Pennsylvania, fewer votes had changed than in Ohio, we would be talking about something entirely different. And we know about Wisconsin and about New Hampshire. So you could always play that game. But, if you step back and look at the big result—the gains in the House, the gains in the Senate, the first time since 1988 that you win a popular majority and improve your performance in forty-eight states. And it wasn't just red states. We got 300,000 more votes in New Jersey, one of the bluest of all states, as compared to last time. The result was very historic. Now I think to over-read that and say this means we have a Republican majority forever is—

GWEN IFILL: Or, say a mandate?

KEN MEHLMAN: I think it was a mandate. Absolutely.

GWEN IFILL: But, wait a second, you just said not to over-read it.

KEN MEHLMAN: Reading it as a mandate is different than saying there is a permanent Republican majority. Republicans have won majorities in the last two national elections—the House twice and the presidency. The Democrats haven't done that in the presidency since 1976 and in the House since 1992. I do think there is a mandate. A mandate is acquired when a political leader runs for office, says he'll do certain things, and wins. If George Bush didn't get a mandate, that means that the only Democrat since World War II who got a mandate was Lyndon Johnson.

MARY BETH CAHILL: Looking at this election, overall, they ran a good campaign. They won and that's a good campaign. From where I sit, I admire the fortitude with which they decided that the only way that they could win was to run an extremely negative campaign and not talk about the issues that were just discussed. First of all, most of the money that was spent in the campaign was spent on negative ads against John Kerry, not about any discussion of the issues.

Second, in terms of what this means, President Bush won by the smallest margin of any president ever reelected. I think 2.45 percent is the most recent number. Woodrow Wilson was the previous low man at 3.2. So, from my point of view, it's not a mandate. Certainly, they did a very good job, a wonderful job, on Election Day. There is going to be a lot of discussion about that and leading up to Election Day, but it was a close race and there is a lot here to build on and a lot to discuss.

MARK MELLMAN: I'm going to say something that will maybe appear radical and also radically self-serving. Forgive me for that. I don't think it's true. I really don't think this was a 50-50 election. I think there was an inherent advantage that this president had, that any incumbent president has. Seventy-five percent of incumbent presidents get reelected. There is a reason for that. You have to have a certain level of pain to unelect an incumbent president.

The truth is, despite our best efforts, they won and that's what counts. They deserve tremendous credit for that. But the reality is the country was not feeling the level of pain that was required to oust an incumbent president. The academic models are saying Bush should have gotten somewhere between 52 and 58 percent of the vote. One way to read that is to say, well, the models are ridiculous. The other way to read it is to say the level of pain is not consonant with what's historically required to unelect an incumbent.

There were tremendous advantages that you have as an incumbent with an approval rating of 50 percent. We could look at that and say half-full or half-empty. The reality is incumbents have been defeated, as Matt [Dowd] rightly said, at approval ratings of 33 and 37 percent. As an incumbent president in times that weren't that bad, they had some real advantages and they used those advantages extremely well. There is no doubt about it.

MATTHEW DOWD: I want to just say one thing. Is there a possibility that we could have lost this race? Yes. We had a president on Election Day that had a 46 percent disapproval rating. No president has ever gotten reelected with a 46 percent disapproval rating. If our approval had been 48 or 47 percent on Election Day, could we have lost? Of course. Did the activities of our campaign and the activities of the Kerry campaign affect that at the margins? You could make an argument that it did, whether it was what we did at our convention, what they did at their convention, or how the course of the year went.

I don't think because our approval ended up—and I've always said the approval rating is very important—at 50 or 51 percent and we won with 50 or 51 percent of the vote that it necessarily means the conduct of each campaign did not matter in affecting what happened on Election Day. We could have had an approval rating of 48 percent on Election Day if we hadn't handled things as well as we did in some cases. The race would have been a very different race if that happened.

So I think the conduct of the campaign was important. I don't agree with the academic models. They were wrong in 2000. The assumptions based on the academic models are so far off with the way modern day is. I don't think somebody's economic factor plays on how people do because the information—

MARK MELLMAN: So, you're saying the economy really was quite bad?

MATTHEW DOWD: No, the economy wasn't— (Laughter.) You can argue it your way which—as I told you about two weeks ago, I never heard you say before Election Day—is how could the President lose?

BOB SHRUM: That would have been his last TV appearance. (Laughter.)

MATTHEW DOWD: The economy and the war and all of those things weren't going so well that the campaign didn't matter or so badly that the campaign didn't matter. We were in this in-between place, which I said all along, where the conduct of the campaign and what the candidates did mattered more than any other presidential campaign for a reelect that anybody in this room has ever seen.

RICK BERKE: Since campaigns do matter and you had two Democratic opponents over these two campaigns with some of the same people this time that you fought day-to-day against four years ago, who was the more formidable candidate in your view, Gore or Kerry?

MATTHEW DOWD: Al Gore had a lot going for him. If you look at what was going on in the country, there was a lot going for him. John Kerry, in my view, worked harder than Al Gore. From my standpoint, he was more disciplined if he wanted to get somewhere. For example, in the debate, by watching his debate prep, he was able to change how he answered questions in a way that made it much more concise and deliberative. John Kerry had different baggage than Al Gore did. He was from Massachusetts and he had his record. But, from a campaign candidate standpoint, I think John Kerry, having watched him, was a better candidate than Al Gore was.

KEN MEHLMAN: I agree with that and I think the Kerry campaign was better than the Gore campaign was.

• THE NADER FACTOR •

GWEN IFILL: If I can direct you to a different question about another candidate who was a factor in 2000 and not as much a factor this year—Ralph Nader. He ended up with a percentage of what he got the time before. He only beat the Libertarian candidate, who got no attention and had no money, by about 50,000 votes.[1]

Theresa, I want you to talk about what you thought the Nader factor was. I also want to ask you guys to tell us what your fears were about what the Nader factor would be and what you did about that.

THERESA AMATO: Ralph Nader wasn't on the ballot in seventeen states. He wasn't on the ballot because of a lot of the activity of the 527s.

GWEN IFILL: Did you sense that the Democrats set out to squash Ralph Nader?

THERESA AMATO: Absolutely. They said it from the get-go.

GWEN IFILL: They did?

BOB SHRUM: Yes. (Laughter.)

GWEN IFILL: How?

BOB SHRUM: Obviously, not only the 527s but also the DNC and other people worked very hard at making sure that if there were ballot requirements, Nader had to meet them. There was no sense in which one could be

---

1. Ralph Nader received 443,830 votes and Libertarian candidate Michael Badarnik received 393,770 votes.

complacent about this, having gone through what we went through in 2000, and given the closeness of the election, Pennsylvania could have moved this way, Ohio could have moved this way. In the end, he didn't matter but he could have mattered and because he could have mattered, you took sensible political steps, in my view, that were very different from what we did in 2000. In 2000, the only thing that happened was at the end—in Oregon where we saw the threat very clearly and in Florida, to some extent—we ran some radio advertising about what was at stake and the choice between voting for Nader or voting for Gore. But, this time, we didn't want it to get to that point.

RICK BERKE: When Kerry made that overture to Nader, did you have any expectation that he could convince him not to run or to pull out of the race?[2] What was that all about?

MARY BETH CAHILL: Kerry knew Nader very well. They had had a relationship over the course of the years. Kerry believed that he could have a face-to-face, real conversation with Ralph Nader and that Ralph Nader would be responsive to the things that they cared about in common. They met in Washington—Theresa and I were there—and they spoke on the phone several times. In between that though, Ralph Nader went around the country and talked about John Kerry a lot more than George Bush, calling him things like "an accordion," which I never really understood. We didn't know where he was going or why he was doing what he was doing. It got to a point where an ongoing conversation was not going to be useful because it wasn't going to lead to anything. In the meantime, the Democratic parties in the states and some of the 527s, we found out later, did their best to make sure that he met the ballot requirements.

GWEN IFILL: You found this out later?

MARY BETH CAHILL: Yes. We didn't know about the 527s. We knew what the state parties were doing. A couple of the state parties on the Republican side actually tried to help, or did help, Ralph Nader meet the ballot requirements.

GWEN IFILL: Did you guys know about the Republican efforts to get Ralph Nader on the ballot?

---

2. On May 19, 2004, Senator Kerry and Ralph Nader met for more than an hour in Washington, D.C. Speculation was rampant that Senator Kerry would attempt to convince Nader to withdraw from the race. However, both sides later claimed that the two candidates limited their conversation to such matters as economic policy and campaign finance reform.

MATTHEW DOWD: Sure. It was public record.

GWEN IFILL: And you said go for it?

KEN MEHLMAN: We didn't say it. They were just doing it. There wasn't huge amounts of money spent on behalf of Ralph Nader by Republicans. When there were Nader rallies, they would sometimes let people know about them. That's what they did.

THERESA AMATO: I would like to go back to the meeting between Nader and Kerry. The overture was both ways. Ralph went in saying, we would like to be a second front against the Bush Administration and that there are a number of issues, especially cracking down on corporate crime and providing a living wage, where there are traditional bread-and-butter Democratic issues that we should stand up and talk about together because they are important.

First, nothing came of the meeting. Then the "Nader factor" was rolled out and efforts were made from the DNC down to not just make sure we met the legal requirements of the ballot but also to intimidate our circulators, to threaten our people, and to make sure that we didn't get on the ballot under any circumstances.

• THE DEBATE OVER THE DEBATES •

RICK BERKE: Let's go on to the debates. You were just complimenting the Kerry team and Kerry for the discipline in his preparations for the debates. I wonder if the President was as disciplined in preparing for the debates. We heard all kinds of reports that said he really didn't spend as much time as some of you would have liked in preparing for that first debate. Can you tell us about that? What preparations went into that first debate?

KEN MEHLMAN: The approach he used was very similar to the approach he used in 2000. That served him well then and I think it served him well in this series of debates. He absorbed a lot of information both by practice—question and answer—and also by a briefing process that occurred. He felt, and we all felt, that what people took out of the three debates was very beneficial to the President.

GWEN IFILL: In that first debate, as you were sitting backstage in your holding room, watching the President sigh and frown and all but roll his eyes, did it strike you that he was a little bit off message or detracting from his message?

*Bush and Kerry communications directors Nicole Devenish (left)
and Stephanie Cutter (right) debate the debates.*

KEN MEHLMAN: I thought that the reaction of the media to the first debate was overstated. That having been said, one of my favorite—and I'm about to ding Nicole—pictures that appeared was in *Time Magazine.* We are all in the room watching the debate, everyone looks very serious, watching the debate seriously—

NICOLE DEVENISH: But it wasn't serious.

KEN MEHLMAN: Yeah, it's not serious.

NICOLE DEVENISH: —like they were going to throw up. (Laughter.)

KEN MEHLMAN: And Nicole—

NICOLE DEVENISH: —I wasn't watching though.

KEN MEHLMAN: Nicole has this huge, incredible smile—

NICOLE DEVENISH: McKinnon was smiling, too.

KEN MEHLMAN: Nicole and McKinnon had these huge, incredible smiles, like, I can't believe they let me in here. (Laughter.) Certainly the President's performances in the second and third debate were better than in the first debate. He made his case better in the second and the third debates. We sometimes make the mistake, and I do it as well as anybody, because we are so into politics, of scoring this from a debating scoring or political perspective, as opposed to what people take away from the debate.

GWEN IFILL: Ken, four years ago, around here, the Gore people were almost saying what you are saying about the debate in which Gore was rapped for sighing audibly.[3] They said this was just something we took away, that these were debating points, but they had an effect on what people did take away from these debates.

KEN MEHLMAN: In the Gore debates, there was clearly a reduction in the numbers. If you look at what happened this time in the numbers, what happened was, before the first debate, Kerry's support was a little bit lower, his base was a little bit dispirited because he had had a tough period during September. His base came back. He didn't gain among Independents. We did not lose among Republicans.

So I'm not looking at it from our perspective but from the perspective of who matters the most—in this case, the American people. Look at the numbers. Look at what they took away. My sense of the debates was that they had a much bigger impact in 2000 against Gore than the first debate had for us. And what the people took away from all three debates was beneficial to us.

BOB SHRUM: As I said in another context, I wish Republicans many more such debate victories. We are not going to agree on this, but I think it is clear that John Kerry won the debates. I think the people were a little startled at the President in the first debate, not just at his affect but at his seeming disconnection and disinterest even in some of the questions.

What I found most interesting about the debates, especially the first one, was that I think George Bush showed up to debate the caricature of John Kerry that the Bush campaign had created. That's not the John Kerry that showed up.

We went through this whole process of working out the rules.[4] We had

---

3. In the first presidential debate of the 2000 election, Vice President Gore was heard sighing audibly during some of Governor Bush's responses. Gore was criticized for showing signs of arrogance, but he claimed that his sighs were not meant to be overheard.
4. In the weeks leading up to the presidential debates, representatives of the Bush and Kerry campaigns met to negotiate a set of rules. The end result was a thirty-two-page document which included, among other stipulations, agreements on the temperature of the halls in which the debates were to be held, regulations governing what type of paper could be used to take notes, the institution of a system of lights to indicate how much time speakers had left to speak, and the establishment of a back-up buzzer system to

lights and he wasn't going to be able to stop in time for the lights. There was going to be a gong if somebody went over three times. The only time that the gong could actually ever have been invoked was against President Bush in the first debate and we got a call saying, no, we don't want to do that. John Kerry prepared in a very thorough, extraordinarily disciplined way.

We could talk about this in a larger context of what I think the campaign ultimately was all about, but I think what people took out of the first debate was a lot of assurance that Kerry could be commander in chief, that he knew what he was talking about, and that he could handle the national security of the country. The Bush campaign wanted that first debate to be on what was presumed to be George Bush's strongest ground and, in the end, that worked for us.

GWEN IFILL: Did Kerry succeed in changing the topic, as he seemed to be striving to do, from Iraq to Osama and the War on Terrorism?

BOB SHRUM: I think that the campaign and John Kerry made, and Mark [Mellman] can talk about this, major progress in separating Iraq and the War on Terrorism. At one point, 70 percent of people thought that they were basically identical and that number came down very substantially.

The thing we had much more difficulty doing, because real events were driving the campaign, was actually getting focused on health care and the economy. Even when Kerry would talk about it a lot, somebody would find a weapons cache in Iraq and that would be the story for several days. Either you were going to be in that story or you weren't going to be in that story. But, in the debates, Kerry made some very real progress in separating terrorism and the Iraq war.

MATTHEW DOWD: Just one thing on the debates. Let's grant the premise that Bob is saying—that Kerry won all the debates and he did great and everything is wonderful.

BOB SHRUM: Geez, I didn't go quite that far. (Laughter.)

MATTHEW DOWD: We were four points up going into the debates. When the debates were finished and everything was done—the vice presidential debate, the three presidential debates, and all of the discussion related to that—we were three points up. So I think we're over-reading. The conven-

---

denote when the entirety of a candidate's time had elapsed. Pundits later suggested that the lights and buzzers helped Senator Kerry rein in his sometimes lengthy style of speech and, thereby, contributed to his strong performance in the debates.

tion speeches by each candidate had more effect than the four debates, watched by sixty million people.

We could argue back and forth whether somebody won it academically. In the first debate, people said Kerry won, but it didn't shift the numbers dramatically. I don't think any of the debates, in total, shifted the numbers dramatically in this race at all. It testifies to how this race was so close and how the people were lined up on each side. In the end, the four debates had an insignificant, if any, effect on this race.

GWEN IFILL: Mark, do you agree with that?

MARK MELLMAN: No. There is a factual dispute. Two sets of data are clear on this. Point one—there are a whole raft of public polls, as well as our own private polling, asking people about the debates and in every poll that was done by every outlet that I know of, including our own, John Kerry won all three debates. Point two—if you look at our data and the consolidated data from all of the public polling, what you see is that John Kerry went into the first debate about five points down and after the first debate was about one point down.

MATTHEW DOWD: That's not what I said. I said that after the series of three debates and the vice presidential debate, what were the numbers when all that was over?

MARK MELLMAN: When all that was over, we were still about one point down. It honestly didn't change.

MATTHEW DOWD: So we did something in the final ten days that changed it from a one-point race to a three-point race?

MARK MELLMAN: To a two-point race, yes.

MATTHEW DOWD: That's totally different than our data. Our data had this race at about a four- or five-point race going into the first debate and when we came out of the last debate, we had a three-point race. This race basically didn't change between the end of the last debate and Election Day.

MARK MELLMAN: Part of the problem in public polling and a lot of the polling that was going on were the assumptions that people were making about what the electorate would look like. That's why I think there was some stuff that was off. Our assumption was, which we hoped to be right, that the same number of Republicans would show up as Democrats on Election Day, which would, therefore, mean we would win by approximately three points.

That's what we thought. Whenever we did a poll, we made sure it was balanced, and it was done with the same number of Democrats and Republicans. We did that throughout the year.

NICOLE DEVENISH: The debates changed the way the Kerry campaign was covered. If you look at the story line that Kerry was dealing with going into the first debate, he was still stepping over all these positions on Iraq. They did a brilliant job in the pre-debate spin and the post-debate spin. You can't say they didn't prepare and do well in the debates. It completely changed the tone, tenor, and substance of their coverage. I don't think that effect waned until the end. It benefited them substantially. There was a new buoyancy, and a new life breathed in, and a sense of momentum. Their press corps felt it and they all felt it. They did a brilliant job spinning the instant polls. Whether you believe them or not, there was spin, supported by coverage, supported by spin, supported by coverage. It was a great period for them. I think they did a great job.

RICK BERKE: One more question about the first debate and then we'll move to the second.

It was widely reported that Karen Hughes, after that first debate, was the only one who could go up to the President and say, this didn't work out very well—here is what you did wrong. What did he learn after that first debate? Did he work harder in preparing for the second debate than he did the first debate, which was widely perceived by some people on the campaign as a lackluster performance?

NICOLE DEVENISH: The words work harder is the wrong concept. Maybe we changed the way we were preparing our answers a little bit. Your first question was, had you not prepared enough? We had prepared for a long time. We had worked very hard and he had worked very hard. But, yes, there were certain adjustments made to how we prepared the message and the substance of the answers. We made some adjustments.

RICK BERKE: What kind of adjustments?

NICOLE DEVENISH: Karen [Hughes] and Dan [Bartlett] worked on that. I wasn't involved.

MATTHEW DOWD: The presumption that Karen was the only person that didn't think he did well in the first debate is—

NICOLE DEVENISH: And that she said that to him is not true.

GWEN IFILL: Well, you all just said he did great.

KEN MEHLMAN: I think what I said was that I thought it was overstated how badly the first debate went. But certainly everybody thought we could improve.

MATTHEW DOWD: When we try to break down each debate, it's a false sense of what the public sees. They don't see a debate and see another debate. They see a total of what happened. If we want to talk about the first debate, did he do worse in the first debate than he did in the second debate? Yes, he did. Was Karen the only person that said to him, you need to do better? There are a lot of things that get talked about in the media that aren't right.

RICK BERKE: So you all knew and all of you said it. Did any of you go to the President and say, you screwed up, or was the Karen the only one who could do that?

MATTHEW DOWD: I'll just say this—he knew how I felt. (Laughter.)

RICK BERKE: So you had that give and take with the president of the United States. That's great. (Laughter.)

MATTHEW DOWD: But, you know what? More importantly, he knew what he needed to do.

NICOLE DEVENISH: Yes, and he did it.

MATTHEW DOWD: One more thing. All the handlers are here and I know this is what we do. John Kerry is a good candidate, a grown-up. He knows when he does right, knows when he does wrong, and knows when he can do better, regardless of who said something to him. George Bush is the same way. He learned in his race for governor in 1994, he learned in his race in 1998, learned in 2000 and learned in 2004. There are not a lot of people that have to go up to him and say, oh, you need to do better. He can figure it out for himself.

GWEN IFILL: The second debate—the vice presidential debate—where was that again?[5]

---

5. Gwen Ifill moderated the 2004 Vice Presidential Debate held at Case Western University in Ohio on October 5, 2004.

UNIDENTIFIED: Incredibly moderated. (Laughter.)

GWEN IFILL: I'll tell you, since we are off-the-record here, that I came away thinking that John Edwards didn't do as well as advertised. What did you think?

MARY BETH CAHILL: I think he did very well. Walking into this, there were a lot of expectations that the Vice President had done this before and that Edwards had done comparatively few debates over the course of his career. But he also prepared in a really tight fashion. He made the decision early on that what he was going to do was not defend himself but rather stand up for John Kerry. He did that. He did it really effectively and it was a very good performance.

GWEN IFILL: Someone who was involved in the debate prep told me, after the debate, that you not only knew that the Vice President and Senator Edwards had met before but you knew there was tape proving that point and that you had advised him not to respond to that because it would be going backward and responding to something that had been said before.[6] So instead what you got, as a reward for this counsel, was a reaction shot of Senator Edwards looking stunned, slightly. Was that good advice, not to respond, when you knew what the Vice President had said was not accurate?

BOB SHRUM: That was non-advice, as far as I know, and I was at the last two days of Senator Edwards' debate prep. In that period of time, this was never discussed and no one gave him that advice. So I don't know what you're talking about.

MARY BETH CAHILL: The recollections of when they actually met were Elizabeth Edwards', post facto. Actually, two times that I was not aware of got added because she sort of ticked through in her mind when Edwards and Cheney met.

GWEN IFILL: So you didn't know in advance that this tape existed of them together?

BOB SHRUM: No, I certainly did not. There are sometimes people who say they know something about debate prep who didn't necessarily know something about debate prep.

---

6. During the vice presidential debate, Vice President Dick Cheney directly rebuked Senator Edwards for his poor record of Congressional attendance, observing that, despite having served as the Senate's presiding officer for nearly four years, "The first time I ever met you was when you walked on the stage tonight." It was later determined that the two had, in fact, met prior to the debate.

GWEN IFILL: Did you guys know about it? Did you cringe when the Vice President said that? I had heard him say it before. It didn't bother you at all that he said something inaccurate in a nationally televised debate?

KEN MEHLMAN: I don't think I realized that it was inaccurate.

NICOLE DEVENISH: I don't think we knew until Elizabeth Edwards had said that.

MATTHEW DOWD: Yeah, later.

GWEN IFILL: Did it bother you once you knew?

MATTHEW DOWD: I thought it was a good line at the time. (Laughter.) Interestingly enough, that line was never practiced.

GWEN IFILL: He had said it before in an interview.

MATTHEW DOWD: I know. But it was never like, in the debate, say this when this comes up, like "you're no Jack Kennedy."[7] It was never a practiced thing. It never came up when I was there for the final three or four days with him.

TAD DEVINE: The standard that we had of success in the vice presidential debate was whether or not the momentum would be stopped. We thought the first debate was a very clear win for John Kerry and that we had momentum coming out of the first debate. It was not stopped because Edwards performed well enough so that people did not have a take-away that this guy somehow was not ready to deal with the responsibilities of the presidency. So, in terms of what we wanted to get out of it—for Edwards to advance the cause of Kerry, to demonstrate his capacity to be president and, most importantly in terms of the politics of it, not to stop the momentum—he met all those standards and did so very well.

KEN MEHLMAN: It's odd that you said that about Kerry because actually watching it, I was surprised that Edwards didn't do more to defend Kerry

---

7. On October 5, 1988, during a nationally televised vice presidential debate, Senator Dan Quayle attempted to defuse concerns about his level of experience by pointing out that he had "as much experience in the Congress as Jack Kennedy did when he sought the presidency." His opponent, Democratic Senator Lloyd Bentsen, retorted, "Senator, I served with Jack Kennedy. I knew Jack Kennedy. Jack Kennedy was a friend of mine. Senator, you're no Jack Kennedy."

and go after the President because a big part of the Vice President's strategy was not to focus on Edwards but to talk about the top of the ticket. It's very easy for these guys to end up in a back and forth and that was certainly the strategy that we had going into it.

GWEN IFILL: So your plan was to be dismissive of Senator Edwards?

KEN MEHLMAN: Absolutely not. It was, in fact, to be very respectful. My point is not to go after Senator Edwards but to point out that Senator Edwards needed to defend John Kerry's record. I was surprised a little bit. My expectation was that Edwards would be more aggressive going after the President and defending Senator Kerry's record than he actually was in the debate.

GWEN IFILL: I got two major responses after this debate from people on the street and in e-mails. One was people saying, gee, that was funny what you did to the Vice President, telling him he only had thirty seconds left. I didn't understand why that was funny but this is what people thought.

The second response I got was from people who were surprised that neither candidate had an answer to the question about black women and AIDS.[8] I got a lot of responses, a lot of op-eds were written, and I was curious about that. I was curious about whether they had been briefed on the subject— whether they honestly didn't know or just couldn't recall.

BOB SHRUM: I don't know the answer to that.

GWEN IFILL: It never came up afterward? Nobody ever said, geez, I wish we had had an answer to that question?

MATTHEW DOWD: No.

GWEN IFILL: I was hoping for something helpful to take back the next time this comes up, but I guess I don't have that.

BOB SHRUM: Gwen, afterwards, there is no question that Senator Edwards, I am sure, found out what the answer was in case he would get asked again. But, did we spend a lot of time on it afterwards? No.

---

8. In the vice presidential debate, Gwen Ifill asked the two candidates about what the government's role should be in ending the spread of AIDS "right here in this country, where black women between the ages of twenty-five and forty-four are thirteen times more likely to die of the disease than their counterparts."

RICK BERKE: While we are talking about veeps and the vice presidential debates, I remember Don Imus,[9] in the middle of the general election, said one morning to Edwards, what happened to you? You're the incredible, disappearing vice presidential candidate. That happened to Dan Quayle when he ran. He was sent out to the regional areas and never heard from again. Why didn't he play a larger, more vocal role in this campaign? Did he bring any added value? Tad, you talked about how he was helpful in some ways but did he bring any added value? Did he help in the actual tally, in the end, in the count? Did he give you added percentage points or was it a wash?

TAD DEVINE: Why didn't he bring more value? Let's answer the first part of the question. In 1988, I had the privilege of being the campaign manager for Lloyd Bentsen's campaign for vice president. As a matter of fact, I think Matt [Dowd] actually worked for me on that campaign. (Laughter.)

MATTHEW DOWD: See what happens? (Laughter.)

KEN MEHLMAN: We paid him better. (Laughter.)

RICK BERKE: Did you two get along?

TAD DEVINE: Very well, and we still do.
   I think it's fair to say that I can't remember a bigger mismatch, in terms of candidates for vice president, than Bentsen/Quayle. It was just night and day. It was clear to everyone and it wasn't just a sound bite—it was everything. Now, did Lloyd Bentsen have a big impact on the outcome of that election? No, he did not. So why did John Edwards not have a bigger impact? Well, it is structural. It has to do with being the candidate for vice president in an election where voters care very much about the candidate for president.
   Part two of your question, what did he add? I think he added a lot. From the very beginning of his selection, he was someone who complemented John Kerry. The visuals of that selection process added enormously, not just to the idea that there was an opportunity for change in an election where change was a very complex issue—and I hope we talk about that later because that was one of the great struggles that we had in this campaign—but also the fact that he brought the best out of John Kerry. When John Edwards and his family and children were there, it really helped people to see a side of John Kerry that all of us could see on a daily basis.

---

9. Don Imus is a nationally syndicated radio host and author.

GWEN IFILL: But, Tad, did it ever give you any concern that, effectively, on the Republican side, both George W. Bush and Dick Cheney spent all day attacking John Kerry, while on the Democratic side, you only ever heard one voice speaking back and that was the presidential candidate?

MARY BETH CAHILL: That's not true.

BOB SHRUM: That's incorrect. I must say, and I say it with all respect, this morning reminded me of a kind of review of Adam [Nagourney]'s and Mark [Halperin]'s writings during the campaign and a checklist to see whether they were right about what was happening at a certain point. The *New York Times* ran a very large story saying this. It wasn't true. He was not being sent to obscure states. He was being sent to decisive places in battleground states. He was going after Bush all the time.

GWEN IFILL: I was making a slightly different point. That point is that when the Vice President spoke, we were much more likely to see him carried live—we were much more likely to hear his comments. We never ever spoke about John Edwards. When John Edwards spoke, he spoke about the President but you never really heard it as much, partly because of the virtue of holding the vice presidency. What Dick Cheney did, and they said as much, is set out to not acknowledge John Edwards. I wonder if that worked or bothered you.

BOB SHRUM: I don't think that played much of a role in this campaign at all. I actually think that John Edwards was a very effective campaigner. He was very effective in the places he went. We'd probably have to reverse roles and get the audience to be the participants and us to be the audience to answer the question of why the media decided that it would put Dick Cheney on live more than it would put John Edwards on live.

MARK MELLMAN: The question is, why didn't you cover John Edwards more? You can answer that question better than we can.

GWEN IFILL: I'm actually asking a more subtle question that nobody is getting.

TAD DEVINE: Can I try to get to it? I think it underlies a fundamental difference between our two campaigns. Strategically, our orientation was to win electoral votes in states that we considered battlegrounds. That's where we spent our time. That's where we sent our most precious resource—our candidates. That's where we spent our money on television. We did not have national cable buys. We did not do national radio buys. We approached the election differently. So the fact that John Edwards was spending time on our targets, that we developed on a very sophisticated model that Mark Mellman can talk about for about five hours if you want to hear it, reflected our strategic orientation towards the race. The fact that you wouldn't see him in some other places was a deliberate choice and judgment that we made strategically to try to win 270 electoral votes.

NICOLE DEVENISH: We did an analysis in September of the network packages because we had noticed there had been about four or five times when we had two bites at the apple—it was a Cheney bite, a Kerry bite, and a Bush bite. All of our messaging was in a dialogue with Kerry and I think Edwards was carrying a different message a lot of days. We certainly noticed that. We did an analysis and tried to maximize the numbers of days or news cycles where we could have two bites, and both of them in a package. We had a lot more cases where Cheney and Bush were in a network package with one Kerry bite. I don't know that we found any instances where Kerry and Edwards were both piling onto Bush. I think it was a different message and that's deliberate.

STEPHANIE CUTTER: That's actually not true. Our messages were coordinated on a daily basis. I think that goes back to coverage. Edwards was out there doing exactly what we were doing in order to have a coordinated message, as were most of our surrogates. It came down to coverage. That was a constant problem.

KEN MEHLMAN: Part of it was there was the bullhorn of the White House. But we tried to do as much as we could to have Cheney and Kerry responding to each other and the President doing something else.

MATTHEW DOWD: That was in the primary.

KEN MEHLMAN: In the general election, too.

STEPHANIE CUTTER: My point is they didn't ever respond to Edwards.

KEN MEHLMAN: Cheney responded to Kerry as much as we could get him to respond to Kerry and the President would be pointing out something else. That also helped a bit.

STEPHANIE CUTTER: Which, Ken, goes back to a previous point you made about how hard it is to run against an incumbent president. That is a huge advantage. Running as an incumbent, you have the bully pulpit, commander in chief, the White House.

KEN MEHLMAN: There's advantages and disadvantages.

BOB SHRUM: Well, we would be happy to take the burden off your hands some time. (Laughter.)

RICK BERKE: Cheney got more coverage but a lot of it was negative coverage. There was Halliburton and his role in the war.[10] It was critical coverage. Were you all hoping to make more of Cheney as a villain in this campaign?

MATTHEW DOWD: The Kerry campaign helped Cheney get more coverage.

NICOLE DEVENISH: It wasn't because of a lack of trying.

This goes back to, what is negative coverage? This is like "ad controversy." Perhaps something we can examine coming out of this election is, when a news judgment is that there was a negative package of all the bad things Cheney said, what did the viewers hear? They heard more about Kerry's record, in our view. Maybe it's something we'll look at for a long time after this.

BOB SHRUM: I thought you were asking a different question—was the campaign or the DNC interested, in its communication, in telling the Halliburton story? Or would Senator Edwards in the vice presidential debate talk about Halliburton? Yes.

RICK BERKE: Do you think it helped?

BOB SHRUM: I agree with Tad. Having seen the 1988 campaign and participated a little bit with Senator Bentsen—and I do think that was the greatest mismatch in modern history—in the end, people vote for president not for vice president.

GWEN IFILL: Theresa, why don't you jump in?

THERESA AMATO: This is one of the things about the media coverage. One person who was taking apart the Bush Administration in very harsh terms was Ralph [Nader]. But, because of the media coverage, any time that he said anything about Kerry that was perceived as negative, that's what got

---

10. Vice President Cheney served as the chief executive officer of the Halliburton Company from 1995 to 2000. Halliburton is the largest military contractor in the reconstruction of Iraq. Democrats frequently accused the Vice President of malfeasance in this regard, but he has denied any wrongdoing on his part.

covered, as opposed to his taking apart the Bush Administration day after day, in venue after venue, in harsh terms that the Kerry camp couldn't use.

GWEN IFILL: So, when Mary Beth says that Ralph Nader was going more aggressively after John Kerry than George W. Bush, you don't think that was the case?

THERESA AMATO: After the meeting between Kerry and Nader, what was printed was that Kerry looked very presidential. The "accordion" comment was about what third parties do—it was about expandability—can you push him to the left on some particular issues?

I don't agree with Mary Beth's perception, but I think that's part of the media's take. They were so fixated on 2000 and fighting the last war and not hearing what he was saying in terms of the Bush Administration.

BOB SHRUM: I'm not sure you two disagree, actually. I think what Mary Beth was saying is what was being communicated to voters through the Nader campaign was more critical of Kerry than it was of Bush. You're suggesting that that's also the case because of what the media chose to cover.

THERESA AMATO: Yes, because the vast majority of his speech was going after the Bush Administration and the Bush record.

GWEN IFILL: It's always a relief to know it's always the media's fault. (Laughter.)

BOB SHRUM: Just sometimes.

GWEN IFILL: I'd like to move on to the rest of the debate coverage, which was the town hall meeting debate.[11] Did that work for you?

KEN MEHLMAN: They both were great.

MATTHEW DOWD: I wish all three were town halls.

KEN MEHLMAN: I felt very good about it. The President did it all the time and I thought it was very natural for him.

MATTHEW DOWD: As I've said, I try to take all the debates as a package. In the second debate, Kerry's troops were motivated by his performance in

---

11. The second presidential debate was at Washington University in St. Louis on October 8, 2004, and was in a town meeting format.

the first debate and there was some slight disappointment among Republicans in our performance in the first debate. For us, that was important because if we assume that this election is a huge part about motivation, how their troops are motivated versus how our troops are motivated becomes very important. The vice presidential debate was important for people to say, okay, we're back at it, Cheney is there. Then, the President's performance in the second debate was important because it took that motivation of our troops back up to where it was before the first debate. That, to me, was the most important thing that came out of the second and the third debate—that the motivation of Republicans, or potential Republicans, was back up to where it was before the first debate.

GWEN IFILL: What about the motivation of Democrats?

BOB SHRUM: Mark [Mellman] said something earlier that I think is very true and that [CNN reporter] Jeff Greenfield and I talked about last night at some length. There now exists polls to prove almost any point you want to make. On the basis of our data, we believe the second debate was a big success. We believe it motivated Democrats. And you could certainly see that in the crowds and in the reaction that Senator Kerry was getting—it kept building from the first debate to the second debate to the third debate.

The oddest thing about the second presidential debate—the town hall debate—was the "DMZ," which was our other point of negotiation, where the Bush people were absolutely insistent that there be some imaginary line drawn down the carpet so that while you were trying to move toward the person, you wouldn't invade Bush's space. The one thing that John Kerry was not going to do in these debates was invade George Bush's space. There had been an experiment in that in the year 2000 that didn't work out very well.[12] (Laughter.) We finally came up with some kind of compromise so that if you went the great circle route, you could get to talk to the people in the audience.

The other thing about that was, once the question was asked, you weren't allowed to have any dialogue with the person in the audience. You weren't allowed to say, how many kids do you have or where do they go to school?

The second debate worked extraordinarily well for us. Mark [Mellman] was very happy after the second debate. And I guess I do understand why you guys want to think about the debates as a package because certainly thinking about at least some of them individually is probably not as comforting for you as it was for us.

---

12. The third presidential debate in the 2000 election between Al Gore and George W. Bush was held in a town meeting format. Vice President Gore was criticized for encroaching on Governor Bush's personal space when responding to questions.

GWEN IFILL: Let me try a package question because there was one issue which both John Edwards and John Kerry brought up separately in two different debates which seemed, in both cases, to be unnecessary—invoking Mary Cheney's sexual orientation.[13] Was that something you talked about in advance and planned to do in response to any question about gay marriage? Did it work?

BOB SHRUM: The answers to that are no, no, and no. It was not talked about in advance, it was not planned as a response to any question, and I don't think it worked. I mean I don't think it was meant to work.

GWEN IFILL: Did it hurt?

BOB SHRUM: I don't think it hurt. The data would appear to indicate that people, especially in the third presidential debate, did not approve of, or were not happy that, Senator Kerry had brought it up. It diverted attention from the momentum of winning the third debate. I went into the spin room after the third debate and, for the first part of that, the basic press take on the thing was, boy, Kerry won again. Then, over a period of time following that, the attention got diverted from that to the Mary Cheney comment.

I want to say, on behalf of John Kerry, and I've said this at least to Matthew [Dowd] before, Kerry thought he was paying a compliment to the Vice President and to his family. He was not trying to do anything bad. You have to put yourself into his mindset and what he thinks about this issue to understand that. But, no, it was not discussed in advance.

GWEN IFILL: Did you guys take it as a compliment?

NICOLE DEVENISH: I want to say, on behalf of Mary Cheney, it wasn't perceived that way. I think it's understandable to be scoring the debates and I think that's fine. But, at the end of it, that third debate confirmed something that I think people were growing uncomfortable with. That was this other story line that was very much present—that Kerry would say and do anything. It was around the same period that Edwards had said that if Kerry

---

13. During the third presidential debate on October 13, 2004, at Arizona State University in Tempe, Senator Kerry made a direct reference to Vice President Cheney's lesbian daughter, observing, "We're all God's children, and I think if you were to talk to Dick Cheney's daughter, who is a lesbian, she would tell you that she's being who she was, she's being who she was born as." In the vice presidential debate, John Edwards responded to a question on same-sex unions by saying, "Let me say first that I think the vice president and his wife love their daughter. I think they love her very much. And you can't have anything but respect for the fact that they're willing to talk about the fact that they have a gay daughter, the fact that they embrace her. It's a wonderful thing."

wins, people like Christopher Reeve will get out of their wheelchairs and walk again. There were all these silos of narratives that were happening in these final weeks of the campaign. I don't question anyone's motives.

BOB SHRUM: But the campaign rather effectively did in the days that followed it.

GWEN IFILL: Well, Mrs. Cheney did.

NICOLE DEVENISH: You've said that it was taken out of context, and I believe you, but it was the combination of Edwards mentioning it, of Mary Beth getting put on the spot to say it's fair and saying she is fair game, and then it was Kerry's comment and the reaction. We couldn't have made up the reaction—it wasn't fabricated. People were uncomfortable with it. Dowd's focus groups, even the ones that said Kerry won, didn't like that answer and didn't like that reference. We didn't go out and talk about it, but I was on the road with our press corps who were all picking up that this was something that the cable shows had been talking about and they talked about it for days.

MATTHEW DOWD: We did not make people uncomfortable with this. People were uncomfortable with this. That's the reality.

KEN MEHLMAN: The discussion of the broad context and the broader narrative is really important in discussing these debates and going beyond the academic scoring. I think there were two things that came out of the debates. One, real concerns about Senator Kerry's effectiveness as commander in chief, as we faced a War on Terror, were reinforced by comments like "global test"[14] and other things he said during the course of the discussions, like the fact that, at one point, on Iraq, he said it was in our national interests and, at another point, he said it was not.

Second was this notion of saying anything to win. During the three weeks of debates, people who were worried about whether John Kerry had the leadership and the strength to lead in this War on Terror had more concerns and people who were worried that the Kerry-Edwards ticket would say anything

---

14. At the first presidential debate on September 30, 2004, in response to a question on American foreign policy, Senator Kerry asserted that, when taking international action, "you've got to do it in a way . . . that passes the global test where your countrymen, your people, understand fully why you're doing what you're doing, and you can prove to the world that you did it for legitimate reasons." The Bush campaign seized on his use of the phrase "global test" to suggest that Senator Kerry would require a vote of approval from foreign leaders before taking action to protect the security of the United States.

to win and use anything for political purposes also had their concerns reinforced. That's the context in which it's worth looking at this.

RICK BERKE: Maybe it's in the eye of the beholder because the Kerry people said that first debate proved that he had the leadership ability to be commander in chief. It sounds like you have totally different views of that.

BOB SHRUM: Frankly, do I wish that Senator Kerry hadn't made the comment about Mary Cheney in the third debate? Of course. Do I think he did it for some planned strategic reason? No. I'll be quite frank about that. Do I think that voters took out of the first debate, because of "global test," some sense that John Kerry couldn't be commander in chief? Absolutely not. I don't think any data that we have would support that proposition. Do I think that Mary Cheney was about "say anything, do anything?" No. I think that's pretty good post-election spin.

What happened after that debate was that the initial reaction was that Kerry had won the debate by a pretty substantial margin and then some people—maybe no one here—associated with the Bush-Cheney campaign pushed that story very, very hard and we dealt with it for three or four days.

TAD DEVINE: These debates have three distinct phases, each one of them. There is the table setting going into it, there is the debate itself, and there is what you say afterwards. In the first debate, we did a good job setting the table, in terms of expectations. Kerry was incredibly effective and made our job of winning the post-debate spin very easy. The second debate was closer, but there were fifteen public polls of the debates and John Kerry won all of them.

With the third debate, again, we went in there, we had raised the bar for the President, Kerry again won, which every public poll said, even though it was much closer. But, in that last phase, the Mary Cheney thing got in the way of us winning the post-debate. That's what happened. I don't think it was such a gigantic issue, but it was an issue.

RICK BERKE: Stephanie and Nicole, can you speak very briefly about the plans, the expectations, the spin before the debates—about you all [Nicole] saying Kerry is a great debater and you [Stephanie] saying that Bush is more experienced? (Laughter.) It gets to the point of being silly, but tell us quickly about your strategies going into it in dealing with the press.

STEPHANIE CUTTER: We looked very closely at what had been done in 2000 and how they had set the expectations game on Bush and Gore, as the sitting Vice President, a champion debater. They set their expectations game very low and we weren't going to allow them to do that this time. We actually started working on it a good six weeks before the first debate, in terms of setting their expectation or, at least, preventing them from lowering their expectation. Kerry is a good debater. Everybody knew that. We weren't ever going to be able to say Kerry was a bad debater, but we could ensure that the expectations were at least kept even.

So that's what we worked hard on, all the way up to the first debate. Then we also studied very closely what they did following the first debate with Gore and how they controlled that first post-debate spin—the sigh or the aggression or whatever it was. Coming out of the debate, those issues weren't very important. A few days later, that's all anybody remembered. We took that to heart. We were going to make sure that that was not going to happen to us this time and worked hard to make sure it happened to them.

RICK BERKE: How do you spin something like that when you don't really believe it? (Laughter.)

STEPHANIE CUTTER: What does that have to do with it? (Laughter.)

RICK BERKE: No, seriously. How do you not look disingenuous?

STEPHANIE CUTTER: I don't mean to be disrespectful, but the President's performance that night helped. A lot of it wasn't that difficult because Bush didn't have his best performance that night and Kerry exceeded expectations.

KEN MEHLMAN: Rick, one of the things I think that also assisted in their effort was that the story line going into the first debate was that Kerry was in so much trouble, which I think overstated where things were, and if Kerry doesn't win this one, he is out of the race.

GWEN IFILL: You're saying that your numbers showed differently?

KEN MEHLMAN: I'm saying that we always said we thought this race would be close—a three-point race. The notion that, in an electorate like this one, John Kerry was, after the first debate, going to be knocked out of the race was inaccurate. Because the media had said this is Kerry's last chance—he is on the ropes—that assisted in their effort.

STEPHANIE CUTTER: But you did say that if he doesn't win the first debate, he will be knocked out and, unless he wins these debates, he has no chance of winning the presidency. That did help our case.

BOB SHRUM: But now we are in the post-election. That was a good pre-debate spin.

MATTHEW DOWD: Keep in mind that this is an incumbent president of the United States, that stood on the rubble on 9/11, that gave various State of the Union addresses, that took the country through two wars. There was no way, in the voters' minds, that we were going to tell them, oh, look at George Bush—this was not like 2000. We did poll after poll and we asked, who do you think is going to win the first debate and they thought George Bush would win the first debate, before anybody started spinning.

NICOLE DEVENISH: As far as what we did, there was still a lot of coverage of Kerry's positions on Iraq and so we tried to set up the debates as an opportunity for him to clarify those positions. We were focused on substance and all the coverage was on style, so it didn't pan out.

MATTHEW DOWD: One thing out of the debates that I have to say is—and I think somebody mentioned this but it's important—that because of the rules and because of how the debates were done, John Kerry came across much different than what people had thought he was, which is that he talks in long things, he can't get to the point, where does he stand and all that. He was disciplined, he got down, and he did follow the rules, one-and-a-half minute answers. The way that worked, in the end, was a benefit to John Kerry.

Stephanie Cutter and Nicole Devenish laugh along with Matthew Dowd.

NICOLE DEVENISH: That was part of our expectations also—that whole fight over the rules game and the lights—

STEPHANIE CUTTER: The stage fright and the notepads.

• THE CHARISMATIC OUTSIDERS: BILL CLINTON AND JOHN McCAIN •

GWEN IFILL: Let's move on to talk about the role played by what we have coined the "charismatic outsiders"—the people on this campaign who weren't candidates but were around the edges, having an impact—Bill Clinton and John McCain.

My first question goes to the Democrats about Bill Clinton. There has been some talk that Bill Clinton's presence at the end of the campaign, before or after his heart surgery,[15] wasn't particularly welcomed by John Kerry—that this was something that was imposed on him, belatedly, by Clintonians who came to the campaign late. You can tell me whether that's true or not. Also, I would like your honest assessment about what you thought, ultimately, Clinton brought or did not bring to the outcome of the campaign. First, what did the candidate think about his coming on?

MARY BETH CAHILL: First of all, we wanted him to campaign for us and we had a plan all along for him to campaign for us. He actually did a fair amount before he went in for heart surgery but, at that point, he was contractually confined by his book contract. He did a lot of meetings and a lot of fundraising for us as he traveled around on his book tour. Then he went into the hospital and, as was on the front page of your newspaper, Kerry and Clinton talked.[16] Clinton talks to every major officeholder and every major candidate within the Democratic party on an ongoing basis. He did that to us. He talked to us at every level of the campaign.

GWEN IFILL: When the phone rings and it's Bill Clinton on the other line, do you snatch up the phone or do you go, ugh, there he is again?

---

15. On September 6, 2004, former President Bill Clinton underwent quadruple coronary artery bypass surgery.
16. On September 6, 2004, the *New York Times* reported that former President Clinton had spoken to Senator Kerry by phone for more than ninety minutes from his hospital bed, offering a wide range of advice on how the Senator should proceed with his campaign.

PBS's Gwen Ifill and the New York Times' *Rick Berke listen to the campaign managers.*

MARY BETH CAHILL: He is very smart, he is very astute, he is a real student of both the news and of politics, and so he is always worth listening to. You always want to talk to him. He entered our campaign at the end, campaigning at an extremely large rally in Philadelphia. If we didn't want to make Clinton a major story, that's not the way we would have done that.

GWEN IFILL: Did his extremely large rally in Philadelphia do anything to not make Pennsylvania a surprisingly close race and did he help in Arkansas when he campaigned there?

MARY BETH CAHILL: We won Pennsylvania.

GWEN IFILL: My larger question is, what did Bill Clinton, in the end, do to help, if he did?

MARY BETH CAHILL: He attracts the Democratic base. People were very happy to see him. He got a lot of news coverage. It was reassuring to the Democratic stalwarts that he was involved in the campaign. At that point in time, we had very large crowds and, for the first event, we had an extremely large crowd.

GWEN IFILL: Mark, did he close the gap in Arkansas?

MARK MELLMAN: There was a pretty big gap in Arkansas, when all was said and done. We were talking before about whether people vote for a president or vice president and we said they don't vote for a vice president. They certainly don't vote for the last president and the next one. There was no reason to expect that Bill Clinton campaigning in Arkansas, or anyplace else, was going to change the fundamental results by big numbers.

As these guys are saying, you're fighting for every vote here—can you turn out an additional 10,000, 20,000, 30,000 votes? If it's that close, that can make a difference. What all that is about is fighting for those last few votes.

GWEN IFILL: Did Bill Clinton's return to the campaign trail hurt among married white women who went so heavily for the President?

MARK MELLMAN: Again, I don't think people were voting for the last Democratic president and I don't think they were voting against the last Democratic president. It did help energize the Democratic base, as Mary Beth said, and that was the goal of having Bill Clinton involved. He succeeded at that goal, but it's not a measurable commodity.

RICK BERKE: Speaking of Bill Clinton, you ended up stocking the campaign with former Clinton people. In those closing weeks, it seemed like every other day there was another Clinton official in your campaign. What did they bring to the campaign and was it a good thing or a bad thing?

MARY BETH CAHILL: Well, I am a former Clinton official. (Laughter.) Stephanie Cutter is a former Clinton official. We had a pretty large assemblage of people in our campaign who had worked with Clinton, in the White House or in the administration. There were a bunch of very experienced campaign operatives—Mike McCurry, one of the foremost—that we actually tried to get to come to us in April and May.[17] My experience with this is people are very willing to give you two months but giving you six months is another matter altogether. So, at the end, we actually had some of the best people in our party out in the states and in our campaign. They were much more available to us post–Labor Day than they had been previously.

RICK BERKE: The way some of those same people characterized it, it was more like, we're coming in late to rescue the campaign. If I were in your shoes, I would be resentful of these people coming in and trying to tell you all what to do, when you've been there from the beginning. How did that all work with Joe Lockhart coming in and people saying that he was running the

---

17. Mike McCurry served as President Clinton's press secretary from 1995 to 1998. He joined the Kerry campaign as a traveling senior advisor in September 2004.

campaign and he was in charge of message now?[18] How did that make all of you feel? Did that really help your campaign, to have so many people try to change the way things were run in those crucial closing weeks of the campaign?

MARY BETH CAHILL: Can I just start with the question on who came in the final days? I just wanted to win so anybody who wanted to help us win was very welcome. The one thing about all of the campaign managers around this table this morning is that they all worked for us. When we talk about our convention, everybody who ran against us spoke at our convention. That was the first time that that ever happened. It's inevitably rocky when there are new entries, but it all smoothed out because everybody who came wanted to win, too.

We had some very skilled people who helped us when we were getting extraordinary amounts of news coverage. When the activity on the plane was absolutely enormous, and Stephanie [Cutter] went out there full-time, Lockhart, [Doug] Sosnick, and Joel Johnson really helped us a great deal in the office.[19] We also had Steve Richetti, a former White House deputy chief of staff, in Ohio. Arnie Miller, who was the personnel director in the Carter White House, was assigning volunteers. It was all hands on deck.

STEPHANIE CUTTER: The thing that was missing in all of this is that we asked them to come on board in late July, early August. They were extremely helpful to us. They were another set of hands, another brain, somebody who has been thorough this before. In terms of the ultimate impact, it made us better and that's what we wanted. In terms of strategy, it didn't change our strategy or day-to-day operation. It was just more people, more experience, doing the jobs.

From my perspective, it made me better so this was a welcome thing. It was always much more interesting outside the campaign, in terms of what was happening inside the campaign, than what was actually happening inside the campaign.

RICK BERKE: How did it make you better? What did you learn from that?

STEPHANIE CUTTER: It took things off my plate. Having Joe [Lockhart] at the headquarters while I was on the plane was extremely helpful. It

---

18. Joe Lockhart served as the press secretary for President Clinton's reelection campaign in 1996 and as the President's chief spokesperson from 1998 to 2000. He joined the Kerry campaign as a senior advisor in September 2004.

19. Doug Sosnik served as a senior advisor for policy and strategy for President Clinton. He served as a senior advisor to the Kerry campaign. Joel Johnson was Senator Daschle's chief legislative and communications advisor and later served as Senior Advisor for Policy and Communications to President Clinton. He was the director of Rapid Response for the Kerry campaign.

meant that I didn't have to plan the next day's message-of-the-day. I could concentrate on what was actually happening in that little bubble. There were a lot of people doing that before, but Joe is one of the best in the business.

BOB SHRUM: This will surprise you, but sometimes you have to not take totally seriously everything you read in the press. I learned that very early in this campaign when the initial transition was made and Mary Beth came into the campaign. There was a lot of stuff written. I had to decide that I was going to either pay absolutely no attention to it and go ahead and do my job or I was going to spend a lot of time on it. I decided that I would just go ahead and do my job.

One of the contributions that Mary Beth made, as some of these stories were written and people were coming in, was she always kept her eye on the ball and got everybody else to keep their eye on the ball. The ball was winning the election.

You would read an account of a meeting you were in and that somebody said something that was never said in the meeting. Obviously, that came from a source who hadn't been in the meeting but couldn't say they were not in the meeting. So what you do is you just blow by it.

GWEN IFILL: Why don't you tell us what was actually said in the meetings then? Instead of telling us that what we read in the newspapers was wrong, tell us what actually was happening. Was it all happiness and goodness and light?

BOB SHRUM: Of course, all is not always happiness and goodness and light, and I suspect that was the case in both the Bush-Cheney campaign and our campaign. But our campaign was remarkably free from a lot of day-to-day internal strain and people pushing back and forth at each other, at least in the way it operated. Debate prep was, as Mary Beth said, small, very contained, and had that same quality of people working together. I should mention, by the way, that Ron Klain did a superb job in that process.[20] We actually managed to get most of the questions that were going to be asked. I hate to say that Gwen, although we missed one, obviously.

GWEN IFILL: You missed more than one.

BOB SHRUM: On the plane, for the last three weeks after the debates, Stephanie [Cutter] was doing a terrific job and people were working together. [John] Sasso and I were talking to Mary Beth everyday about the polling. I found the process to be very integrated. I've been in too many of these where

---

20. Ron Klain served as chief of staff to former Vice President Al Gore and played a leading role in Senator Kerry's debate preparations.

the process is not integrated and there are about nine different theories of the case running around.

GWEN IFILL: Let me just read you the words from Tony Coelho, who ran Al Gore's campaign, on September 15, 2004.[21] He said, "There is a civil war going on inside the campaign, there is nobody in charge, and you have these two teams that are generally not talking to each other." He said, "You need a campaign boss, somebody who says 'Shut up, we are going to work this out,' not someone who can go around to Kerry, and that's Shrumy's forte."

BOB SHRUM: Yeah, Coelho doesn't like me because he blames me for his being asked to leave the Gore campaign. I don't really have any comment on that except to say that he had no idea what was going on in our campaign and he had nothing to do with our campaign.

TAD DEVINE: I went to the campaign every day to work. I was there almost every single day—other days we were traveling. I don't remember ever seeing Tony there once, so his insight as to the rival camps and who was doing what is something he derived from a distance, not having actually seen any of this.

GWEN IFILL: Sour grapes?

TAD DEVINE: You are going to have to speak to his motivation. I can only speak to the facts. The facts are the people who could have understood whether that was true or not were the people who were actually there and saw what was going on and all the days that I went there, I never saw Tony.

RICK BERKE: Tad, one point you mentioned a little while ago was the debate inside the campaign over change and whether Kerry was bringing change. Can you tell us a little about that and where the camps were on that?

TAD DEVINE: Again, I don't think there were a lot of camps. (Laughter.) This is sounding more like a civil war than the campaign I was involved in. Mark [Mellman] may have a lot of really good insight on this as well.

The issue of change was an enormously complicated issue in this election, in my view. The country wanted a change in policy, without a doubt, but there were real questions about whether or not they wanted a change in leadership. That, in part, was due to the fact that the President, in the aftermath of the attacks of September 11, surprised a lot of people.

---

21. Tony Coelho is a Democratic political strategist who ran Vice President Gore's campaign in the early stages of the 2000 election.

He won a disputed election. He came in with a cloud over his head and, for the first nine months of his presidency, that cloud persisted. Then it changed because he exceeded the expectations that voters had of him and his performance as president.

In terms of the policies, the country clearly wanted to go in a different direction. When we talked about change, which we did a lot in the research, whether it was in the polling or the focus groups or other places, people expressed some resistance to actually engaging in the idea of real change. Again, I think it's because it was the first post–September 11 election and because we were so close to those events. That's what made change complicated—wanting to go in a different direction and yet being resistant to change.

I've been involved in some change elections, certainly in 1992. I wasn't involved so much in the general election, but that was a change election—this country wanted change and that's why Clinton said the word change, over and over again. I've done a lot of them in Latin America. You say "cambio," you win. If it's a change election, that's the way it works. This election was much more complicated, so what we had to do was to speak to change without using the vocabulary of change. That's why it got nuanced a little bit, in terms of admitting to what they accused us of. That's why we moved to rhetoric which talked about moving the nation in a new direction—about strengthening America, making it stronger, restoring respect for the nation in the world, and, ultimately, moving it in a new direction. We hovered around change without really being able to run a change campaign because we felt if we offered change overtly, rhetorically, and in terms of our messaging, then it would repel too many of those voters who were our principal targets who were uncertain about the President's policies but really not quite ready for a change in leadership.

KEN MEHLMAN: It's interesting you say that because we also recognized the need for change and, in fact, we embraced it. What was unique about this election, among the other things that were unique about this election, was the fact that you had an incumbent running a change platform. If you look at the last four years, a lot of what the President did was to ride a change government, reform government, to deal with all these new challenges we face. If you look at our agenda for the future, you may agree or disagree with it, but it involves a lot of changes. We didn't have a debate internally. We clearly embraced change and reform as one of the big common denominators to a lot of the policies the President put forward.

MATTHEW DOWD: Ken is right, but Tad is also. There was a big reluctance in this country, and specifically among suburban women voters, that might not have agreed with the President on all the policies but were very worried. They trusted the President, they liked his strength, they thought he would protect them. They at least knew he had a clear idea of where he wanted to go, and they were very reluctant to make that jump between, "I may not like all his policies" to "I want to replace him with X."

That existed for the entire election cycle. We had to make voters more comfortable, make them connect with the President, show them that he will continue to do what he needs to do. That was always the razor's edge that existed.

NICOLE DEVENISH: We did that with the President. He started saying every day on the campaign trail, you may not always agree with me, but you'll always know where I stand. That was our way of bridging. He, in his own words, in his own way, and with his own ability to connect with people so effectively, was able to say, I understand you don't always agree with every little thing, but you know me, you know the guy, you know where I stand.

MATTHEW DOWD: We also had a constant push from folks that were asking, why aren't you guys running a "Morning in America" campaign? Why aren't you guys saying how great everything is? Why aren't you doing this and why aren't you doing that? Why aren't you talking about all this stuff?

GWEN IFILL: Who were the folks applying that pressure?

KEN MEHLMAN: Tony Coelho. (Laughter.) And Tony Fabrizio.[22] (Laughter.) The two Tonys.

MATTHEW DOWD: It's just that there are a lot of folks that are inside the 202 area code that do a lot of this and they never understood this situation that we were in. You all, at times, took advantage of some words that we used that were probably not the right ones at the time. "Turning the corner" was a bad phrase because voters were not completely happy with the way things were, whether it was Iraq, the economy or whatever it was. They wanted to know that there was a light at the end of the tunnel, but they didn't want to be told everything was fine, don't worry about it, whether it's from a terrorism standpoint or an economic standpoint. We had a balancing act on that—to run as an incumbent president and not be able to say reelect us, everything is great. We couldn't do that.

RICK BERKE: Tad, on your balancing act, how much pressure was there to be more overt about change? You said you all were cautious, but there were different points of view.

---

22. Tony Fabrizio is a pollster and political pundit who served as the chief pollster to Senator Robert Dole (R-KS) during his 1996 presidential campaign.

TAD DEVINE: This was an ongoing discussion within the campaign. There was more pressure, if you talk about political pressure, from within the ranks of our own party and party structure. I actually had a rule—I called it the two Tonys rule—which was if Tony Coelho was on the front page of the *New York Times* or the *Washington Post*, we were in trouble and if Tony Fabrizio was on the front page of either newspaper, they were in trouble. That's how I could measure the progress of the campaign.

This idea that we needed to embrace change overtly resonated much more powerfully within the ranks of our own core supporters. But we were not running a campaign—that's the campaign, fundamentally, I think that they ran—which was very much directed towards the core supporters. We were running a campaign directed towards other people, the people Matt just alluded to, who were much more uncertain about it. That's why we made the decision to speak more to them and to be less overt about our call for change.

GWEN IFILL: We promised to talk to you about both of the "charismatic outsiders."

RICK BERKE: The other one is John McCain. I'm a little confused because Mary Beth said last night that you got some bad advice from someone to put him on the ticket.

MARY BETH CAHILL: That was a joke.

RICK BERKE: Okay, that was a joke. (Laughter.) Can you tell us about the overtures from Kerry to John McCain to be on the ticket?

MARY BETH CAHILL: Kerry talked to McCain in an ongoing fashion, up until pretty late in the campaign. It was a conversation they had started a long time ago. Actually, he was one of the senators that Kerry spoke with most often. McCain played the role, from my point of view, of an old-fashioned—like Walter Lippmann or someone like that—somebody who was an arbiter and who called both sides to attention in a way that the press would have done in previous generations, and who said, okay, this is in bounds, that is out of bounds. Kerry wanted advice from McCain in an ongoing fashion. He has a lot of respect and affection for the guy.

GWEN IFILL: Are we talking about policy advice or strategic advice?

MARY BETH CAHILL: McCain had run for president before. Kerry talked to a lot of people who had run for president—Clinton among them—and said, okay, I'm at this point, what do you think, what did you hear, what would you recommend I do here? A lot of it was about his personal performance and that was an ongoing conversation.

GWEN IFILL: At what point did that conversation turn into, it would be really great if you were on my ticket?

MARY BETH CAHILL: This is something that was hugely overblown in the press.

GWEN IFILL: It didn't happen?

MARY BETH CAHILL: I was not present, if it did. I was present pretty often when John Kerry talked to John McCain and I don't believe it happened. I believe that it was hugely overblown. This is a fascinating story line and it was something that got so much more play than actually existed, at least within our campaign.

RICK BERKE: *Newsweek* said there were about a half dozen overtures and it wasn't done explicitly but it was done very clearly so he could say it but not say it, like a wink-and-a-nod, so everyone knew what was going on.

MARY BETH CAHILL: Are we going to go through the *Newsweek* list— (Laughter.)

STEPHANIE CUTTER: I want to play, if we do. (Laughter.)

RICK BERKE: Let's not. Bob, as a true liberal Democrat over the years, would you have been comfortable with McCain on the ticket?

BOB SHRUM: Sure, but I didn't think it was going to happen. I never thought it was going to happen and I don't think John Kerry believed it was going to happen. I'm in the same position as Mary Beth. While I heard a number of these conversations and was present when he was talking in a number of these conversations, I have no reason to believe that he ever asked John McCain or that John McCain ever answered the question.

RICK BERKE: What about McCain's pretty conservative positions on a lot of issues?

MARY BETH CAHILL: Sure, that would have been a huge problem.

BOB SHRUM: It would have been a problem and we would have won the election. (Laughter.)

GWEN IFILL: Ken, do you think that's true?

KEN MEHLMAN: I don't know how it would have played. But I do agree that he would have been certainly formidable to put on the ticket and, partly, he would have been because of how you covered him. I also agree and, as I said last night, I think that he did end up being—a lot of it was because of the press—an arbiter for both campaigns and for the media.

• THE ROVE FACTOR •

RICK BERKE: We talked about all your help from Clinton and some of how your campaign was organized. The one person we haven't heard about in this whole two days is Karl Rove—the Mr. Mastermind, political genius, whatever. Ken, would you say he is your mentor?

KEN MEHLMAN: He is a mentor, absolutely.

RICK BERKE: Can you talk a little about his role in this campaign and your role and how all of you worked together?

KEN MEHLMAN: One of the things that was nice about this campaign, and useful in this particular team, is that the same folks that worked on the 2000 campaign were largely present for 2004. Matthew [Dowd] and I had worked with Karl since 1999 on the Bush for President campaign. Having been at the White House as a political director and then going over to do the campaign, there was a natural flow to a lot of the things we had been building—whether it was the "72-hour effort," the stuff we did with the media, or the targeting stuff.

All that stuff had been occurring at the RNC and, as political director at the White House, I had been involved in it so there was a seamlessness to the effort that was really useful. Karl Rove being at the White House was very important in helping manage what otherwise would have been a very difficult process of dealing with the White House, which a lot of reelection campaigns have to deal with because you had someone over there who had been so central to everything and who had a history of working with the key players in the campaign. That helped make things very well organized and effective and really helped make things seamless.

RICK BERKE: What kind of decisions did he make? Was he the broader thinker? Or how did it work? Did you carry things out? Can you give us some examples?

KEN MEHLMAN: A couple of things. One, we set up a system by which it wasn't just I decide or you decide, things were discussions, usually. We had a system by which the three of us and Karl and Dan Bartlett and others were able to talk about and discuss things. It was reported in the *New York Times* that the "Breakfast Club" was a tool by which a group of people could help plan the coming weeks and how things would work. We also had a series of calls in the morning to talk about—

NICOLE DEVENISH: We talked a lot.

KEN MEHLMAN: —message of the day, plan of the day, attack of the day, what we were likely to hear, and what our plan was. All that helped. If you build all that stuff into the process, then it works really well. People feel like they are a part of things and, ultimately, you are able to execute very well. One of the great things about Karl, and the President too, is that they trust people to make decisions. When I was first asked to do this, I said I want to make sure that while we talk about everything, I'm the campaign manager— I'm making, in consultation with other people, decisions about how we spend money and decisions about who gets hired. If I can make those decisions, then we are going to have a system that works. One of the other good things we have is—this is certainly true of Matthew and Nicole, I hope it's true of me, and it's true of Karl and others—we are people that are not worried about personal credit. That's really important. We are worried about sharing credit.

If you add all those factors together—a history of working together, doing a lot of planning and getting a lot of people's input up front, trust in people they put in charge and giving them real authority, and people that are not trying to hog credit—you end up having a system that works pretty well.

GWEN IFILL: It seems like it comes in handy that you don't care about personal credit because Karl Rove has gotten all the credit for this campaign. (Laughter.) He has risen to kind of god-like, little "g," proportions in the political pantheon. How much of that is overblown?

MATTHEW DOWD: The media, and Karl has talked about this before related to White House stuff, and folks find it a convenient thing to say, okay, this event happened and, therefore, that changed the nature of the campaign, or this person is the one that controls all the stuff under here. It's much more difficult to say that campaigns are about big waves that include a lot of different things and that campaigns are about a lot of different personalities that give a lot of advice on different things. That's what this campaign was.

Karl has been close to the President for more than twenty years. He is his right-hand man on political advice. But, like a lot of things in life, they are much more complicated than one person or one event.

GWEN IFILL: But doesn't his right-hand man status make him first among equals?

MATTHEW DOWD: Yes, obviously. If push came to shove and there was a disagreement on political advice and Karl has got it one way, the President is going to take that to heart when he makes a decision. But it's not that Karl says, we need to do X, we need to do Y, and we need to Z, and minions, go take care of it. It just doesn't work like that in life, in any way. You can't enter a presidential campaign with $300 million and expect that when decisions are made every two seconds. It just can't work that way. It works for the media to just have one person—to say we have a name, a person, we can describe them, this is how it is, and we got the picture and here it is. It's much harder to say there are seven people here, and the decision was made this way, and things flowed this way and it worked. It's much harder to describe unless you say "Karl Rove."

NICOLE DEVENISH: I think the reason people have written so much about the "Breakfast Club" and those eggs we ate all year is that it took longer to run the campaign that way. It takes longer when you bring seven people along every step of the way, but everybody did it everyday. A lot of the magazines are writing these year-end who-did-what articles and a lot of people have asked me. It's very hard to go back and recollect a single decision and assign it to one person. Between Ken [Mehlman], Matthew [Dowd], and Karl [Rove], it's hard to know, in the key decisions, strategically, where each one of them ended.

When people look at the campaign and it being a reelect, there is not a lot of focus on the reelect. The focus is on the White House and on the White House infrastructure and that was perfectly fine with all of us. When you look back and try to figure out who made those key decisions, as a lot of people are doing in their year-end coverage, it's very difficult. I can't even go back, and I was there every week at the breakfast and know what any individual thought of anything. We took this path and we stayed on it.

There were certainly times where it was like, oh, let's just do it, you know, there are 175 of us over here. But, at every step, it was this process and this live wire of Dan [Bartlett] and Karl [Rove] at the White House, Karen [Hughes] on the road, and those of us in the campaign.

RICK BERKE: One of the striking decisions early on that was an undercurrent or a theme for the whole campaign was the decision by the President to be overtly political, very early on, in striking contrast to Clinton's reelection campaign. He was out there criticizing the Democrats, criticizing Kerry. There were very hard-hitting ads with him in there. Was that a uniform agreement or was there real discussion?

NICOLE DEVENISH: Can I take on the notion of early? There was also Fox News every Sunday for months, and a lot of commentary about how we had been very slow to respond to this Democratic primary that had beaten up relentlessly on Bush. In every Democratic debate, they didn't go after each other, they went after us. The candidate who was often deemed the winner of those Democratic primary debates was the one that had gotten tough on Bush. I know you're asking about the Rose Garden strategy. Look at the coverage in March and April. There was a lot of coverage about how slow we had been to respond to all the attacks on Bush from Dean, from Gephardt, and from the whole field.

KEN MEHLMAN: Two points that are different from 1996. The central question of the 1996 campaign was answered when Bill Clinton won the battle over the government shutdown.[23] That battle had occurred at the end of 1995, the beginning of 1996. You had [Senator] Bob Dole, who was ultimately the nominee, in the middle of negotiations. Congress said they accepted Clinton's approach. From that point forward, the definition of Bob Dole and the definition of the Republicans occurred through television ads, which occurred more than a year before the Clinton campaign ran. That definition was baked in the cake that year in a way that it was not in this election.

The second difference is what Nicole just said and that is the first ad which the Kerry campaign ran against the President was in September of 2003—it was the first ad criticizing the President. While we did respond to those ads, we had been attacked for a very long period before we responded. I think he always responded in a way that was appropriate—that was consistent with being presidential—and he didn't let it interfere with other duties that he had. So there are clear differences from 1996, in terms of definitions.

RICK BERKE: Was there anyone disagreeing with that or was that sort of a unanimous decision?

MATTHEW DOWD: That was a unanimous decision. The only question was the day—not even the month. It was, do we do it this day? That was the

---

23. In December 1995 and January 1996, Democratic and Republican leaders were forced into a partial shutdown of the federal government as a result of their inability to resolve an ongoing budget dispute.

only discussion. It wasn't if and it wasn't generally when, it was how. Do we do it in a funny way? How do we start that process?

NICOLE DEVENISH: It was the RGA speech, I think.[24]

MARY BETH CAHILL: I think it was the President in the Oval Office in March. Bush really went at Kerry in the Oval Office.

NICOLE DEVENISH: That was after the RGA speech though.

RICK BERKE: Matt, what was the funny way you were thinking?

MATTHEW DOWD: I forget how he did it in the RGA speech. We thought the best way to start this process was to poke fun at the fact that he was somebody that's taken every side of every issue. It was a two-line thing. We thought the best way to start this process was not a two-by-four to the head, but a funny way to start this process moving and that's what happened in the RGA speech. I forget exactly what the line was.

NICOLE DEVENISH: It might have been, "If you don't like the position, wait—"

KEN MEHLMAN: No, it was something, it was a good line. (Laughter.)

GWEN IFILL: Memorable as well.

KEN MEHLMAN: I remember it.

MATTHEW DOWD: The first two or three times he did it was a funny way to do it and that's what we thought was the most appropriate way to start.

NICOLE DEVENISH: Funny is obviously in the eye of the beholder.

GWEN IFILL: We discussed this before, haven't we?
    I would like to flip-flop the Karl Rove as god idea for a moment to the Democratic side. If Karl Rove is the great, all-seeing genius, that makes Bob Shrum what?

BOB SHRUM: Certainly not that. I actually was uncomfortable with a lot of the stuff. I tried to disappear during the campaign.

---

24. On February 23, 2004, President Bush gave a speech to the Republican Governors' Association in Washington, D.C., in which he criticized the Democratic candidates for president.

GWEN IFILL: Not successfully, Bob.

BOB SHRUM: I stayed off television for a year and went away and wouldn't talk to most press people. I agree with what they were saying about any good campaign. When they were describing how their campaign operated, in terms of getting people in a room, talking about ideas, then making a decision, they are describing very much how our campaign operated. I don't believe that there are campaigns in America that are successful, where there is one person who is sitting there saying, we are going to do this, we are going to do that, we are going to do the next thing.

What does it make me? It makes me somebody who works on spots, who has ideas about strategy, and who works on debates. I think I had a couple of good ideas and I had a couple of bad ideas during the course of the campaign.

GWEN IFILL: Would you do this again?

BOB SHRUM: I am absolutely determined that there will be a Democratic president of the United States in 2008, and if someone wanted me to help, obviously I would help.

GWEN IFILL: What if somebody thought your presence would hurt?

BOB SHRUM: That's their decision.

• THE SPOUSES •

GWEN IFILL: The next outsiders who have played a role in this campaign are the spouses.

MARY BETH CAHILL: They didn't think they were outsiders.

GWEN IFILL: Well, not the principals. How's that? Unless, depending on how you interpret that, actually. (Laughter.) Teresa Kerry had a lot to say during the campaign, in different ways, but the one thing that seemed to catch at exactly the wrong time was on October 19 when she said to *USA Today* that First Lady Laura Bush never really had a real job. When you heard that, Republicans, did that sound like a gift to you?

KEN MEHLMAN: It sounded like something that a lot of people would have scratched their head about, think it was not reflective of their view of the world, and would find to be condescending. We didn't do anything with it.

NICOLE DEVENISH: That's not true. We did. Karen Hughes responded.

GWEN IFILL: Yes, she did.

NICOLE DEVENISH: Mrs. Bush then accepted the apology and that was the end of it. But we did respond.

GWEN IFILL: On morning television—it wasn't just an incidental response.

KEN MEHLMAN: I stand corrected.

GWEN IFILL: Okay.

KEN MEHLMAN: I thought it was a revealing comment. It was something that she said she regretted and I think, to a lot of people, it indicated a different approach to looking at the world than they had.

MATTHEW DOWD: I also think that, like a lot of things, Teresa is a quilt of many colors and so that was just one part of her, over the course of that campaign. I don't think that was problematic on its own. There were a lot of things.

GWEN IFILL: How many of those colors were in her Apple file?

MATTHEW DOWD: We never had an Apple file on her. She was herself and we were fine about that.

NICOLE DEVENISH: I think she suffered. Laura Bush was a star of this cycle. People were drawn to her as the first lady and, on the campaign, her star rose. I think that maybe made the press or people harder on Teresa.

MATTHEW DOWD: I also think what has happened, and whether it's because of 9/11 or a new environment, people are voting more for a family in the White House. Maybe it's post-Clinton, or whatever it is. In our research, the perceptions of the first ladies and the family mattered more. Whether it's the 9/11 environment, care and comforting, who the person is matters because now you see a first lady much more on television than you did ten or twenty years ago. They are much more of a political presence. As we look forward, the first lady or first man, first husband, or however we're going to describe that person, will matter more than it's ever mattered before because it's a family now in the White House that deals with the nation, as opposed to just a president.

RICK BERKE: Did your research show that Teresa was detrimental to the Kerry campaign?

GWEN IFILL: And the same question to Mark.

MATTHEW DOWD: Among women voters, there was a big concern when they saw Laura Bush and they saw Teresa Heinz.

RICK BERKE: That what?

MATTHEW DOWD: Laura Bush was much more readily accepted as a first lady than Teresa Heinz was potentially.

RICK BERKE: Mark?

MARK MELLMAN: A very different view on this. The reality is Teresa Heinz Kerry is an extraordinarily accomplished person who has done a tremendous amount in her own right. There is a prescription drug program in Pennsylvania because of Teresa Heinz Kerry. There is a prescription drug program, I believe, in this state because of Teresa Heinz Kerry. There is all kinds of environmental activism around the world because of Teresa Heinz Kerry. So there are a whole group of people—a whole group of women in particular—in our party, in our base, for whom she was absolutely a role model, and people would die and kill for her, are in love with her.

There are also a group of people who didn't like her. Those people, by and large, are people who would never have voted for John Kerry under any circumstance. I don't think that she had that kind of effect. In another context, we did see people reacting to Laura Bush very positively. But one of the reasons that people respond positively to Laura Bush is they have this view, which may be right or wrong, that she will keep the President from doing bad things.

We did focus groups around the country with women talking about the issue of choice. We asked, will George Bush appoint a Supreme Court justice who is going to overrule *Roe* or make abortion illegal? They responded, he would like to but Laura won't let him, pillow talk. Now, I don't know whether that's true or not. I certainly have no idea what their pillow talk is and no idea what her view is on the subject. But people have invented this story for themselves that Laura Bush keeps the President from doing bad things and that's one of the reasons that people like her.

RICK BERKE: Is it true, Stephanie, that Teresa was a pain in the ass for the staff to have around but that she made the candidate much more relaxed, that he liked her and they had a good relationship, except they were fighting openly? Tell us what really— (Laughter.)

STEPHANIE CUTTER: You must have read that somewhere. I'm just going to build on what Mark said. Teresa had an enormous amount of assets and it was much more effective for us to have her campaigning someplace else—

GWEN IFILL: Now wait a second, do you want to rephrase that?

STEPHANIE CUTTER: —in another battleground state, getting votes for us. It was a divide-and-conquer strategy. There were moments where they wanted to be together, and so that's when we brought them together, like right after the convention, which has been slightly mischaracterized in the press coverage that followed.

There are certain instances, like the Laura Bush comment, where I think that Teresa is very accomplished and she is proud of her accomplishments, and I don't think she meant any harm by that comment. Certainly, if I were on the other side of it, I would have done exactly the same thing that they did. That's why we jumped on it pretty quickly and Teresa was adamant about putting out an apology and saying that's—

NICOLE DEVENISH: Immediately.

STEPHANIE CUTTER: Yes, immediately.

NICOLE DEVENISH: Laura Bush accepted it immediately and that was the end of it.

STEPHANIE CUTTER: She did, absolutely. So, in terms of how the staff would handle Teresa, she had her own staff and, by and large, they had their own schedule and it worked out well.

GWEN IFILL: I'm curious whether Teresa's coat of many colors, to use Matt's phrase, contributed to the nagging question of elitism when it came to John Kerry. The windsurfing, the Sun Valley vacations, the SUV which they did or did not own. How did you strategize around that to appeal to this middle ground that you were hoping for? The people who Mark said think of Teresa as a role model were not the voters you needed to win over.

MARY BETH CAHILL: First of all, some of this about a candidate's family are just facts—you don't strategize around them, you accept the facts of people's lives. We were going to appeal to middle-class and lower-middle-class voters by talking about things that were of concern to them, not about John Kerry's personal circumstances. So that was what he did, day to day, on the stump. John and Teresa Heinz Kerry got married when they were older, both very accomplished people, both had very separate lives, and they came together with those different accomplishments. That was the thing that he loved and admired about her the most—that she had her own life and that she did things that she thought were really important. That was important to him and it was something that he talked about in an ongoing fashion during the campaign.

RICK BERKE: What did you think when you saw those pictures in the paper of him windsurfing? Did you say, oh my God, this is not good for us? (Laughter.)

GWEN IFILL: For the record, Mary Beth rolled her eyes. (Laughter.)

MARY BETH CAHILL: I didn't think it was a good idea.

RICK BERKE: Did you tell him that?

GWEN IFILL: And with how much force?

MARY BETH CAHILL: I had a lot of conversations with John Kerry every day. The moment in time was the first day of the Republican convention. We were in Nantucket doing debate prep. He had two hours off and had gotten some new equipment and wanted to try it out. Then there was video.

RICK BERKE: You knew beforehand and were not able to stop him?

MARY BETH CAHILL: I thought that he was not going to windsurf.

RICK BERKE: He just did it? Did he not realize how it would look or did he say, to hell with it, I am who I am?

MARY BETH CAHILL: He very much had an "I am who I am" attitude. He was not going to change who he was. He was not going to be wearing browns or beiges or earth tones.

GWEN IFILL: He was going to be wearing spandex. (Laughter.)

MARY BETH CAHILL: Well, naturally, he stopped wearing spandex. (Laughter.) And this was something he had been doing over the course of fifteen years, so it's not as though he took things up for the course of the campaign. He did the things that he had done through the course of his life.

RICK BERKE: So he did have fair warning and he just chose to do it his way? Ken Mehlman, when you saw the pictures of Kerry windsurfing—

KEN MEHLMAN: We actually paid for the equipment. They don't know that we bought him new equipment—it was a birthday gift—sent it overnight. (Laughter.)

RICK BERKE: What did you think? Did you really think ad?

KEN MEHLMAN: Yes, I thought we might have a good ad here.

NICOLE DEVENISH: Didn't your press go crazy though because they didn't know—they didn't get to go? We found out he had gone from your press corps.

STEPHANIE CUTTER: Yes. We preferred that it didn't get into the press because we understood what it meant. He went windsurfing, there was no pool there.

MARY BETH CAHILL: And they went nuts and they told us.

STEPHANIE CUTTER: It was a local camera crew, who just happened to be there, that got the coverage. It was a day from hell.

GWEN IFILL: So the lesson you've learned from this is tell the press everything.

BOB SHRUM: Can I say something about both of these things? The windsurfing footage gave them some decent visuals for an ad. The amount of time we've just spent on this is massively disproportionate to its impact on the campaign and it illustrates a lot of what's wrong with the way we think about politics in this country today.

On Teresa, in the very dark and difficult days, and they were literally dark in New Hampshire and Iowa, she went out on her own and did an extraordinary job. She had people in those states, who were very much working-class people, lower middle-class people, who related to her and who understood that she related to them. I think she had a good deal to do with us winning the Iowa caucuses.

I also reject the whole notion that a lot of the people who were offended by her accent, her independence, or her prominent role in life were likely to vote for the Democratic nominee for president. They weren't. She is an extraordinary person and, having worked with her a good deal during this campaign, I did not find her difficult to work with.

• BUSH'S VIETNAM WAR RECORD •

GWEN IFILL: We'll move on from the personality, even though that was a lot of fun, and back to a little bit of policy.

One of the things that John Kerry seemed hesitant to do during his campaign was to openly and directly question the President's war record—something which CBS tried and failed and maybe now we know why John Kerry resisted.[25] On one occasion, the final night of the Republican National Convention, John Kerry and John Edwards had a midnight rally in which Kerry said, "I will not have my commitment to defend this country questioned by those who refused to serve when they could have and who have misled America into Iraq. I'll leave it up to the voters to decide whether five deferments makes someone more qualified to defend this nation than two tours of combat duty."

Why didn't we hear him on that theme more?

MARY BETH CAHILL: Part of it was what we've discussed through the course of the afternoon, that voters really did want to talk about the current state of affairs and where both sides wanted to lead the country. So, at a certain point in time, discussions about their pasts became something that the voters just washed out because they had had enough of that. That statement came after the Vice President's speech at the convention, which was a pretty unfair excoriation, and that was his response to it.

We talked in an earlier session about Kerry's time protesting the war and, during that period of time, he had refused to question the service or decisions made during that period by other people who made the same decisions as him or others. Part of this was just the way that he and the Vietnam vets against the war had acted over the course of years. That was one singular departure from that in response to a great deal of provocation.

GWEN IFILL: Were you surprised at all that you didn't get more attacks from the Kerry camp on the President's war record?

---

25. In September 2004, CBS broadcast a story on *60 Minutes II* which alleged that President Bush received preferential treatment during his stint with the Texas Air National Guard and failed to complete his required duties. It was later determined that several of the memos on which the story was based were forgeries.

KEN MEHLMAN: As I recall, he did it twice. He brought it up once, I think it was on the *Today Show,* when there was a question about his own record, and he did it the night of the convention speech. I was surprised about it from a couple of perspectives. First, the Vice President had, during the course of his speech, actually praised John Kerry's record of Vietnam service, as had Rudy Guiliani and John McCain, and the convention floor applauded three times.

I thought that night was really important to the campaign because the President had just let out a future-looking agenda and, in response to that, John Kerry talked about an issue, and divided Americans over an issue, that occurred thirty-five years ago. A lot of people said, particularly in the press, they were attacking on the Swift Boat thing. On the other hand, they were making the same attacks, just from a different perspective. I felt that that made him much more amenable to the argument that the Swift Boat folks had had. To a lot of people, it said that George Bush is future-oriented and is focusing on solving problems, and this guy is focused on the past and on dividing people. I thought it was a bad night for him. I was surprised that he did it and the way he did it. I don't know why you do a midnight speech anyway.

NICOLE DEVENISH: I don't think it was as much the substance as it was his own statements about Clinton, which were so eloquent. Kerry had said, "we should never divide the nation over who served and when," which is what we fed back to the press to help blunt this very attack. It was about the past and it was also that it contradicted a very eloquent position he had taken when Clinton was running. He had been out there very prominently saying we should never divide the nation over who served and when or how.

MATTHEW DOWD: [DNC Chair] Terry McAuliffe, for forty-something days, had this stupid website thing going and was feeding it to the press. I was like, fine, because if you are not talking about the cost of health care and you are not talking about the loss of jobs and you are talking about George Bush's service thirty years ago, whether or not he served or was in the Guard or not, it was meaningless to people. This is a post-9/11 president. The people whose votes you could influence on this could care less whether or not he had served in the National Guard thirty years ago and whether or not he showed up in Alabama. This President had already passed the threshold of, he is a commander in chief, I trust this guy, he has done what has needed to be done, let's talk about X. So every day that was spent either talking about John Kerry's Vietnam service or George Bush's Guard service was a waste of time.

RICK BERKE: What was the thinking behind that midnight decision?

GWEN IFILL: And then respond to it, Matt, just whether that was a waste of time.

MARY BETH CAHILL: Once again, another view of the Republican convention. It was all about trying to make a case that Kerry was unfit to lead the country, and whether it was Zell Miller's "defending the nation with spitballs," that was a constant theme of all the speakers at the Republican convention. After four days of that, Kerry wanted to say something back. The other thing is he was in Ohio, which turned out to be ground zero, right after the Republican convention stopped at 11:00. At 11:30, he was in Ohio. That was the beginning of the general election campaign. We were both on the same playing field, we were both under the same counts, and now we are off to the races. That was a natural response from a veteran and somebody who was very interested in foreign policy and defense to what had been said about him by a cast of Republican speakers over the course of four days.

RICK BERKE: Was there any hesitation about upstaging the nominee on his big night? Did it look desperate or unseemly?

MARY BETH CAHILL: No. When everyone was calling us and asking for the response to his speech, Kerry gave a response to his speech, instead of Stephanie [Cutter] or Tad [Devine] giving a response to the speech.

TAD DEVINE: A guy, who had a real record, watched a Republican convention where people were walking around with band-aids with purple hearts on them. He heard people attack him, attack his character, attack his service, attack his life in very personal and bitter terms. I think it's understandable that he would want to say something about it.

Why didn't we say something about it for eleven months or why did we only sporadically say something about it? Exactly for the reason that Matt [Dowd] pointed out. If we talked about that all the time, we were not talking to people who were going to decide this election about the issues they care most deeply about. That's why.

We had just gone through this period where the Kerry campaign spent $400,000 in August on television and the Bush campaign spent $32 million. The DNC independent expenditure spent a lot, but that wasn't us. What we needed was John Kerry standing there, making his case directly to the people, and we didn't have that for five weeks. At that moment in time, did he try to turn the page, vividly, by standing up at midnight and moving us ahead? Yes, he did and, to some measure, he had some success in moving the campaign to a different place after the convention.

RICK BERKE: On the other side, related to that somewhat, we had Bob Dole step out and question John Kerry's war record. Did you all know that was coming?

KEN MEHLMAN: Bob Dole was a surrogate for us in a number of occasions and was a great surrogate. He did a very good job. But obviously Bob Dole says what Bob Dole wants to say and I don't recall knowing about it specifically beforehand.

NICOLE DEVENISH: I had a thing on my door for a long time where Dole said, there are these dumb conference calls to go over what we were supposed to say on the Sunday shows and I never get on them. He wasn't someone that called in to find out what the message of the day was and he certainly didn't take his cues—

GWEN IFILL: Just for the record, let me just read what Dole actually said so you can respond and refresh your memory. He said, "He is a good guy, a good friend. I respect his record but three purple hearts and never bled that I know of. I mean they are all superficial wounds. Three purple hearts and you're out." I could do my Dole impression here but that wouldn't be right. "One day he is saying that we were shooting civilians, cutting off their ears, cutting off their heads, throwing away his medals or his ribbons. The next day he is standing there, I want to be president because I'm a Vietnam veteran. Maybe he should apologize to all of the other two and a half million veterans who served. He wasn't the only one in Vietnam."

KEN MEHLMAN: I would say, in response, that was not something we had planned with him beforehand and we did not expect him to say that, necessarily. But, I will tell you, talking to a lot of veterans, that reflected what a lot of veterans thought, not about the awards but about the statements and testimony afterwards.

GWEN IFILL: Bob Dole was the nominee of your party not very long ago. He is still a major spokesman for your party. When your candidate is saying, I respect his record and leaving it there, when your vice presidential nominee is saying the same thing, and then Bob Dole says something this harsh, you are saying it just came out of the blue?

KEN MEHLMAN: You know Bob Dole and I know Bob Dole.

MATTHEW DOWD: We had a concerted effort to tell people that were at all associated with the campaign, or came to ask us our advice, don't talk about John Kerry's Vietnam service at all, and if you talk about it, praise it and move on and talk about his votes on defense or—

NICOLE DEVENISH: The $87 billion.

MATTHEW DOWD: Anybody that we talked to, we said, don't question his medals. So, if he did it, it was done. If he asked for advice, we would have told him not to do it—

GWEN IFILL: It was probably Wolf Blitzer's fault. (Laughter.)

MATTHEW DOWD: This wasn't a wink-and-a-nod. I would prefer it never had been raised. I would have preferred that nobody ever raised questions about John Kerry's medals in Vietnam. I would have preferred that, from a person that wanted to have an impact on the voters.

KEN MEHLMAN: As I recall, I think Bob Dole called afterwards and said, yeah, I probably wasn't supposed to say that but I did say something along those lines. That's what happens, as I'm sure the Kerry campaign will tell you, with surrogate programs. People sometimes say things that are not exactly consistent with the message you are putting forward.

RICK BERKE: Mark?

MARK MELLMAN: I'd just like to ask you guys a question in that respect. I heard what Matt said, so I have two questions. Number one, are you saying that you thought the Swift Boat ads in August were not damaging to John Kerry? Because you said you preferred no one ever talked about his record. Number two, had those ads not been aired, did you guys research this? Did you look at ads and decide you weren't going to do that? Did you look at ads and decide you were going to do it, if they hadn't done it?

MATTHEW DOWD: As Shrum or somebody said, there was always a ton of research—newspaper articles—available that said what John Kerry's record was. We looked at that and came to the quick conclusion that we were never going to question John Kerry's service in Vietnam.

GWEN IFILL: Did that question come after April 25 when Karen Hughes, also talking to Wolf Blitzer, said, something is building here, he only pretended to throw his medals away?

MATTHEW DOWD: Let me finish, Gwen.

GWEN IFILL: Oh, okay.

MATTHEW DOWD: There were two questions in our campaign. There was the question of questioning his medals and his service in Vietnam and then the question of what he did after he came back from Vietnam. We always said, on the first part, we didn't want anybody to do anything except praise him for his service. The second part, which we never talked about, was something that I thought was completely fair game because you were using his own words and what he said. Kerry was out there. He was on the front page talking about what he did and what he said. The medals and his service were completely different than what he did when he came back from Vietnam. Those were two separate issues.

GWEN IFILL: So that remained fair game throughout?

MATTHEW DOWD: In my view, if you want to talk about the Swift Boat ads, if the Swift Boat ads had an effect—and I've said this from day one—it was because they highlighted something people didn't want to talk about which was, why are we talking about Vietnam? Why aren't we talking about issues that matter to us? The controversy that brewed about the Swift Boats was going back to Kerry's convention speech. What did he talk about? He talked about his Vietnam service and that's all we were hearing. Who is John Kerry? What is he going to do? All we hear is Vietnam, Vietnam, Vietnam. What more is there?

GWEN IFILL: In your minds, did it all get conflated like that?

BOB SHRUM: Number one, let me say that, whether or not the campaign or anybody associated with the campaign had anything to do with the Swift Boat ads, I think they helped the President in the sense that they did take the discussion off onto a track that the voters were largely uninterested in.

Number two, we generally discovered that Kerry's opposition to the war when he came back, while it enraged a number of people on the right, didn't actually have much impact on voters.

The first Swift Boat exchange actually was the most important Swift Boat exchange. At the end of it, in the data we saw, people decided that Kerry had served honorably and they believed that the Bush campaign had had something to do with the ads. They said, please stop talking about this, please talk about health care, please talk about jobs, please talk about the economy or Iraq. So, in that sense, I think they served the President's purpose.

RICK BERKE: Mark Mellman, is it not true that you were pushing aggressively inside the campaign for the campaign to respond more quickly, or more swiftly, to the Swift Boat ads?

MARK MELLMAN: There are two ways to look at this and we will never know, in retrospect, which was the better course. One argument is hit the thing quickly.

RICK BERKE: This is the Mellman argument.

MARK MELLMAN: Your words, not mine. The other side of the argument was, you don't want to make this a bigger story than it is.

RICK BERKE: There is a reason why you and Bob Shrum are on different sides of the table. (Laughter.)

MARK MELLMAN: No, it's not. (Laughter.) Just because one reads it somewhere doesn't mean it's true.

RICK BERKE: That's why we are trying to get to the bottom of it.

BOB SHRUM: The reality of this is that there was a phone call made to John Kerry after Mark's polling, for about a day and a half, had shown that this was hurting us and the cable had taken on a life of its own. Kerry was going to speak to the firefighters the next day. There was a recommendation, from about five or six people sitting in the room, to him that, A, he take it on with the firefighters in Boston and then, B, we decide, since neither the independent expenditure nor a 527 had figured out that they should respond to this, that we would go on the air and do it. That recommendation was unanimous and he accepted that recommendation.

JEFF GREENFIELD (CNN): Went on the air in what way? I don't understand.

BOB SHRUM: We put ads on the air.

TAD DEVINE: In the markets where they were advertising, we responded.

• THE WAR IN IRAQ AND THE WAR ON TERROR •

RICK BERKE: It's not quite related, but it's a good jumping off point to talk about Iraq because during this whole campaign there was this whole backdrop of the war and our soldiers getting killed, and the 9/11 Commission and terror reports coming out that were critical of the administration. How concerned were you all about these outside events and crises affecting this campaign and things that were maybe beyond your control?

KEN MEHLMAN: That was a big concern. The fact is that you were the incumbent president at a time when there was a war going on overseas and war is always very difficult. There is always a lot of uncertainty associated with it. You had an economy that was recovering but, in some places, the recovery hadn't been going on as long as you would have liked it to have been. There were a lot of outside factors that were a concern. You couldn't do a lot about it in terms of affecting the outcome of the war.

NICOLE DEVENISH: There were also a lot of books that came out. At one point, we had a calendar with all the books on them that were coming out.

KEN MEHLMAN: We had to determine how to deal with it and we thought that the best way to deal with it was to remind people why we went to war, remind people about the War on Terror, remind people this was a central front in the War on Terror, and remind people about Senator Kerry's, shall we put it, complicated record on discussing these questions.

RICK BERKE: What were you all thinking? Were you thinking, there is going to be a point where there are so many fatalities here that it's going to turn against Bush—as sensitive as this is an issue, it's a very real thing out there—that people were dying and that could affect the campaign?

MARY BETH CAHILL: It did affect the campaign. The nightly news coverage and what people were seeing, especially during Fallujah, and when things really spiraled out of control, the day when we passed the threshold of 1,000 fatalities. They were real benchmarks where there was a lot of coverage. People talked about it a lot. People talked about it at town hall meetings, they talked about it in focus groups, they talked about it everywhere Kerry went. So there was no way that you could run the campaign, day-to-day, and not be talking about what was moving into the forefront of the voters' minds.

GWEN IFILL: You don't think, in the forefront of the voters' minds, was Social Security and jobs?

MARY BETH CAHILL: The thing about voters is it's not mutually exclusive. When the news coverage, and particularly the television news coverage, was really graphic, of armored vehicles blowing up and all of that sort of thing, the war really moved to the front. But underlying everything was always, what about my life? What about Social Security? What about keeping jobs in this country? All this stuff that we, frankly, wanted to have more of a discussion about but because 9/11, security, and terror were always present, you couldn't not discuss it.

MARK MELLMAN: You can see the difference here in the way you asked the question. If you asked people what they were concerned about personally, health care costs and jobs going overseas were at the very top of the list. If you asked them what the President should focus on, they said terrorism and Iraq. There were two forefronts, three forefronts, of voters' minds. The truth is they had different judgments about what concerned them personally, on the one hand, and what they thought the fundamental role of the President was in these times, on the other.

RICK BERKE: As a purely political matter, was your calculation that, no matter what happens or how bad it gets, people are going to want to stick with their commander in chief?

KEN MEHLMAN: It comes to something I said this morning and that is if Iraq is the concern—if people think this battle is tougher than they originally thought—what were they likely to be looking for if they don't want this incumbent president to be reelected? What they are going to likely be looking for is strong leadership. What was always important to us was that we always won on the strong leadership question and, because of John Kerry's complicated record on the issue, this was not seen as a strength that he had.

So part of the challenge that they always faced was the more they talked about Iraq and how tough the battle was, the more the American people said, we want to make sure we have a strong and resolute commander in chief—attributes in which the President had a much stronger position than Senator Kerry.

BOB SHRUM: I disagree with that. I think a lot depended on how you asked the question. If, for example, you asked the question, can Kerry handle terrorism? Is he strong enough to be commander in chief? The answer was yes. The President had a comparative advantage, especially on terrorism.

I also believe, and Mark can supply the numbers, that among people whose first concern was Iraq, John Kerry won on Election Day. Among people whose first concern was terrorism, George Bush won, by a pretty decisive margin, on Election Day. That's why I suggested earlier that I think there was some separation of these two issues over the course of the campaign.

GWEN IFILL: Unless they accepted that Iraq was the front of the War on Terrorism.

BOB SHRUM: I'm saying there was a very large group of people, and Mark can give you the numbers, for whom Iraq was the first issue and those people voted for us. There was a large group of people for whom terrorism was the first issue and those people voted for Bush. Obviously, the voters could draw some distinction.

MATTHEW DOWD: We could have an interesting poll discussion, but that's when you separate out and say, what's your number one issue and how did you vote? On Election Day, the people that said Iraq was their number one issue were, by and large, predominantly Democrats. People that said terrorism was their number one issue were predominantly more Republican and more likely to support the President.

If you ask all voters—which is, I think, what we got to in this campaign—who they trust more to deal with Iraq, who they trust more to deal with the economy, who they trust more to deal with terrorism, on Election Day, we were tied on the economy, we were ahead on Iraq by ten or eleven points, and we were ahead on terrorism by seventeen or eighteen points. What I think ultimately happened was Iraq was a concern in everybody's mind.

Kerry was never able to present an alternative on Iraq that people wanted to choose more so than sticking with the President. There were a lot of people that never knew if Kerry wanted to cut and run—they didn't know what he wanted to do. On Election Day, a lot of them questioned whether or not he had any different plan than the President. In the end, the majority of voters said, I trust the President more than John Kerry on Iraq. Even with the fatalities, even with all of that, Kerry never presented an alternative plan that people sided with.

GWEN IFILL: Mark?

MARK MELLMAN: There is, once again, some difference of opinion here. I think the reality is fundamentally that people, at the end of the day, did see big differences between John Kerry and George Bush on Iraq. Overwhelming numbers saw big differences between the two on Iraq.

MATTHEW DOWD: That's actually not true.

MARK MELLMAN: It's true in the public polling. It's true in the private polling.

MATTHEW DOWD: No, it's not, Mark.

MARK MELLMAN: It is.

MATTHEW DOWD: Take out Democrats, take out Republicans, look at people that are in that in-between world. They didn't see a big difference and said, why should we switch?

MARK MELLMAN: I would tell you that most people—the large majority of Americans—saw fundamental differences between George Bush and John Kerry on Iraq, number one.

MATTHEW DOWD: Not when you factor out partisanship.

MARK MELLMAN: Hold on.

Number two, when you asked people who they agreed with more on Iraq, John Kerry had a small but real advantage.

Third, and I think most important here, we are missing the point on this issue. The fundamental issue on Iraq was people agreed with the decision to invade Iraq. They do to this day and did through the election. No dispute about that. What they also said, very clearly, on Election Day and all the way leading up to it is they thought the current situation was a mess and that the administration had not planned well, had not dealt well with the current situation in Iraq. There was also no question that that sense of failure hurt George Bush.

GWEN IFILL: But ultimately—

MARK MELLMAN: Ultimately, it was not enough. That we know definitively. It was not enough, but there is no question that that sense of failure hurt George Bush in this election.

MARY BETH CAHILL: The constant reappearance of acts of terror on the news, during the course of the campaign, really accrued. Nobody had anything to do with it, but it accrued to stability and keeping, not changing, leadership.

The two things that I think made the most difference were, first, the terrorist attack at the school in Beslan immediately before the Republican convention.[26] It was Americans' worst fear—seeing schoolchildren being held hostage by terrorists, in the most graphic way, over the course of three days.

Secondly, the appearance of the Osama tape just before the election really brought terror back into the campaign in a very real way.[27] I think that that contributed to a real fear of changing leadership.

MARK MELLMAN: Just to underline one point, agreeing totally. When we talked about the convention before, no one even mentioned Beslan which, to me, is incredible. There is just no question, in my mind, from the data that we saw, that that had a profound and powerful effect. Here you

---

26. On September 1, 2004, a group of Chechen terrorists seized control of a school in the Russian town of Beslan. After a tense standoff, which lasted several days, more than two hundred people died after Russian troops stormed the school.

27. Three days before the 2004 election, a videotape featuring Osama bin Laden was circulated to the media. On it, bin Laden renewed his warning to Americans and insisted that they change their policy toward the Muslim world, claiming, "Your security is not in the hands of Kerry or Bush or al Qaeda. . . . Your security is in your own hands."

have a convention, the goal of which is to say the most important issue is terror, and, at the same time, you have a real event where children are being shot in the back as they run from school. There is no question that that powerfully interacted with that convention.

RICK BERKE: Do you all agree?

MATTHEW DOWD: I agree with that. If the day was spent on the campaign trail and the discussion was about Iraq or the War on Terror, and that's the political discussion of the day, from my vantage point, I would prefer that day than if the day was spent on Social Security or the cost of health care. We can dispute the numbers, but if it's Iraq or if it's the War on Terror being talked about on a day during this election, or if it's Social Security and the cost of health care, we would prefer the former and I'm sure the Kerry campaign would have preferred the latter.

KEN MEHLMAN: At some level, what Iraq presented for the Kerry campaign was an attractive nuisance. I remember I was stunned that last week when Senator Kerry kept discussing the size of the weapons cache around Baghdad.[28] It seems to me if I had argued, which he did in the debate, that Iraq was a distraction from the War on Terror, the size of the weapons cache is not something I would be discussing the last week of the campaign, as opposed to discussing health care or the economy or jobs. I was surprised at the extent to which, often, he seemed to go back to that, as opposed to trying to define the terms of the debate.

GWEN IFILL: Why did you?

BOB SHRUM: Most of what he talked about in the last week was health care, the economy, and Social Security. The press of real events meant that you were constantly being asked to comment on this.

When I first entered this business, there was a doctrine that political consultants could tell the voters what the election was about and then the voters, whomever controlled the definition and asked the question, would get the answer they wanted. It probably was never true, but what has clearly happened over the years is that real world events shape the questions that voters are asking. So there were real world events.

I have to add one thing for Matthew. I'm very glad you said that you didn't want a day discussing Social Security because one of the points I think

---

28. On October 25, 2004, it was reported that nearly four hundred tons of explosive materials were believed to be missing from a former Iraqi military facility south of Baghdad. Prior to the weapons' disappearance, the site was thought to have been under American control.

that's important to come out of this election is the President does not have a mandate to privatize Social Security. (Laughter.) Because, A, you didn't want to discuss it and, B, you didn't put a single ad on saying privatize it.

MATTHEW DOWD: Granted that we don't want to privatize it. We are not going to do that.

BOB SHRUM: It probably has more consequence for the next election.

• THE BATTLEGROUND STATES •

GWEN IFILL: I want to take you back to a week before the election, when almost all that you thought you could do had been done, aside from raising money for lawyers. If you could go back to that day a week before votes were cast, where was your head at that point?

KEN MEHLMAN: I thought that it would be a very close election. I thought it would be decided by a couple points. Therefore, I felt the ground game would be decisive and I had a lot of confidence in the ground game we had put together. I also thought momentum would be very important and the fact that we spent the last week discussing the weapons cache and discussing the new tape I thought was also important, in terms of the final discussion of the campaign.

RICK BERKE: What states were you most worried about?

KEN MEHLMAN: The states that we were most focused on—I don't know about worried about—were Ohio, Pennsylvania, Florida, Wisconsin, Iowa, New Mexico, and New Hampshire.

TAD DEVINE: We were looking at the same geography. We knew ten months before that this thing was about winning two out of three of Ohio, Florida, and Pennsylvania. It wasn't that complicated. You can do it six ways to Sunday and that's the way it comes out. So we were focused, in terms of our most important resources—our candidate, our candidate for vice president, their spouses, and the other key surrogates—and all of our efforts on trying to effect the outcome in those places.

GWEN IFILL: In your decisionmaking moments in your meetings and your hydra-headed conference calls, what did you decide? How did you divide your days between the priorities that you had to set for yourself that last week, whether it was turnout or shifting resources from one state to another?

TAD DEVINE: We did a lot of work, and Mark [Mellman] and other pollsters did an awful lot of this work, trying to develop formulas, in terms of resource allocation. Those formulas targeted individual media markets and led to decisionmaking in terms of resource allocation of television coverage. One of the big differences, too, that we had, in terms of our approach, was that we very much were trying to talk to individual voters in individual states. For example, we had an Ohio jobs ad. They were running a different kind of campaign where, for the most part, their advertising was national advertising—the same ad in almost every place. We had different ads in almost every place around the country. We were taking a different approach and our targeting was driven by our understanding of the election on turnout models. In retrospect, it turns out 500,000 more votes in Ohio than Gore got wasn't enough. We needed 600,000.

GWEN IFILL: Why was that? How did you end up being off on that? Did they just beat you at your own game?

BOB SHRUM: They did an extraordinary job on turnout. I believe they spent four years putting it in place. I believe they tried it out in the 2002 election. And I believe it was built in a network that was not simply sending organizers in. It was built through networking people who lived there and institutions that existed there and an awful lot of work went into doing it.

GWEN IFILL: How much of that did you see in advance?

BOB SHRUM: You could see some of it in advance. The truth of the matter is, let's be honest, on Election Day, most people in the press corps that I talked to as the reports were coming in that there was high turnout thought that meant we were going to win. I didn't assume that if there was a high turnout, they would win.

MARY BETH CAHILL: The other thing about Election Day, in hindsight, is it seems as though it was much harder to vote in Democratic precincts, in some parts of the country. The article that was on the front page of the *Washington Post* yesterday about the difference between resource allocations made in Ohio for certain Democratic precincts versus other, more Republican-leaning precincts is something that we are going to spend the next four years on so we have more parity of equipment and trained staff in different areas, regardless of the tax base in those areas.

RICK BERKE: You said earlier that you had planes waiting on Election Day. Where were they waiting? How many planes? Where were they headed for?

MARY BETH CAHILL: We had four teams of lawyers—on the West Coast, in Minnesota, in D.C., and in Florida—and to go wherever anybody had to go. The states that were close were the states that were close, so we would expect New Mexico, Iowa, and Ohio.

RICK BERKE: Did you think that there may be a repeat of 2000? Were you expecting it to be that close?

MARY BETH CAHILL: We've all talked, over the course of the day, about the data that we all looked at, that this was an extremely close race, that it could go any given way in any of the most closely contested states, and that you just had to be ready for that eventuality. Life is the matter of learning the lessons from the last campaign, and so we were very well prepared for the problems of the last campaign.

RICK BERKE: Just to be clear on that, you did have planes?

MARY BETH CAHILL: We did. We had private planes that were available to us to carry tons of lawyers.

KEN MEHLMAN: We all had similar planes and similar lawyers, sometimes from the same law firm and billing the same clients. (Laughter.)

GWEN IFILL: That's where tort reform comes in. (Laughter.)

MARY BETH CAHILL: There actually was a sign on Election Day at one lawyer's office that said, "All lawyered up and no place to go." (Laughter.)

MARK MELLMAN: In terms of the turnout, I think the Republicans did an extraordinary job. Frankly, I think the Democrats, all told, did an extraordinary job and I think both sides did a great job in turning out as many voters as they could. There were a few more of theirs than of ours, at least there were a few more of theirs willing to wait in line in Ohio than of ours, and that's the tale of the day.

There was, in fact, a tremendous effort, organizationally, on the Democratic side to turn out the vote, and I think it was extraordinarily successful. You look at most of these states and the Democratic vote is way up, and that's certainly true in Ohio, and the Republican vote is up, too.

MATTHEW DOWD: One thing I want to say on turnout is I totally agree with Mark on this. But Election Day was not a surprise to us. Election Day was not like, oh my gosh. We had assumed that as many Republicans would turn out on Election Day as Democrats, nationally, and then we had different calculations in individual states.

BOB SHRUM: We had the same assumption.

MATTHEW DOWD: And, by and large, it was true, which gave us a 2.7 percent national victory and gave us what we thought. We thought we were going to win Ohio by two or three points, we thought we were going to win Florida by four or five points, we thought New Mexico was going to be very close, we thought Wisconsin was dead even, and we thought, in Iowa, we were going to win by one.

What was so different than 2000 is that what we did, and what our calculations were, and what happened on Election Day, and what the Democrats did, was about what we thought was going to happen. A week out, this was about where the race was.

KEN MEHLMAN: Let me just add something to what Mark said. Both sides did a very, very good job on the ground game this time. I have Republican friends who say, we sure showed them, we understand and they don't. They are completely wrong. There were better things about what we did than what they did, but they did a fantastic job. They were incredibly effective at targeting their voters and were incredibly effective at turning them out. Both sides really worked this process over.

What Bob said is right—that is what we worked very hard to build. We did not have outsiders come in. This was bottom up, not top down. What we tried to do was to provide channels for those people all over the country that supported this president to get their energies and their enthusiasms involved, and to figure out metrics by which we could figure out resource allocation. It really was remarkably bottom up.

One of my favorite stories is what happened in two states—in Maine and Pennsylvania. There had never been a real serious, grassroots political organization in Maine for Republicans before. In Maine and Pennsylvania, when the polls closed, no one left the call centers to go home or to the election night victory party. They called into New Mexico. And in Florida, all over the state, when the polls closed, volunteers stayed in the call centers and called into the panhandle part of the state. These are just incredible stories— the extent to which people were willing to, and proud of, doing that.

My other favorite story is Peggy Noonan and Don Evans,[29] independently, were out campaigning and normally, as you all know, when you have surrogates out there, they want a plane, they want all this stuff. They went

---

29. Peggy Noonan was a speechwriter for President Ronald Reagan. Don Evans served as the secretary of commerce during President Bush's first term.

anonymously door-to-door because that became the cool thing to do among Republicans. I have been stunned by the number of people I've seen on K Street and on Capitol Hill talking about the great time they had going door-to-door and participating in call centers.

GWEN IFILL: Those poor people who answered their doors. (Laughter.)

MATTHEW DOWD: One thing is you can't do mechanics without message. We talk about phone banks, but you can have all the mechanics in the world and if you don't have a message— It helped that we had a candidate with a 93 percent approval rating among 46 percent of the country. That was helpful.

• ELECTION DAY •

RICK BERKE: Matt, when you saw those first few waves of exit polls, what were you thinking?[30]

MATTHEW DOWD: Well, I was thinking maybe I shouldn't have told the President at 7:00 in the morning that he was going to win by three points. (Laughter.)

GWEN IFILL: Wait a second. You told the President at 7:00 in the morning he was going to win by three points?

MATTHEW DOWD: On Election Day.

GWEN IFILL: What did you base that on?

MATTHEW DOWD: The data that I had.

GWEN IFILL: Did he believe you?

MATTHEW DOWD: Yes. He said, I'm a five-point man, and I said, well, I'm sorry, I don't think you are going to get there.

NICOLE DEVENISH: He was talking about Florida. I was there. (Laughter.)

---

30. On Election Day, a series of exit polls predicted a resounding victory for Senator Kerry.

*The Kerry campaign staff listens to the Bush campaign
staff explain how they won the election.*

MATTHEW DOWD: Here is what I thought. I had a judgment on what the electorate would look like and, when the first exits came in, I thought one of two things. I had so misread what I thought was going to happen, it's completely different than anything we thought, it's a completely changed electorate, we misjudged everything and, boy, did we screw up. Or I thought the alternative, these are totally messed-up exit polls. I went with the totally messed-up exit polls.

GWEN IFILL: Where else were you going to go at this point, really?

MATTHEW DOWD: Because it was so far off from every piece of data that we had seen in individual states. The fact that South Carolina was dead even and we were losing Pennsylvania by eighteen points. We had felt we were going to win, nationally, by two or three points on Election Day, if all was right. The fact that 59 percent of the country that voted was female and that we were only winning men by four points. All of those sorts of things were so far off that I thought this has got to be messed up and, as soon as the first votes came in, we saw that they were messed up. By and large, every state was messed up.

RICK BERKE: Ken, what were you thinking? Were you so sure things were messed up?

KEN MEHLMAN: I also thought that there were a couple of different things because, remember, this happened in 2000 and 2002. In the last two elections, the exit polls were wrong. So Terry [Nelson] had put together an operation to go over where turnout was up and where turnout was down. For instance, in Lancaster County, Pennsylvania, in terms of our numbers, we hit our goal at 2:00 in the afternoon. So, if you compared the actual data with the exit poll data, the actual data looked right and the exit poll data looked wrong.

I actually had a conversation with the President and former President Bush right after the first numbers came out. They called together and said, what do you think? I went over where turnout had been and said, I don't think these numbers are right because it is inconsistent with all of the on-the-ground data that we're getting, and this is why it's wrong and this is why it's right.

RICK BERKE: Was the President nervous? What did he say?

KEN MEHLMAN: He didn't sound nervous. Actually, it was funny. After that, Mary Matalin called and said call the V.P. with what you just told the President—he was fired up by it.[31] So I said to someone—it may have been Nicole—either I'm really right about this or else. Oh well.

NICOLE DEVENISH: We probably had a similar Election Day. Ours was just inverted. We had a terrible afternoon.

MATTHEW DOWD: I pick ours.

NICOLE DEVENISH: I pick ours, too. But I know exactly how it feels. There was a point in that night, I'd say from 6:00 P.M. to 8:00 P.M., where Matthew [Dowd] was the mad scientist in his office, trying to crack the code. Our press was downstairs thinking they were covering a losing campaign. Ken really put the campaign on his back and went down and did cable interviews for about two hours, when we really didn't know what was going on.

There was a moment, around 8:30 or 8:15, when the mad scientist cracked the code, came running down to my office, and said, you've got to go tell the press. I didn't know what the heck he was talking about. I said, well, you come, and we went down there and at 8:15 or 8:30, we said to our press, cheer up, you are covering the winning campaign. There was certainly a point in the night when I'm sure this was conveyed to the operations set up

---

31. Mary Matalin is a Republican political strategist who served as a senior advisor to the Bush campaign in 2004.

at the White House, when we knew that the numbers looked the way we had thought they were going to look.

GWEN IFILL: Mark, did you tell John Kerry at 7:00 in the morning that he was going to win by three points?

MARK MELLMAN: No. (Laughter.)

MARK MELLMAN: The first time I thought we really were going to win this election was about 5:00 on Tuesday afternoon.

NICOLE DEVENISH: When we thought we were going to lose.

MARK MELLMAN: Yes. The first wave of exit polls came and, having the honor of working at CBS before and watching these things come in, you know that they don't mean very much. In fact, we had put out a memo the day before—which looked at the previous exit polls—that said, don't pay any attention to the early numbers because they are always way off, so you can't get that excited about the first wave of exit poll numbers.

By the time you have the second wave come in and, as a statistical matter, you have separate national polls, separate state polls, and then you have an *L.A. Times* national poll and *L.A. Times* state polls, at a certain point, you start to say all this evidence is identical. There are separate, independent observations and, yes, you look at the female numbers, but, as that closed, it didn't really change. We reweighted the numbers, the 52-48 female-male, and based on the numbers we were getting, in terms of the internals, it made a half a point difference. So, at that point, you start to develop a little bit of false confidence, as it turned out.

RICK BERKE: Mary Beth, what were you thinking?

MARY BETH CAHILL: I was in Boston on Election Day and spent most of the day upstairs. We had a boiler room at the Copley Plaza Hotel. I spent most of the day there getting information in and talking to our people around the country. We got the same exit polls that everybody else did and the thing that was really interesting to me this year was the extraordinary reach to everybody in the country of the exit polls. Everybody in the country was e-mailing and calling about them, but they were so out of whack. Being so far ahead in Pennsylvania was nothing that we ever thought was going to happen. But it was fairly euphoric there for a little while.

RICK BERKE: Did John Kerry see all the same numbers and think, obviously, he was going to win?

MARY BETH CAHILL: We have talked about this in a bunch of forums over the course of the campaign. John Kerry actually pays less attention to polling than any other candidate that I've ever met in my life—except, of course, when he is losing and then, like any candidate, he is paying a great deal of attention. But, unlike other people who really consume the data, he wanted a critique of how he was doing on any given day, he wanted to know about his performance, but he did not want to discuss the ins and outs of the poll. He was much more concerned about the policy, the speech, and his performance than he was about the polling.

RICK BERKE: But, on Election Day, though, that's different.

MARY BETH CAHILL: Election Day is completely different and he did what he always does. He goes to lunch at the Union Oyster House on every single Election Day of his lifetime, with his family. Then he went home and we talked over the course of the afternoon.

BOB SHRUM: At 7:30 that night, Mary Beth and I rode over to his house with him. We had been given the last round of exit polls.

MARY BETH CAHILL: And I should also say that he spent the afternoon in a satellite chair.

STEPHANIE CUTTER: For three hours.

MARY BETH CAHILL: Five hours.

STEPHANIE CUTTER: I had the pleasure of sitting with him for those five hours and he never even asked about exits, for five hours.

TAD DEVINE: He worked it.

BOB SHRUM: But he knew them at 7:30. I don't think he was prepared to assume that he had won but— He knew the exits, and we went in and we talked about a number of different things. We were there about an hour and a half when Tom Kiley called and said you guys better come back.[32] Then, over the course of the evening, he called Mary Beth a number of times, he called me a number of times, and it slipped away. The way it slipped away was, initially, we would be told by the people who were analyzing the numbers, well, you know, Florida is going to be tight but we are probably going

---

32. Tom Kiley is a Boston pollster who served as an advisor to the Kerry campaign.

to make it, well, Florida is gone but Ohio is fine, well, Ohio is getting really tight.

MARY BETH CAHILL: But Ohio was long.

BOB SHRUM: Yes, Ohio was long. It was about 2:00 in the morning—I don't know what Mary Beth said in her call with him—he said to me, what do you think the bottom line is? I said I think the bottom line is that there is significantly less than a 50-50 chance that you will win this election.

RICK BERKE: Let me just ask one thing, when you were sitting there in the living room, was there a time when you said, Mr. President, or toasted?

BOB SHRUM: No, we didn't.

RICK BERKE: He would know you were too cautious or superstitious?

MARY BETH CAHILL: He is very superstitious. He is very aware of the power of who has the office and he would never allow that.

BOB SHRUM: It was much like the night of Iowa. I think he felt good about it. On that day in Iowa, when Mary Beth and I went out and got a cup of coffee and I came back, he called me on the phone and said, do you have the other statement, if I need it? I said yes, and he said, I don't want to see it, just have it.

MATTHEW DOWD: Where did you all think the race was in the last four or five days? Did you all go into Election Day thinking the odds are we are not going to win? Because, for us, in the last four or five days, honestly, we thought if we follow through on everything, we are going to win this race by two or three points. All our data, everything, showed that if we followed through on what we thought was going to happen, we were going to win by two or three points.

BOB SHRUM: Matthew and I always have this fight because we've done several of these forums. I thought it was going to be a very close race and, ultimately, I believe you won by a margin of about 50,000 or 60,000 votes switching in Ohio. I don't think you would have been on very high moral ground to say the winner of the popular vote gets to be president. What I felt in the last few days, on the plane, with the crowds and everything else, is I thought that we were probably going to win. Then the Osama bin Laden tape comes and we just flatline. We don't go down, we flatline. I think Mary

Beth is right that it reintroduced into the election, in a very powerful way, the terrorism question.

By the way, I think it's very important, at least from my perspective, to understand that the President's strength on terrorism was not just a mechanical or efficient strength of office and how he was prosecuting the War on Terrorism. It was an emotional identification with him from what happened in the days after 9/11. People felt, on that issue, very, very comfortable with him and, in many ways, it was a dominant issue. We live in a transformed America now and this was the first election.

RICK BERKE: We have one last question for each of you.

GWEN IFILL: You can address these questions to each other if you like. What hit didn't your opponent take against you that you expected to get?

BOB SHRUM: None. (Laughter.)

KEN MEHLMAN: I can't think of any either. Honestly, twice I mentioned the times Kerry brought up the record of what Bush did during the time of the Vietnam War. But I can't think of any either that we expected, that we didn't really get hit on. Can you think of any?

MATTHEW DOWD: No.

GWEN IFILL: It's nice to know it was such an exhaustive campaign.

RICK BERKE: You were criticizing them for negativity. Do you think they played fair?

KEN MEHLMAN: I think that there were a number of attacks—and Nicole alluded to them—like the statement about the President wanting to end stem cell research and the comment about people walking again, preying on people who are ill or who are injured's false hopes. I thought the comments on the draft were just totally factually inaccurate. Those were two examples of things that were just, in fact, wrong.

MATTHEW DOWD: What are you going to do, start whining? I can't believe they said that, they took it out of proportion. You would rather spend your time saying, why did John Kerry vote for taxes twenty-seven times, instead of whining about the hit you took.

KEN MEHLMAN: The only thing we can agree on whining about is the media. No, I'm kidding.

GWEN IFILL: No, you're not.

RICK BERKE: I do have one final question, and I think I know the answer, but I'm curious. Did you see any press, in your estimation, any favoritism, Nicole, to one candidate or the other, overall, in how the press covered the campaign?

NICOLE DEVENISH: No, I was too close to it to offer an analysis like that. There were some stunning stories, but I was too close to really assess.

RICK BERKE: Would you say it was pretty even-handed, in your view?

NICOLE DEVENISH: I don't want to go that far. (Laughter.)

RICK BERKE: Stephanie, what would you say?

STEPHANIE CUTTER: I would say, for a long time, it was hard to get covered, but when you're a challenger against a sitting president, that's somewhat expected, although frustrating. I don't want to go as far to say that the press was even-handed. There were moments where I do think that we were much more scrutinized—whether it was the Swift Boats, the continuation of that story, Iraq. We were held to certain standards that were different than the President. In many ways, the President was covered as the President and not a candidate, but, by and large, I don't think that there was a huge tilt one way or the other.

TAD DEVINE: I'll just say, at the risk of suffering the consequences of what I'm about to say, that I do a lot of work outside this country and when you work in different countries, you see that the press is partisan. Basically, in South America, we've got our newspaper, we've got our TV station, they have their newspaper, they have their TV station and their radio station, and that's the way the game is played. Everybody knows who is on whose side. I do believe that in our country, while we're a long, long way from that and there is no doubt about it—there is still an awful lot of independence and integrity in the press—I sense the movement in the organizational press is more towards what I've seen in other countries, which is the press having partisan institutions and broadcasting their side of the story institutionally.

KEN MEHLMAN: Is that on both sides?

TAD DEVINE: Yes, on either side. We could say who has got the most of it right now—I'll leave that to others to decide. But I do think that that's happening right now and I think that could become a bigger phenomena in our elections in the future. Campaigns will recognize that and we will attempt to exploit it to our advantage.

NICOLE DEVENISH: I think that must be occurring, otherwise, how would you explain the emergence of the power and influence of the blogs?

RICK BERKE: Theresa?

THERESA AMATO: I would agree with what Tad said, and certainly, from our perspective, we suffered a barrage of negative press from the get-go. It was like, how dare you think about running again this year. All the questions were about 2000.

GWEN IFILL: Did that surprise you?

THERESA AMATO: No. But do I expect more? Yes.

MARK MELLMAN: I certainly don't subscribe to press conspiracies of any kind—I think the press is, ultimately, more or less fair—but I think there were differences. I'll give you two examples from the debate. I don't want to re-fight the campaign. We had both the president of the United States and the vice president of the United States say things that were flatly untrue in the debates—the Vice President's comment you referred to before about never having met Senator Edwards and the President saying he never said that he wasn't concerned about Osama bin Laden, or whatever that exact quote was. There is just no question that what was said in both cases was completely untrue. In my mind, that did not get the level of scrutiny that somebody standing on the stage in the presidential or vice presidential debates, saying something that wasn't true, would normally get. It didn't get the level of scrutiny, say, that mentioning Mary Cheney got after the third debate. Ultimately, I think it was a little more important when the President and Vice President said things that aren't true, but it got a lot less attention than, for example, the Mary Cheney piece.

GWEN IFILL: Why do you think that was?

MARK MELLMAN: I think it has to do with the way in which people approach the story. I think there is a story line that people find interesting and compelling and they follow that story line, as opposed to necessarily looking at each incident individually and saying, how important is this? How much attention does it deserve?

GWEN IFILL: We want to thank you all for being so forthcoming and at such length.

Outside Influences: 527s, McCain-Feingold, and Message Politics

5

> "The problem with campaign finance, and with a lot of the coverage of it, is that it's always dealt with as a black-and-white issue. Money is seen as evil, per se. There are different kinds of money and there are different kinds of groups. . . . It's a much more complex issue than McCain-Feingold was going to clean up."
>
> —*Washington Post* Reporter Tom Edsall

PHIL SHARP: Tonight is our concluding session. Recognizing that there was a new phenomenon in these campaigns, the 527s, we thought it was very important that there be some clear discussion about that so we've invited some folks engaged with the 527 organizations.

We're very fortunate tonight to have as our moderator David Gergen, who is a professor of public service at the Kennedy School of Government, director of the Center for Public Leadership, a commentator at CNN, editor-at-large at *U.S. News & World Report*, and a former speechwriter and advisor to several presidents of the United States.

DAVID GERGEN: Our effort tonight is going to be to focus on those outside influences in the campaign, especially the 527s. I hope we will have a somewhat broader discussion before we conclude about some of the outside influences that shape the campaign. Let's start with the 527s. Hopefully, you can really let go tonight. This is a time when we really want to get down to the nitty gritty. I will start by calling on Ben Ginsberg, who has spent a lot of time thinking about why 527s were important and framing what the 527s were doing this year.

• THE LAWYER'S VIEW •

BEN GINSBERG: It's always good to talk about 527s, or the new third rail of American politics, as we call it in the Ginsberg household now. They were a real phenomenon in the 2004 election campaign as a direct result of McCain-Feingold, the campaign reform bill. That was largely because

*David Gergen listens on as Ben Ginsberg explains his role with
the Swift Boat Veterans for Truth.*

McCain-Feingold took a large chunk out of what national party committees could do. All money that had been legal under state law became soft money. Parties couldn't use it. As parties or participants on both sides were looking at 2004, that put a huge gap in a couple of parts of party operations. One is the messaging that had been done through issue ads, and the second was the voter registration and Get-Out-The-Vote programs that had become pretty much the mother's milk of the political parties.

The Republicans and Democrats took different strategic approaches to 527s at the start of this election cycle. Republicans had a popular president who was a proven successful fundraiser. Therefore, our feeling was that we would be able to raise sufficient hard dollars through the party committees to be able to do what needed to be done.

Democrats faced a different challenge. They had historically always relied more on the now banned soft dollars for party operations. While Republicans had one candidate who was clearly going to get the nomination, there was a split field on the Democratic side. That meant there were a lot of very good political operatives who didn't necessarily want to choose sides, because they were friendly with a number of them. It was clear that there was going to be more money in 527s than in the Democratic national party structure, at least for the beginning eighteen months, until a nominee was chosen on the Democratic side. The Democratic groups, through the Media Fund and America

Coming Together,[1] did a very robust fundraising effort that caught the attention on our side because it was so robust. As a result of that, Republicans actually tried to shut down 527s—to get the Federal Election Commission [FEC] to act like a grown-up enforcement agency.[2] Big mistake on our part. By May of 2004, it was pretty clear that the FEC was not going to do anything to stop the very proficient fundraising that the Democrats had done.

That led to a lot of 527s in two areas. Number one, television. The Democratic 527 groups seemed to do a great deal to supplement the Kerry campaign once Kerry was the nominee in the spring. Again, that got a lot of attention on our part.

Republicans held back on television advertising and on Get-Out-The-Vote and voter registration activities through 527s, for the most part, until after the conventions. I know Steve Rosenthal will talk about the really terrific operation that they put together. Republicans used the party structure, which was well-funded. You heard the discussion today about the grassroots party operations. The Democrats, to steal Tom Edsall's word, outsourced the program to the 527s. That was the basic parameters under which the operation operated.

DAVID GERGEN: To follow up on your comment, why did you think it was a mistake to have taken this to the FEC? Should you just have gone on the counter-offensive and started raising a lot more money without going to the FEC? Was that the mistake?

BEN GINSBERG: The mistake was thinking that the FEC was actually going to do anything. The reality was that Republican donors were tremendously reluctant to give to 527s. The corporate community, the traditional source for Republican soft dollars through the party committee, just didn't want to give.

DAVID GERGEN: Why?

BEN GINSBERG: Legal caution, for the most part. The rule of thumb amongst Republican lawyers was that there was something illegal about giv-

---

1. The Media Fund and America Coming Together (ACT) are two Democratic-leaning 527s that were created in the 2004 election cycle. Media Fund ran issue ads and ACT worked to register and turn out voters.

2. On March 31, 2004, the Republican National Committee and the Bush-Cheney campaign filed a complaint with the Federal Election Commission (FEC) alleging that liberal advocacy groups, most of which are 527s, were engaging in "unprecedented criminal enterprise" to circumvent campaign finance laws.

ing corporate dollars to 527s, or at least they became convinced of that. I think, frankly, organized labor did not operate under that particular restraint. The corporate community just wasn't giving.

DAVID GERGEN: And then it started giving heavily, or big givers came in heavily in the months that followed, because the Democrats were getting such an advantage?

BEN GINSBERG: Well, George Soros was a tremendous fundraising boost.[3]

DAVID GERGEN: For Republicans. (Laughter.)

BEN GINSBERG: Yes, George Soros was absolutely the best fundraising tool the Republican 527s had going because he had given so much money in such a way and he was so dogmatic in his views. In May, when the FEC didn't do anything, the corporate community never did anything throughout the cycle, but individual Republicans saw George Soros and Peter Lewis and Steve Bing as really funding the Democratic effort.[4] At that point, Republican individuals thought, well, you've got to have a level playing field to balance out the issues debate.

• A HISTORY OF 527s •

DAVID GERGEN: Let's go to Tom Edsall then, who has carved out a profile for himself as someone who's thought a lot about money in politics and has written about this subject extensively. In one of his more recent pieces, he has written that the 527s are widely thought to have had a major influence on shaping the outcome of the election.

TOM EDSALL: First, let me correct my good friend Ben on a couple of things. He and I play poker and he doesn't know how to lose.

He described the Republican position as being kind of self-righteous at the beginning—that they were going to fight the 527s. In fact, both parties, early on, met secretly and tried to set up 527s. Terry McAuliffe, while he was promoting the McCain-Feingold bill, created a special McCain-Feingold task

---

3. George Soros is a multimillionaire international financier who gave more than $20 million to 527s working to defeat President George W. Bush in the 2004 election.
4. Peter Lewis, chairman of Progressive Car Insurance, donated more than $20 million to 527s, and Stephen Bing, a movie producer who heads Shangri-La Entertainment, donated more than $10 million.

force. The purpose of that task force was to find ways to get soft money back into the system. The Republicans were doing the same thing. They created a group called The Leadership Forum. The Republican Congressional Committee gave $1 million to this group. They ended up having to give it back because it was too blatant. Then the Republicans discovered that because of all the corporate scandals that had been going on, corporations were reluctant to give money to these 527s without authorization from the FEC. So they then abandoned going the 527 route and tried to get it barred by the FEC.

On May 13, the FEC ruled that they were not going to regulate 527s and it was open season. At that point, the Republicans joined together with the Democrats, much later in the ball game. They did a very good job and raised a lot of money. Progress for America and the Swift Boat Veterans for Truth were the two that did it.[5]

The 527s clearly did play a major role. Steve Rosenthal's group has to be credited with a significant amount of the turnout increase on the Democratic side. On the Republican side, studies of the ads that were done show pretty consistently, and I think Steve and others will support this, that the ads by the Swift Boat Veterans for Truth were a devastating factor in this election and really changed the ball game for Kerry in a way that was very hard to correct.

Later, the Progress for America group ran an ad called "Ashley." It was about a young girl whose mother, I believe, was killed on 9/11 and Bush takes her under his arm and sort of adopts her. They really fulfilled the "compassionate conservative" role for Bush while he was doing all these attack ads. Odd reversal of roles, interestingly, but it was a very effective ad and all the surveys showed that it was significant. I think in the end run these 527s were very influential in the outcome.

DAVID GERGEN: In politics, we're always trying to look and see what the tipping point was. What was the decisive factor? Had there been no 527s, do you think the outcome of the election would have been the same?

TOM EDSALL: I think the 527s played a significant role during that one first window, after March 2, when Kerry had locked up the nomination, was broke, and Bush had $104 million in the bank and spent a big chunk of it, something around $50 million, largely defining Kerry in negative terms. The 527s did not do what the Kerry campaign wanted, which was to basically present a different image of Kerry. They attacked Bush. But at least they kept

---

5. Progress for America is a Republican-leaning 527 led by Brian McCabe and Swift Boat Veterans for Truth is a 527 organization of Vietnam veterans opposed to Senator John Kerry.

another message afloat. They probably did keep Kerry afloat at a time when he could have been pretty devastated.

In the same way Clinton defined Dole in 1996 with his whole secret program that Dick Morris was running outside of Washington, the Republicans had hoped to do to that to Kerry. But the 527s protected him then. So they were quite significant in the outcome.

DAVID GERGEN: As you talk about Terry McAuliffe assembling his group and looking for loopholes in McCain-Feingold, I'm reminded of W. C. Fields on his deathbed. After living a very rollicking, secular life, a friend came to him and he was madly flipping through the Bible, looking at it very intently. The friend said, what in the world are you doing? He said, I'm looking for loopholes. (Laughter.) Before we leave you, Tom, given the Republican success toward the end of the campaign, after all of the push by the Republicans to shut these things down and then their success toward the end, where do you think that leaves prospects for 527s in the future? [Senators] McCain and Feingold are back at it now trying to rein them in.

TOM EDSALL: In terms of Congress, the air went out of the Republican sail on reform as soon as Progress for America and Swift Boat Veterans for Truth proved to be very effective vehicles, so it was no longer a purely Democratic thing. I don't think there's the sentiment in a Republican Congress to pass a campaign finance reform bill.

The one area where these groups may run into trouble is that the courts are pushing the FEC to take much stronger steps and may force the FEC to adopt the kind of regulations that Ben at one time wanted and now probably doesn't want. We'll see what happens.

• SWIFT BOAT VETERANS FOR TRUTH •

DAVID GERGEN: Let's look for a few moments then at the message side of the 527s. Ben said there were two things they were doing. They were trying to get messages out and they were trying to get voters to turn out. Let's first look at the message side.

Chris LaCivita was the senior advisor to Swift Boat Veterans for Truth and everyone has agreed that they had an enormous impact. Public Opinion Strategies (POS) interviewed voters in six battleground states after the campaign was over and found they were most strongly influenced by three advertisements. First and foremost on the list was the Swift Boat ads, second was the "Wolves" TV ad that was produced by the Bush campaign,[6] and third

---

6. On October 22, 2004, the Bush-Cheney campaign issued a new television ad showing wolves circling while the narrator criticized Senator Kerry for voting against defense appropriations.

was the "Ashley" TV ad produced by the Progress for America Voter Fund. Two out of the three most memorable ads—all three were on the Bush side—came out of 527s. So, Chris, tell us about your efforts. Did you have any idea that this would take off in the way it did?

CHRIS LaCIVITA: A couple of things. One, the POS poll actually had—I know people find this strange—the "Ashley" ad first and the Swift Boat ad second. Then there was a Fabrizio poll which came out that had the Swift Boat ad first and the "Ashley" ad second. It just depends on who you believe.

DAVID GERGEN: But you guys were both together at the top.

CHRIS LaCIVITA: Yes. The Swift Boat ad wasn't a specific ad, because we did eleven, but I think it was the entire campaign effort.

Basically, the bottom line was this. In June, about ten of these guys came to me and said, hey, we held a press conference in May and no one bothered to give us any attention. The *New York Times* dismissed them. Most folks just didn't pay any attention. How do we get attention? I said, the only way you can essentially get attention is if you raise enough money and put it on TV. And, I will tell you this, for the record. That first ad was a buy of a half-million dollars. The intention was not to generate repetition through gross rating points—that was probably the one aspect that Shrum had right. Where they underestimated was that it was nothing but an earned media play, plain

Representatives from Republican-leaning 527s—Brian McCabe, Ben Ginsberg, and Chris LaCivita (left to right)—talk about their election efforts.

and simple. The pure intention of that first ad was to generate earned media about the message that we were conveying. And yes, it was in your face. There was no other way to communicate it.

The *New York Times*—not the *Washington Post* but the *New York Times*—reported daily that these claims were debunked. None of the claims that had ever been made had been debunked. The second ad that we ran actually had Kerry's voice. *Newsweek* said we used an actor. Well, it wasn't. It was actually Kerry's voice.

It's hard to get three hundred guys in a room and get them all to agree to lie—to flat out lie. That's the greatest conspiracy ever. I'd like to meet somebody who could pull something like that off. These guys had two perspectives—one was based on personal experience and fact, and one was based on personal opinion. There shouldn't be a person in this room who doesn't say they have a right to express their opinion, on paid TV, no matter how distasteful some may find it.

But the fact of the matter is that—granted, I need to say this for the record because my lawyer's here—our intention was never to influence the outcome of the election. (Laughter.) We are an issue advocacy group and the purpose of our organization is to educate the public about issues. Never once in our ads, or in the $3 million worth of mail that we did, did we ever say, "defeat John Kerry" or "vote for George Bush."

We reiterated a common theme and the common theme was trust. Trust, trust, trust. That was essentially the theme that we wanted to build through the entire cycle, the entire ad campaign. We assumed the Kerry campaign knew that somebody would come after him on the testimony. I just can't imagine them not knowing that that was going to be an issue. There are a whole host of issues that were never answered. I listened to the panels earlier today. Some folks are saying the Kerry campaign was under greater scrutiny than the Bush campaign. Well, the press never asked the question of the Kerry campaign why they only released six pages out of a hundred of Kerry's military record. Why was John Kerry's discharge signed in 1978, seven years after he got out of the Navy, and why was it based on a board of review of officers? It's an important distinction.

The point is that it was a very thought out, methodically planned effort. We had a story to tell and we did it through sixty-second commercials as opposed to thirty.

DAVID GERGEN: Where was all the thinking about this occurring? Was it in Texas or in Washington? Where was all of the planning on this taking place? It didn't spontaneously happen.

CHRIS LaCIVITA: No. Actually, the Kerry campaign should probably thank Douglas Brinkley for writing his presumptuous presidential biography of John Kerry, *Tour of Duty*. Admiral Roy Hoffman, who lives in Richmond, about three blocks from where I live in Virginia, read the book, was incensed by a lot of things, and started calling everybody. This seventy-eight-year-old rear admiral corralled everyone and they held their press conference in May. These guys actually did it on their own. They came to me in June.

DAVID GERGEN: In Richmond?

CHRIS LaCIVITA: Actually, I met with John O'Neill and a couple of other guys in D.C. in June.[7] The planning was done in a number of places. When I got all the guys in, we were always at the Key Bridge Marriott in Virginia.

DAVID GERGEN: As you planned this out, how sensitive were you to who knew what you were doing? You had to assume that the word got back to the Bush campaign about what you were up to, without knowing how it happened.

CHRIS LaCIVITA: No. We didn't give a whole lot of thought to what the Bush campaign was thinking or what the Bush campaign was doing, quite frankly. About half of these guys were Republican, about a quarter were Democrats, and about a quarter were Independents. Granted, we were predominantly funded by Republicans. I'll give you that. But in terms of what the Bush campaign thought, you're always cognizant of that and you try and keep that in mind, but we didn't care, quite frankly.

DAVID GERGEN: If the Bush White House press office had said in a press interview, we'd like to see these called off, what would you have done?

CHRIS LaCIVITA: I would have increased the buy.

DAVID GERGEN: Really? I'm talking seriously about this.

CHRIS LaCIVITA: I'm dead serious. Let me give you an example of why.

DAVID GERGEN: Because the assumption in the public was all they had to do was wink and you guys would stop.

CHRIS LaCIVITA: Well, you know the world is filled with people that make a living out of making assumptions. The general sentiment was that the

7. John O'Neill is the author of *Unfit for Command*, an anti-Kerry book published on August 15, 2004. O'Neill was the spokesman for Swift Boat Veterans for Truth and he commanded the same Swift Boat Senator Kerry previously commanded in Vietnam.

Swift Boat Veterans for Truth would not air any TV ads during the Republican National Convention, in fear that we would step all over the President's message. That's what everyone was saying. We laughed at that. We produced that second ad with Kerry's voice and we bought about $2 million worth of national cable. I couldn't think of any other way to really demonstrate that we're not going anywhere and we're not going to be dictated to, whether it be from the Republicans or the Democrats. We put the ad up on national cable, predominantly on Fox.

DAVID GERGEN: Let's get a couple more facts on the table. The Center of Public Integrity today released that Swift Boat Veterans for Truth raised $17 million. Is that number correct or was it understated?

CHRIS LaCIVITA: It was understated. They actually raised $27.8 million. They spent $19.6 million on paid TV.

• PROGRESS FOR AMERICA: THE "ASHLEY" AD •

DAVID GERGEN: The Center listed Progress for America as raising around $44 million and it also, of course, produced the "Ashley" TV ad. Brian, as executive director, tell us about your group and also about the "Ashley" ad and how much influence you thought you had.

BRIAN McCABE: As Tom [Edsall] talked about before, the FEC passed on May 13. We didn't jump in right away. It wasn't until May 27. We still had that moment of hesitation.

Progress for America, the 501(c)(4), had been around since 2001 as an issue advocacy organization. The question we had was, do we continue on as PFA or do we also get into the 527 game? It was pretty clear, when you looked around, that we were already $100 million behind what the Democrats had raised at that point. We went ahead and figured we'd better file as a 527. At that point, we didn't know if we'd succeed or not with our donors, but we wanted to have as many vehicles as possible.

Early on, fundraising was very difficult. We ran our first ad right before July 4 and right after July 4 in Nevada and New Mexico, purely as a marketing opportunity. We had raised some early money. We needed people to see Progress for America Voter Fund out there and show people the kind of message we would do. That's really where we set the tone on the War on Terror. Our first two ads, "What If" and "Why Do We Fight," were really to lay down the marker that the issue we were going to focus on was the War on Terror.

From there, we focused heavily on fundraising. It was in July when we cut the "Ashley" ad. What was interesting about that is we had the ad in the can the whole time and we used it as our fundraising tool, knowing we were never going to run it until the end. We built our advertising campaign working backwards, knowing that Ashley's story would be the highlight for us. Once we cut the ad, we traveled around the country and started to meet with donors.

I was talking to Tom [Edsall] when we got going. I told him that I thought the mix of donations would be 60 percent corporate and 40 percent individual. It turned out it was about 99.5 percent individual. Ben [Ginsberg] was right when he said that general counsels were telling their companies not to give. That became apparent pretty quickly. So we changed our focus to Republicans who really believed in getting the message out about the War on Terror. We had some success in July. Once we got some big names and some big donors in, that's where it started to take off and we were able to build from there.

Most people want to focus on Ashley's story and don't really focus on the eight other ads we did. The origin of Ashley's story was at a campaign event in Lebanon, Ohio. The President was working the rope line and this woman yelled to the President, "Mr. President, this young girl lost her mother on 9/11." The President turned around, stopped, talked to the girl, Ashley, for a minute, and her dad snapped the photo and sent it to seven of his family members. It was from there that a couple of family members sent it on to a couple of people and it appeared in a local paper in Ohio. We actually saw it on Drudge. The picture ran like crazy on Drudge.[8]

We tracked down the family and we told them about Progress for America Voter Fund. They wanted to know a bit more about us. We spent some time talking to them. We spent three days out on location in Ohio filming. Once the ad came back, we knew we had a gold mine. It was such an emotional ad that the difficulty we had was getting it down to a sixty-second spot.

Since then, Eileen Scheffler, who works for Larry McCarthy, has actually put a sixty-minute film together for the family of all the outtakes.[9] There's just so much emotion because the Faulkner family is so real, and the President stopping, hugging, and having an emotional exchange was really believable. What helped us out in the whole thing is that people believed, and they could see, that the President would do this. It reinforced the character, compassion, and leadership they saw in George Bush after 9/11.

We took that ad out and showed it to donors. The emotional response from donors was amazing. We had 50 percent of the people cry the first time

8. Matt Drudge operates the website DrudgeReport.com.
9. Larry McCarthy is a Republican media consultant who produced the "Ashley" ad.

they saw the ad. One gentleman in New York City who saw the ad said, "now that's a close." We would always just show the ad and hope they gave money to it.

We ended up buying TV time because we knew, as a 527, we couldn't just reserve the time. If the Bush campaign or the Kerry campaign came in, they could bump us out. So we were wiring money starting in late August and placed $14.2 million of TV time by about the end of September, before the first reporter called us and asked us about this buy. It hadn't really popped up on anyone's radar screen.

We didn't want anyone to know we were buying it because it was so back loaded and so big that we figured if the 527s on the other side saw it, they would just go in and match it. To be honest, our idea was just to lock up as much of the time in the states as possible.

When we launched Ashley's story on October 19, we went with the whole "surround" campaign. It was actually a trick. We looked at what the Democrat, the liberal, 527s had done with the Internet, which was amazing. We ran a banner ad campaign that did about 75 million impressions. We e-mailed out 20 million copies of the ad. One of the unexpected consequences was that within days, we had raised another $6 million. We were only able to place $2.5 million of it. The total amount that we ran on TV was $16.7 million. The rest of the "surround" campaign was $20 million of the $35 million we spent all behind Ashley's story.

DAVID GERGEN: Brian, if you look at the "Ashley" ad, the other ads that you ran, and the ads that were running by the Swift Boat folks, how much impact do you think they had on the campaign outcome?

BRIAN McCABE: We think Ashley's story was an ad that cut through the clutter at a time that there was obviously a lot of advertising going on. It was pretty high risk going with the positive spot at the end. Everyone assumed when we placed this buy, especially the press, that it had to be just unbelievably negative. We got the sense that people were out selling that it was a pretty negative spot. The whole time we knew it was incredibly positive.

You mentioned the POS survey. Bob Moore did one. Fabrizio did one. The interesting thing across all the surveys is it's the same three ads that had the most impact. It really cut through. The verbatims afterwards that POS did were unbelievable—they were just giving our storyline right back to us. When asked, what ad made the most impact, they would respond, when the President hugged that girl. They just kept coming back to it. When you followed up and asked them why, it was because it was believable and it reminded them what they liked about the President. In this little girl, Ashley Faulkner, the President was able to connect and remind people that he's protecting us as a nation and as individuals.

DAVID GERGEN: It goes to the point that Ken Mehlman was making earlier today that the ground game is essential, but you've got to have the message to go with it to make it work. Is that what you all think happened in the end—that the impact really helped to sharpen the message?

BRIAN McCABE: We think we sharpened the focus on the issue of the War on Terror. From when we ran that first ad in June all the way through for us, it was the War on Terror. We wanted to compare different people's policies and issues and beliefs on the War on Terror. Ashley's story fit right into that.

DAVID GERGEN: Good. Thank you. I think others will probably want to come back to you.

• THE MEDIA FUND •

DAVID GERGEN: Let's move on now to Erik Smith, from the other side, with the Media Fund. The Media Fund is listed officially as having raised some $59 million, with Harold Ickes who helped pioneer 527s for Democrats.[10] The Media Fund got into massive television advertising. Tell us about your efforts.

ERIK SMITH: We raised a little over $60 million and, of that, a little more than $50 million went into ad time. We're proud to say that eighty-five cents of every dollar went on the air. That doesn't include production and research, so we really were moving a lot of money out the door.

Our 2004 is easiest to explain in three phases. The first was the spring—March and April—a time that everyone knew that the eventual Democratic nominee would be tremendously outspent. The Bush campaign had made no secret of the fact that the nominee was going to emerge from the primaries and hit a wall of money. The *New York Times* reported that there was a ninety-day strategy to define John Kerry and win the race early. We worked to prepare for that. We ended up, in those first eight weeks, doing $25 million of national ads, running in eighteen states, to the tune of roughly $3 to $4 million a week.

In the second phase, during the summer months, we had a lot less money to spend.

In the first eight weeks, the Bush campaign ended up spending $40 million nationwide. We spent $25 million. I believe our research showed that

---

10. Harold Ickes served as deputy chief of staff for President Clinton and was president and founder of the Media Fund during the 2004 election cycle.

Washington Post *reporter Tom Edsall listens on as
Media Fund President Erik Smith explains his group's ad strategy.*

the Kerry campaign spent somewhere in the neighborhood of $12 million. We worked very closely with the 527s on our side—the AFL-CIO and MoveOn.[11] There was another $9 million spent by the AFL and about $3 or $4 million by MoveOn during that period. In the end, you had the Bush campaign spending somewhere around $51 million and the combined Democratic spending at $48 million. During those first few months, when the Bush campaign set out to take Kerry out early, we did essentially spend to parity.

One thing Tom [Edsall] mentioned was that we learned over the course of this program that we may not have been doing exactly what the Kerry campaign wanted. I hope the record reflects that. I'm going to FedEx that to my lawyers for Christmas. That's one of the pitfalls of not being able to coordinate. You may not always be able to do what the campaign wants you to do.

Let me try to shed some light on what was going on in the spring for us. We were starting up in January and February, at a time where we did not actually know who the nominee might be. When it became clear who the nominee was, we were preparing to make sure the Democratic message was competitive on the airwaves. But we did not know exactly what we wanted to say.

Chris [LaCivita] and Brian [McCabe] were in a different situation where they came in later in the year, as Ben Ginsberg said. You started in July, Brian?

11. MoveOn.org is a progressive grassroots 527 that was started in 1998 in response to the impeachment of President Clinton.

BRIAN McCABE: Late June.

ERIK SMITH: Late June. They've got three or four months of Bush advertising, knowing very clearly what that campaign wants, what they're saying and what their message is. We were in a different situation. We were, by three or four weeks, out in front of the Kerry campaign, trying to anticipate where the holes might be and what message might need to be communicated.

We had a circle of advisors, a lot of them with presidential experience, who said there were two main tasks—one is a negative track, one is a positive track. Fairly easy stuff. We felt that we were better prepared, certainly at that point, to do the negative track. We did not know enough about how the Kerry campaign was going to develop and what their message was going to be and what they wanted or what they were doing or saying to be able to help in that endeavor at all. We felt that we were better suited for the negative message, which we embraced and did. We did that for, as I said, eight weeks. The hope was that through our actions, we would show very clearly what we were setting out to do.

DAVID GERGEN: Let me ask you this. What you said was very interesting. You had a choice about whether to go negative or positive and you didn't know enough about what their positive message was for you to build on something—that there was not enough out there for you to develop it. They were complaining earlier today that it would have been a lot better if you had gone positive rather than going negative during that particular cycle—if you'd helped to build the profile of John Kerry and what he stood for. But, you all, yourselves, didn't know what they were trying to say, and you're their friends.

ERIK SMITH: Well, it was early. You have to keep in mind that we were developing these ads while the primaries and caucuses were still going on. We were writing scripts and producing at a time before the nominee had emerged and before we really knew what was going to come out of that campaign.

One of the brilliant things about the Republican side is that if you look at every one of their ads, whether it was a Bush-Cheney ad, a Swift Boat ad, or Progress for America, they used the same message frame, same character frame—what Kerry says and what he does and you can't trust him in the War on Terror. Can't trust him.

DAVID GERGEN: They had more cues?

ERIK SMITH: Yes, absolutely.

DAVID GERGEN: From within the campaign to frame the conversation?

ERIK SMITH: Because of schedules, the Bush campaign was essentially able to put the playbook on the air and that helps the allies out.

Getting to the other two phases quickly. In the summer, we had fewer resources. We tried to do more targeted stuff and tried to be a little more experimental in what we were doing. What we learned over the summer is that some targeted ads worked—some very geographic and demographic specific advertising. In the fall, we did about another $15 million in advertising. When I say fall, I mean the last four-and-a half weeks. Unlike the Republican stuff at the time, and unlike our stuff in the spring, we did, in October, more than a dozen different commercials in different markets.

DAVID GERGEN: What was your central pro-Kerry message?

ERIK SMITH: Our central message was that the Bush Administration had the wrong priorities.

DAVID GERGEN: So it was an attack?

ERIK SMITH: Yes.

DAVID GERGEN: What was your central pro-Kerry message?

ERIK SMITH: Like I said, we didn't view it as our job to do that. We chose one path and took it. If we had $8 million a week, maybe we would have done both tracks. But we had enough resources in eighteen states and seventy-something media markets to do one track effectively and we chose that course, thinking that that was a place that we could be most effective.

DAVID GERGEN: Mark, for all of us to understand this, would you be willing to respond to what you've been hearing about from the Kerry campaign perspective?

MARK MELLMAN: First of all, without refighting the campaign, it just needs to be said, for the record, that the stuff that Chris [LaCivita] was talking about was demonstrated to be false. It is not true and that just needs to be stated for the record very clearly. Let's not refight the campaign.

Let me make a couple points. If you walk down to the business school here, they will tell you that all the research suggests there's absolutely no correlation between the memorability of an ad, on the one hand, and its persuasiveness, on the other. So the fact that after the fact—weeks after the fact in some cases—people say, I remember this ad, is really not proof of its persuasiveness.

DAVID GERGEN: You don't think that the Willie Horton ad had an impact on that race?[12]

MARK MELLMAN: I didn't say that. What I'm saying is that there is no correlation. There are ads that are very memorable and that may be one, but the fact that an ad is memorable does not mean it's persuasive. There is a difference. Don't ask me. Walk down the street to the business school people. They'll all tell you that.

The second point I want to make is in terms of the "Ashley" ad. We did see that that ad was very effective in Ohio. It was an Ohio-based story. It did have an impact. Frankly, we did not see the effectiveness of that ad in other states. And, frankly, if hugging were a clear signal of leadership, there's no doubt John Kerry would be president today. It did have an impact in Ohio because it was an Ohio-based story.

DAVID GERGEN: How much impact, Mark? Was it significant or modest?

MARK MELLMAN: You were talking about movements of a point or two or three, so significance is a hard word to attach here. But there's no question that it moved the numbers up for Bush in terms of his favorabilities. There's no question it moved the poll numbers to some extent. There's no question that lots of people responded to it. There's no doubt about that. Again, that's because it was an Ohio-based story.

As far as the Swift Boat ads are concerned, we talked about that this morning. If I can ask Chris a question. This afternoon, Matt Dowd said two things very clearly—not necessarily my opinion, his opinion—A, that the Swift Boat ads had no impact, on the one hand, and, B, he said, and I think I'm quoting him, they were a distraction because if you were talking about Vietnam, that was bad from their point of view. My question to Chris is really threefold. One, do you agree with Matt? Second, if you disagree with him, why do you think he said what he said? And third, if you knew at the time that they felt that the ads were harmful and not helpful, would that have affected anything you did?

CHRIS LaCIVITA: Someday you'll have the pleasure of meeting the Swifties who drove the message and who we took our orders from. These guys

---

12. In September 1988, a group called "Americans for Bush" launched negative attack ads against Democratic presidential candidate Michael Dukakis to portray him as soft on crime for allowing furloughs of convicted criminals. The ad used the example of Willie Horton, an African American Massachusetts convict who was released from prison on a weekend furlough while Dukakis served as governor of Massachusetts. Horton used his furlough to travel to Maryland, where he assaulted a couple and raped a woman.

were determined to get their message out and they insisted on getting their message out and there was nothing that was going to get in their way. So, regardless of what Matt said, it's really, quite frankly, not relevant to the discussion. Whether it had an impact or not, I'll let the academics take a look at that. I think on the issue of trust, which is again what we were focused on, it had an impact. But the bottom line was these guys had a message to get out, they wanted it heard, they wanted it told, and they did it. And that's what the spirit of the First Amendment is about and that's what the spirit of 527s is about.

DAVID GERGEN: Mark, as you look back on the campaign and the lessons, without pointing fingers at anybody individually, I'm just curious, what runs through your mind when you hear that the three most memorable ads were all on the Republican side?

MARK MELLMAN: Well, I note those were also all Republican pollsters. I think it's fair to say, in my view, that the Swift Boat ads, not directly but as a result of the conversation they spawned, did have an impact. But, the truth is, and I think Chris just said this, it wasn't the ad these people remembered. They couldn't have remembered the ad because they didn't see it. It was the conversation that had been started. So, in fact, all these people that are saying they remember the ad are not even telling the truth to the pollster about remembering the ad because they hadn't seen it. The conversation did have an impact.

As I said, the "Ashley" ad had an impact in Ohio. It was memorable because it was different. What's interesting to me is the "Wolves" ad—one of the last ads in the campaign. It was a metaphorical story. You had these wolves running around the screen. It was certainly different, certainly memorable. I don't think there's any evidence that we saw that that ad was persuasive to anybody in any way, shape, or form. The truth of it is they didn't even stick with it. They announced that it was going to be their closing ad and they took it off within a couple of days. I'm not sure they believed it was all that persuasive, ultimately.

What's interesting to me is the two most influential ads in this race, which I would say are "Ashley" in Ohio, because Ohio was the ballgame, and the Swift Boat discussion, were not ones by the Bush campaign. To me, that's an interesting fact.

DAVID GERGEN: That's true. But help me understand. Here's the Democratic Party, which is very close to a lot of a creative talent in Hollywood and in the country. I'm just curious what has happened that the people affiliated with the Republicans have come up with the ads that are more memorable. Why is that?

MARK MELLMAN: Again, I go back to two points. First, there really isn't a relationship between memorability and persuasion. We were not in the business of creating ads that were going to be memorable. The goal of the campaign was not to have ads that were memorable. The goal of the campaign was to win the election.

DAVID GERGEN: Right. But obviously you would have preferred to have your ads being the ones discussed on cable rather than their ads.

MARK MELLMAN: That's true. We had plenty of ads and a lot of them were discussed.

The other point I want to make is that we felt there was a strategic imperative that we had for people to get to know John Kerry, to get to be exposed to him, and to find out what kind of person he was. That was a process that was going to happen through John Kerry appearing on television talking directly to people. Most of the advertising from our campaign was John Kerry speaking directly to people.

One side of that is, by definition, it's not going to be terribly memorable. It's not going to stand out. You're not going hear people say, oh, I remember that ad when John Kerry said X. None of the three ads that you're focused on have any candidate talking in them. But we think that they were serving a strategic purpose. That purpose was for people to get to know and get to be comfortable with John Kerry and for them to have a very different impression about him than they got from the negative advertising from the Bush campaign.

Second, we wanted to talk about our agenda and, the fact is, hundreds of millions of dollars were spent communicating an agenda. Most people thought John Kerry was better on health care. We talked about that and most people came to that conclusion. Most people thought John Kerry was better on education. We talked about that.

I don't design ads for a living, but the ads did have an impact on people. In fact, what we saw at the end of the campaign was that in the battleground states, taken as a whole, where it was campaign versus campaign, ad versus ad, John Kerry actually won the majority of votes in those states. They weren't optimally distributed, to be sure. We could have used a few more people moving from Michigan and Minnesota down to Ohio—we would have had a different outcome. But where the campaigns were really engaged ads against ads, John Kerry actually won the majority of those votes.

• AMERICA COMING TOGETHER •

DAVID GERGEN: I want to move on now to the organizational side of this and the registration and turning out the votes because there was obviously

*ACT's CEO Steve Rosenthal addresses David Gergen's questions
about turning out Democratic voters.*

a very dramatic effort in that regard. We're fortunate tonight to have Steve Rosenthal here from America Coming Together—ACT—which was given a very high profile during the campaign. An awful lot of young people signed up with you. From your point of view, Steve, tell us the story briefly and what you thought you accomplished in the end.

STEVE ROSENTHAL: Thank you, David, and thanks to the Kennedy School for pulling this conference together. I do want to take one second and say that I thought, by and large, the Swift Boat ads were immoral, outrageous, and effective.

DAVID GERGEN: Which one's the most important?

STEVE ROSENTHAL: The bottom line is I think they gave all the 527s a very bad name from their activities, and I would be remiss if I didn't say that.

And, by the way, not to contradict Mark, who I think is a brilliant pollster and one of the best in the business, certainly one of the best on our side, they were memorable and effective from the standpoint that we just did focus groups last week in Ohio with exurban voters[13] who not only remembered the ads, chapter and verse, having seen them or not, but would recite directly from the ads and say, how could I vote for John Kerry when people who

---

13. "Exurban" is a region lying beyond the suburbs of a city.

served with him—which wasn't the case, by the way—didn't think he was fit to be commander in chief? So I think they were extremely effective ads.

DAVID GERGEN: Did you hear people reciting ads on the Kerry side from memory?

STEVE ROSENTHAL: No. Erik [Smith]'s point would be that there were different messages in different states and different ads running at different times. It was probably a much more targeted effort. I would agree with some of the points that Mark [Mellman] made that, overall, the ad campaigns were aimed at bolstering and introducing John Kerry to voters and also making the case on Bush. But I'm no expert on ads, so you're talking to the wrong guy about ads.

America Coming Together. I come from the labor movement. I had spent a lifetime organizing workers, both into unions and politically. I got to the AFL-CIO as political director in 1996. In the 1992 election, about 19 percent of the electorate were voters from union households. In 1996, if you took the whole pie of everybody who voted and sliced off 23 percent, those were the union household voters. By 2000, in the last presidential election that I was there, we drove that up to 26 percent. At a time when the labor movement was getting smaller, we were bringing more and more union members into the political process, to the point where more than a quarter of the electorate came from union households despite the fact that we were representing about 16 percent of the voting age population in the United States.

I don't know about any secret meetings with Terry McAuliffe. I never would doubt the facts that Tom Edsall gathers, but I was never part of any secret meetings. I came out of my experience at the AFL-CIO feeling we needed to set up something for this election on a parallel track to what the labor movement was doing, to better reach that 74 percent of the American electorate that wasn't in the labor movement, or some part of them, in these battleground states.

The notion was that the way we were able to get more union members to participate over those elections was by talking to them, very simply, one-on-one—beginning to engage people where they work, engage them where they live, talk to them by phone, talk to them one-on-one about the issues that they cared about. We set out with ACT to try to do the same thing—to go into the battleground states and put together an organization. Then we began to talk to voters again.

Frankly, it's pretty outrageous that in America, about a third of those who are eligible to vote aren't even registered. Usually about half of those who are registered turn out. We set out to try to figure out how to begin to create dialogues with people. What we found was that the number one reason that people weren't registered to vote was because nobody had asked them. And the main reason people weren't voting was because nobody was asking them. So we said, well, we're going to try to see if we can't change that.

The organization was grounded by George Soros. I know that he certainly helped fundraising for the Republicans, but, in fact, he was an enormous asset on our side. He was a person who had donated millions of dollars over the years to fight for democracy around the world. He saw democracy and human rights eroding here at home and decided to help center an organization like ours with contributions that would attract other donors at a time when the Democratic community overall was pretty despondent and beaten down, and probably thinking that Bush could not be beaten.

We set out with three goals—one, to bring people into the political process; two, to help defeat George Bush; and three, to elect progressive candidates up and down the ticket in the states where we were active. We put state directors in very early, almost a year before the November election, in most cases around January, February, March. We had them put together plans and vote goals in each state and begin to hire a staff. We hired a firm to do opposition research. We put communications directors in each state and essentially built an entire field structure.

Part of it came from my frustration overall with the Democratic Party for not having done this work for so long. Not, in fact, in coalition with Terry [McAuliffe] but, rather, out of frustration that the state parties and the Democratic Party overall had failed in a lot of ways to build the kind of infrastructure that really was needed to begin to engage voters again. We ended up with about 2,000 paid organizers on the ground and we had another 3,000 paid canvassers.

As Ken Mehlman said earlier today, it was fashionable to canvass on their side. We found the same thing. We had built plans, for example, in the state of Pennsylvania that called for somewhere in the neighborhood of 12,000 paid workers on Election Day. We ended up with 17,000 volunteers on Election Day and didn't have to pay a single person.

Having experienced campaign after campaign with no volunteers, on Election Day this year, we had somewhere in the neighborhood of 75,000 people on the streets—almost all knocking on doors, some making phone calls, some providing rides and doing other things. It was just an enormous effort.

DAVID GERGEN: Do you have a sense of how much you might have increased the turnout on the Democratic side?

STEVE ROSENTHAL: We're going to be doing a detailed precinct-by-precinct analysis of places that we worked. Overall, the Kerry vote totals were about 10 percent higher than Al Gore nationwide. In the states that we were in, the turnout was about 20 percent higher than Gore. It's too bad we weren't running against Al Gore because I'm certain we could beat him. (Laughter.) We actually exceeded our vote goals in every state and found certain formulas for contact with voters. For example, we had run tests over the last couple of years leading up to this election with new registrants and we knew, when we registered groups of voters, how many times we needed to contact them to try to then make sure that they turned out to vote.

DAVID GERGEN: In a moment, I'm going to ask two of the nation's best journalists, Walter Shapiro and Roger Simon, to give us their thoughts on this. But, before you sit down, I have a question for you that I am really anxious to ask. You were out organizing. We've heard many times now that the goals were exceeded on the Kerry side and yet the turnout on the Republican side was even bigger and was unexpected. As you think about what you did with your group, how do you compare that with the organizing that was underway in this campaign within churches, especially the Evangelical churches and the Catholic churches, on the other side? Could you describe what you saw and what your conclusions were after that?

STEVE ROSENTHAL: It's a very interesting question. We've taken a pretty hard look at the organizing that was done on the Republican side. We did some post-election polling among exurban and rural voters in Ohio and some focus groups there—outside Columbus and outside Cincinnati. This would have been a tough target for the Republican Party and not so much for the Democrats. What we found was that they were contacted as much by the Democratic side as the Republican side—almost as much with a couple of points different in mailings, phone calls, and personal contact.

The level of contact and the discussions that we've had with voters was no more personal on the Republican side than it was on the Democratic side. By the Republican side, I'm including the churches, Evangelical churches, anti-choice groups and others.

What I believe generally happened is that, and our Republican colleagues in the room have to forgive me for saying this, I don't think they really had a huge organization driving the vote on the ground in states. We didn't see it in terms of voter registration. We didn't see it in terms of absentee ballot requests. We didn't see it in any of the measurable things we'd see leading up to an election. Granted some of the work was done over four years, particularly the registration in some of the exurban and rural areas. But, in the election year itself, except for an occasional spike up around the Republican convention, you didn't see a huge increase in any of the measurable things on their side.

What they are doing, though, is they're generally changing the culture. The first time I was at the AFL-CIO, we didn't reach as many union members as we would have liked. In 1996, we were only getting through to about 11 percent of union members with a one-on-one campaign. But we talked about it a lot, we built the organization, we showed that we valued that work, and we increased it in the next election to 22 percent and then 45 percent and so on.

I think the Republicans are doing essentially the same thing. They're talking about it a lot right now, but they're not doing it much. What the voters would tell you is that every time they turned on the TV, turned on the radio, opened a magazine, and opened the newspaper, they heard about the election. There were kids talking about the election in school and co-workers talking to each other about it. Being in the center of the storm of the election, in Ohio, the entire level of activity was driven up. I think there was some evidence of contact on their side, but not nearly as much as they're claiming—and certainly not as much by Evangelical churches.

DAVID GERGEN: Do you then tend to discount the stories which say that moral values, the churches, and the ban on gay marriages were not a driving force? The stories say that they were driving forces in this election. Are you saying they were not?

STEVE ROSENTHAL: Absolutely not.

DAVID GERGEN: They were not?

STEVE ROSENTHAL: No. Both the exit polls and some of the post-election polling, and the discussions we've had with voters, would indicate that it was not. When you ask voters what are moral values, in these target areas that are Republican, they talk about having a core, standing up for what you believe in, fighting for what's right. They rarely turn to gay marriage or abortion.

DAVID GERGEN: Brief response from Ben and then back to Walter.

BEN GINSBERG: Let me agree with part of what Steve said and disagree with another part. I don't think moral values was what truly drove the Republican Get-Out-The-Vote effort. I think Steve's response to that is correct. It is fundamentally wrong to say that there was not a Republican organization that drove turnout. In point of fact, even if you didn't see it, somewhere along the line, 3.4 million new Republican registrants were put on the books. That just doesn't happen by osmosis. That happens because of an organization. The turnout was there.

But it is also true that you guys did a great job of hyping that. On Sunday, September 26, the *New York Times* said there was a big increase of new voters in swing states—a sweeping voter registration campaign in heavily Democratic areas has added 100,000 new voters to the rolls in Ohio and Florida, a surge that has far exceeded the efforts of Republicans in those states. The *New York Times* story sent a great deal of optimism, from what I've heard through the Kerry campaign and Democratic ranks, about the turnout. The fact was the *New York Times* just flat out missed the story. In the sixteenth paragraph, they allowed the Republican officials to say they remain confident that their voters will prove easier to get to the polls.

It was a phenomenon in Republican organization. There were precinct captains in every target precinct and in every target state, and an elaborate organization. They really did a superior job of turning out the vote. That is not to say that in years when the party committees are as well funded as they were in the hotly contested 2004 race, your model of paying workers by the hour won't be the better model in the future, but it wasn't this year. The Republican organization in 2004 was there and delivered the vote.

STEVE ROSENTHAL: Can I say one thing?

DAVID GERGEN: Yes, please.

STEVE ROSENTHAL: I have no doubt there were places where there was a Republican organization, and I have no doubt they're building that. It is frankly worrisome. I give them a lot of credit for driving the vote. But I think the way the vote was driven, as I said, was largely through message, with an excellent campaign buying cable TV and radio, getting local newspaper ads, and a very local campaign that got people excited and energized. And there was registration done.

DAVID GERGEN: You ran the ground effort, but you say the vote was driven more by the message?

STEVE ROSENTHAL: Absolutely on the Republican side. I would say on our side that we do have to work harder to turn out a lot of the votes that we registered.

DAVID GERGEN: Great response. I'll keep on trying to get back to you. Karen Hicks, you were the national field director at the Democratic National Committee.

KAREN HICKS: I think the Republicans started trying to run a good turn-out operation in 2000 and found out that it was harder than they originally anticipated. They learned a bunch of stuff that they wrote up in a "72-hour report." We heard this morning from Ken Mehlman that they spent unprecedented resources—$50 million is what he said—studying tactics and figuring out exactly the voters that they needed to move. They tested it in 2002. One of the legacies of this election is that we both ran different kinds of campaigns that involved many, many more people and focused on building leadership. I think that's frankly good for democracy.

The myth that I think we need to say for the record is that politics is all about addition. It's great that 527s were out there getting people involved. But the two parties really did an unbelievable job. The Democratic National Committee, where I led the field effort, spent about $45 to $50 million in 2000. We spent $80 million getting out the vote, investing in leadership, training and reaching out to new voters. It was an unprecedented effort and people deserve credit all around.

Ultimately, I think it was matched fairly evenly down the line. I think the Republicans had some advantages on the targeting that they had tested earlier on. In a race that came down to so few votes, any one of these things could have made the difference. But, on both sides of the equation, we deserve a lot of credit for just involving many, many more people.

• THE INFLUENCE OF 527s •

DAVID GERGEN: Walter, the influence of 527s?

WALTER SHAPIRO: Two questions come to my mind. One is for Erik [Smith] and the people on the national security oriented side who did the "Ashley" ads. What is the challenge of a 527 doing a positive ad when you cannot get the normal biographical film archive material from the candidate, which is the staple of positive ads that we know? And, for Steve Rosenthal, what I really want to know is, had the money been there, would the Democrats have been better off if your operation and Karen Hicks' operation was the same operation, under the Democratic National Committee or the Kerry campaign?

DAVID GERGEN: Excellent questions. Roger, why don't you chime in here now while you have the microphone.

ROGER SIMON: I think we've reached the point in the evening where everything has been said, but not everyone has said it, so I'll keep this even briefer. It's really in the nature of a comment, since Walter's handled the question side.

If the FEC was really a truly first-rate organization, it would probably subpoena the tape of this evening. I'm not an expert in campaign finance reform, but it seems to me the whole point of ending soft money was to end the unrestricted flow of money to candidate advocacy. You can't listen to the candid and honest comments made by both the Republicans and the Democrats here tonight and say that their ads, especially those discussed in the early part of the evening, were about anything other than candidate advocacy. They worried from day one to the last day about getting their candidate elected.

That seems to me to fly in the face of what finance reform was all about. I was going to say I really wonder if Congress will let it continue, but because the Republicans turned out doing so well with 527s, I'm sure Congress will let it continue. I think it's part of the wink-and-nod game that makes some part of the public so contemptuous of politics in America today.

DAVID GERGEN: Roger, let me ask you this question. If you think about the health of democracy, what is it about the 527s this past year that troubles you versus what you would find actually healthy for democracy? Is it the amount of money that some of these large givers give? Is it the advertisements? What about this Get-Out-The-Vote? One could look at that and say, wow, they've got a lot more people registered. They got a lot more people to the polls. Isn't that worthwhile?

ROGER SIMON: Some of it is worthwhile and it shouldn't trouble you if you believe that there is no undue influence of money on politics. If you simply listen to all the debate and argument on McCain-Feingold, you find that perhaps money, over the decades, does produce an undue influence on politics.

DAVID GERGEN: Would you assume that someone who gave lots of money to a 527 would have the same amount of influence within the party structure than if he had given the money directly to the party in years gone by?

ROGER SIMON: Well, Ben Ginsberg could probably answer that better than I. I did want to ask a question to Ben Ginsberg, who is a good and honorable man and who has worked very closely with the Republican party structure. Did it give you any pause, or did you think anyone would see there was any kind of appearance of a conflict, to then work with the Swift Boat Veterans for Truth?[14]

---

14. Ben Ginsberg resigned his position as the lawyer for the Bush-Cheney 2004 campaign after it was disclosed that he had advised the 527 organization Swift Boat Veterans for Truth.

DAVID GERGEN: If you want to. You've had to answer that on many occasions.

BEN GINSBERG: I have had the honor, thank you. (Laughter.) The simple matter is when I started representing the Swift Boat Veterans in July, my colleagues on the Democratic side had already been representing MoveOn and the Media Fund and ACT since March, and $60 million had been spent with nary a peep from those of you in the media who were watchdogging this sort of thing.

I don't think it was illegal for my colleagues on the Democratic side to have dual representation like that for the simple reason that the law itself says that legal services don't fall under the prohibited consultant activities. From my reading of the law and my Democratic colleagues' reading of the law, as well as the practice that had been in place for four months before I ever talked to the Swifties, no. We give legal advice. We don't do message.

ROGER SIMON: That was a good answer to some questions but not my question. The question wasn't whether it was legal or not. The question was, did you think it gave the appearance of a conflict?

BEN GINSBERG: The answer is no because I was not involved, nor were any of the lawyers, in the message of it. The goal of the lawyer is to keep everyone complying with the law. It is a tricky law and all of them wanted to comply.

I think the appearance about the Swift Boat ads, in particular, is frankly more a comment about the subject the Swift Boat Veterans were talking about. I trust that that's not a purely subjective question that you're asking because you, and the media at large, felt differently about the Swift Boat Veterans on Vietnam than about MoveOn, who compared the President to Hitler without anybody objecting to it, or about the Media Fund who talked about President Bush's ties to the Saudi royal family in a negative way with nobody commenting about that. So the answer is that's a subjective question with which the topic that the Swift Boat Veterans were dealing.

DAVID GERGEN: We have two Walter Shapiro questions that are on the table that I think do deserve answers. Brian, you go ahead on the question about the positive ads.

BRIAN McCABE: Walter's question was, I think, about the positive nature of the ads. People forget that the same person who did "Willie Horton" also did "Ashley." You have someone who's been accused of doing one of the toughest ads who also did one of the most positive ads. There were a lot of times when we were going on with our comparison ads on the issue. They got a little tougher as we went along. There were times we thought of going with something positive. As I said earlier, it was pretty high risk. We didn't know if we would cut through. It was high risk, but we did it and we think it worked, whether it's just memorable or persuasive. What matters for us is that it was about issues. We did want people to remember the issue and that's why we know it was a winner. Ours was about issues. We were an issue campaign.

ERIK SMITH: Just to echo something. I don't want to repeat Brian [McCabe] and Chris [LaCivita] so much, but I do have to agree that we were also an issue advocacy organization that didn't call on people to vote or come out for anyone or against anyone.

DAVID GERGEN: When the tape is subpoenaed, that will be shown.

ERIK SMITH: If we could have done true express advocacy, we would have been a lot more effective. But we were doing issue advocacy, which is something different. That gets to Walter's question. He was essentially putting a finer point on what I was trying to talk about earlier, as far as what we saw our mission as and why we felt we were better suited for putting one set of information out there over another.

John Kerry had a great story to tell and he had a good message. But we didn't feel it was our job to figure out what part of his message or history he wanted out week by week. We believed the best thing we could do was to put out information about George Bush to try and combat all the negative information he was putting out about John Kerry, in the hopes that by taking on that responsibility, others would be able to go communicate John Kerry's story and John Kerry's message. Like Mark [Mellman] said, John Kerry is his own best messenger. I totally agree with that.

DAVID GERGEN: If there had been an interview in the newspapers with someone high up in the Kerry campaign saying, gee, we're really trying to get a positive message out about Kerry, we've got a lot to talk about and we're not anxious to go after Bush, and we sure would like to get more of a positive message out, would that have changed what you were doing?

ERIK SMITH: Yes. If it was in the public domain and it was public information, it would have been instructive.

DAVID GERGEN: Wasn't that kind of informal communication going on? That's what I don't get.

ERIK SMITH: No. I was up here a couple of days ago meeting with some students who said, come on, you guys talked all the time, right? The truth is, no. One thing McCain-Feingold did was make criminal penalties for this stuff. I think John Kerry would be a great president, but I'm not going to jail for the guy. (Laughter.)

DAVID GERGEN: But if it had been in the newspapers?

ERIK SMITH: There was no wink-and-nod. The open secret about was there coordination or was there not coordination is that the more information you put out in the public domain, the more information everyone has. So, if we're making a media buy and we say that we're going up in these ten states with this ad for this much, everybody has it and that's not coordination.

I know we're trying to finish, but if I could just comment on one thing Roger [Simon] said about the effectiveness of campaign finance reform. I come at this from having served in 2000 at the Democratic Congressional Campaign Committee (DCCC) where Tom [Edsall] watched us very closely and we broke a lot of soft money records. I then went back into the Congress and worked on the team to try and pass campaign finance reform.

There's oftentimes some mission creep here. The goal of campaign finance reform was to separate federal officeholders from the raising of large, unregulated soft money checks. That was a success. If we had had a Senate leader or a House leader raising seven or eight figure checks for us, we would have been a lot more successful. We would have raised an awful lot more money.

The assumption was that if you separated federal officeholders from the raising of this money, there would be less money in the system. The unintended consequences was that none of us realized that that was actually not true. Even though the Time Warners of the world disappeared and didn't give a lot of soft money contributions to anyone, ideological donors, who didn't care about access to Senate or House leaders or to a president or a White House but just simply had an ideological agenda, filled the void and then some.

DAVID GERGEN: Brief intervention here with Tom Edsall.

TOM EDSALL: Roger's question about money is a very interesting one. The problem with campaign finance, and with a lot of the coverage of it, is that it's always dealt with as a black-and-white issue. Money is seen as evil, per se.

There are different kinds of money and there are different kinds of groups. Some kind of groups can only finance their activities with large donations. Unions, for example. Most of these groups tend to be on the left, not on the right. The large donors are the ones that are needed to get across a message that money is a form of speech and that when you start restricting it, it is a First Amendment issue—you are restricting the ability of people to speak.

It's a much more complex issue than McCain-Feingold was going to clean up. McCain-Feingold, as Erik [Smith] pointed out, only sought to separate politicians from big money. It did not seek to separate organizations from being able to represent themselves. That's another issue that may have to be taken up by further legislation. I just would caution that there's a tendency, especially in groups like academics, to see money as an evil in and of itself.

DAVID GERGEN: That's the Harvard $21 billion endowment. (Laughter.)

THERESA AMATO: I want to put on the historical record that, although I agree with a lot of what Steve Rosenthal said, there was no monopoly on offensiveness with the Republican 527s. The Democratic party used 527s to undermine and keep the Nader campaign off the ballot, in a very anti-civil libertarian way.

DAVID GERGEN: That's helpful. Steve, and then Mark, and then we're going to finish.

STEVE ROSENTHAL: A couple of things quickly. Somebody on my staff was married in July. She had worked with a lot of people from the DNC and the Kerry campaign, so there were people from the DNC, people from the Kerry campaign, and people from ACT there. I told people it was the first time I've ever been at a wedding where we all danced around each other instead of with each other. (Laughter.)

In all honesty, I talked to Mary Beth [Cahill] the day she got the job as campaign manager to wish her good luck, and then I called her on election morning, per my lawyer's advice, saying it was okay, to wish her luck again, and that was it. There were a lot of times when I would have loved to have talked to people at the DNC and the Kerry campaign to try to tell them what we were doing.

In answering the question about whether or not this would have been better combined with the Democratic Party's activity, yes and no. Yes because, in the long run, there's nothing I would love to see more than the Democratic Party really rebuild its organization, build the state parties, make them into a real force of neighbors talking to neighbors. That is the most effective type of communication in politics. So, yes, I would like to see that.

But, on the other side of it, something happened this year. We had small donors who contributed $25 million dollars to ACT. Between ACT and the Media Fund, we raised about $205 million. It began to come in in small donations from people who could have contributed to the Democratic Party very easily, could have contributed early on to the Kerry campaign, but chose instead to contribute to this organization. That was just extraordinary.

When I said that there were upwards of 70,000 volunteers on Election Day, those were people who could have gone to the Kerry campaign, could have gone to the Democratic Party, but instead decided that they wanted to do this work in a different way. I think there's an opportunity out there right now to really build and engage and develop organizations that talk to people and get them involved in politics again.

Per your comment, David, that this is very good overall for our democracy—that, as you pointed out, we played a role in registering voters. We registered about 450,000 voters on the Democratic side in this election. It's extraordinary. I don't believe that work would have been done had it not been for organizations like ours.

Finally, on the donor access point. We had no nights in the Lincoln Bedroom to offer. We had no access to changes in legislation or regulatory changes. We didn't even have cufflinks and little pins that we could give people. Donors came forward in big numbers this year because they believed that the direction the country was headed in was the wrong direction. There's an enormous opportunity to build on that in the coming years.

DAVID GERGEN: Thank you. Last word, Mark.

MARK MELLMAN: You finally asked the question that I wanted to answer, so I wanted to take that opportunity. You asked what the impact of this is on democracy. I don't know what the answer is, but we really do have to understand there are competing considerations. We do have our First Amendment. It's vital to the functioning of this country. The question of campaign finance reform is always the balance of the First Amendment on the one hand versus the manipulation of the electoral process on the other. What we saw in some of the 527 advertising—I'll use Swift Boats as an example here—is a set of accusations that were made that the Bush campaign said today they would never have made because they were, in their view, not factual and it would have rebounded to discredit George Bush. You have a situation here where people are free to say things, have free speech, but no one is held responsible for the consequences of that speech. That is a problem. The solution is not to abolish the First Amendment, to be sure, but some balance does need to be struck.

DAVID GERGEN: In fairness, do you want to respond?

CHRIS LaCIVITA: Yes. Mark, I won't get into a tit-for-tat, but that's not what Ken [Mehlman] or Matt [Dowd] said. Actually, what they said was they couldn't comment on the accusations regarding collaborations. Then, the secondary point they made was that the testimony John Kerry gave and the fact that John Kerry met with the enemy in Paris were issues they felt were fair game. That's what was precisely said. If you check the tape, that's exactly what was said.

BEN GINSBERG: I have one thing to say to your point about 527s and the role that they play. It is beyond a doubt that 527s are probably, all things considered, not good for the American system because they take away from the campaigns. It is not the candidates that drive the message in the same manner that they would be able to were it not for outside groups and 527s.

Having said that, as long as the notion of campaign finance reform is to cut back what the political parties can do because of the money that they can raise, you are always going to have either 527s or their equivalent out there in the game as long as the parties and candidates don't have more money than anybody else.

DAVID GERGEN: With that, ladies and gentlemen, the battle is over but the war obviously goes on. In the meantime, we want to thank those who've paused here and put their shields and their swords down for a short while to come together and break bread. Most of all, we want to thank those of you who have come here from these campaigns—not only for contributing your thoughts but for being in the arena. We salute you for being out there in the arena. I know you fight hard for what you believe in and, yes, there are differences, but this country gains enormously from your participation and we're just delighted and proud to have you here.

Thank you.

PHIL SHARP: To echo what David Gergen said, this program could only be successful with the interest and the participation of those of you who are willing to come together and talk through these critical developments and events in America. I know that this book will be the kind of thing that others can draw on for the next round of campaigns. We really are grateful for your participation.

2004 CAMPAIGN TIME LINE

· 2002 ·

May 30	Governor Dean became the first Democrat to create a presidential exploratory committee.
July 29	Senator Lieberman pledged he would not seek the Democratic nomination for president if Al Gore decided to run again.
October 11	Congress passed a war resolution to give President Bush the power to compel Iraqi disarmament.
December 1	Senator Kerry announced that he was forming an exploratory committee.
December 14	Former Vice President Gore announced that he would not run for president again.

· 2003 ·

January 2	Senator Edwards announced he was running for president.
January 5	Reverend Sharpton told the Associated Press that he intended to run for president.
January 13	Senator Lieberman announced he was running for president.
February 17	Congressman Kucinich announced he was setting up an exploratory committee.
February 18	Ambassador Moseley Braun filed papers forming an exploratory committee.
February 19	Congressman Gephardt announced he was running for president.
February 21	Governor Dean gave a speech to the DNC's winter meeting blasting Democrats for not standing up to President Bush.
February 26	Senator Kerry hired the political consulting firm Shrum, Donilon, Devine.

February 27	Senator Graham filed papers to run for president.
March 19	The United States went to war against Iraq.
March 31	First quarter FEC numbers showed Senator Edwards and Senator Kerry raised the most money.
May 16	President Bush filed papers for reelection.
June 17	Governor Dean aired first TV ads in presidential campaign.
June 23	Governor Dean formally announced he was running for president.
June 30	Second quarter FEC numbers showed Governor Dean raised the most money.
August 1	Congressman Gephardt was endorsed by the Teamsters union.
August 23	Governor Dean began "Sleepless Summer Tour."
September 2	Senator Kerry formally announced he was running for president.
September 4	General Clark said he was a Democrat. Democratic candidates participated in a debate at the University of New Mexico.
September 11	Governor Dean reportedly asked Wesley Clark to run as his vice president.
September 16	Senator Edwards formally announced he was running for president.
September 17	General Clark announced he was running for president.
September 23	Former New Hampshire Governor Jeanne Shaheen endorsed Senator Kerry.
September 25	Democratic candidates participated in an MSNBC debate at Pace University in New York.
October 6	Senator Graham withdrew from the race.
October 10	Democratic candidates participated in a CNN/NAACP debate in Phoenix, Arizona.
October 15	President Bush raised nearly $50 million in the third quarter.
October 16	Third quarter FEC numbers showed Governor Dean raised the most money among the Democratic candidates.
October 19	General Clark and Senator Lieberman announced they would not compete in the Iowa caucuses.
November 4	Senate passed a bill authorizing $87 billion for war in Iraq.
November 5	Democratic candidates participated in MTV's Rock the Vote forum in Boston, Massachusetts.

November 8	Governor Dean announced he would opt out of public financing.
November 10	Senator Kerry fired his campaign manager Jim Jordan and replaced him with Mary Beth Cahill.
November 12	Governor Dean was endorsed by AFSCME and SEIU.
November 14	Senator Kerry announced he would opt out of public financing.
November 17	Governor Dean launched negative television ad aimed at Congressman Gephardt.
November 19	Massachusetts Supreme Judicial Court ruled that a ban on same-sex marriages is unconstitutional.
November 21	The Republican National Committee ran its first television ad.
November 25	Democratic candidates participated in an MSNBC debate in Des Moines, Iowa.
November 28	President Bush visited Iraq.
December 9	Al Gore endorsed Governor Dean.
December 13	Saddam Hussein was captured in Iraq.
December 17	A 527 organization began running a negative ad attacking Governor Dean on foreign policy.
December 19	Senator Kerry mortgaged his Beacon Hill home in Boston to finance his campaign.
December 29	Senator Edwards unveiled "Two Americas" stump speech.

• 2004 •

January 8	NBC news aired footage of Governor Dean criticizing the Iowa caucuses on Canadian television.
January 9	Iowa Senator Tom Harkin endorsed Governor Dean.
January 11	*Des Moines Register* endorsed Senator Edwards.
January 13	Iowa Governor Tom Vilsack's wife Christie endorsed Senator Kerry.
	Governor Dean won the nonbinding Washington, D.C., primary.
January 15	Ambassador Moseley Braun withdrew from the race and endorsed Governor Dean.
January 19	Senator Edwards and Congressman Kucinich agreed to share support in Iowa caucuses.
	Senator Kerry won Iowa caucuses and Senator Edwards came in second.
	Governor Dean "screamed."

January 20	Congressman Gephardt withdrew from the race.
January 22	Democratic candidates participated in the final debate before the New Hampshire primary.
January 27	Senator Kerry won New Hampshire primary.
January 28	Governor Dean fired campaign manager Joe Trippi.
January 30	Democratic candidates participated in a debate in Greenville, South Carolina.
February 3	Senator Kerry won five of seven primaries. Senator Lieberman withdrew from the race.
February 6	Congressman Gephardt endorsed Senator Kerry.
February 7	Senator Kerry won Michigan and Washington caucuses. AFSCME withdrew endorsement of Governor Dean.
February 10	Senator Kerry won Tennessee and Virginia primaries. General Clark announced he would drop out of the race.
February 13	General Clark endorsed Senator Kerry. AFL-CIO endorsed Senator Kerry.
February 14	Senator Kerry won Nevada and Washington, D.C., caucuses.
February 17	Senator Kerry won Wisconsin primary.
February 18	Governor Dean withdrew from the race.
February 22	Ralph Nader announced he would run as an Independent.
February 25	President Bush endorsed a constitutional amendment banning same-sex marriages.
March 2	Senator Kerry won nine of the ten Super Tuesday primaries.
March 3	President Bush unveiled first television ads.
March 17	Senator Kerry said, "I actually did vote for the $87 billion before I voted against it."
March 21	Richard Clarke's book *Against All Enemies* was released.
March 25	Governor Dean endorsed Senator Kerry.
April 2	First quarter FEC numbers showed Senator Kerry raised more than $50 million.
April 8	National Security Advisor Condoleezza Rice testified before the 9/11 Commission.
April 28	Prison abuse at Abu Ghraib facility in Iraq reported.
April 30	President Bush and Vice President Cheney interviewed by the 9/11 Commission.
May 3	Senator Kerry launched $25 million positive ad campaign.
May 13	FEC released decision allowing unlimited spending by 527s.

June 2	"Swift Boat Veterans for Truth" protested Senator Kerry's television ads.
June 11	Press reports said Senator John McCain refused an offer by Senator Kerry to be his vice president.
June 25	Michael Moore's movie *Fahrenheit 9/11* opened nationwide.
June 28	The United States turned over sovereignty in Iraq to the interim government headed by Ayad Allawi.
July 6	Senator Kerry picked Senator Edwards as his running mate.
July 22	9/11 Commission issued report.
July 26–29	Democratic National Convention held in Boston, Massachusetts.
August 4	"Swift Boat Veterans for Truth" launched advertising campaign against Senator Kerry.
August 19	Senator Kerry gave a speech attacking "Swift Boat Veterans for Truth."
Aug. 30–Sept. 2	Republican National Convention held in New York City.
September 9	CBS News reported that President Bush shirked National Guard duty.
September 21	CBS News admitted that the memo about President Bush's National Guard service could not be authenticated.
	President Bush met with Iraqi Prime Minister Ayad Allawi.
September 30	President Bush and Senator Kerry participated in the first presidential debate, focused on national security, in Coral Gables, Florida.
October 5	Vice President Cheney and Senator Edwards participated in the vice presidential debate in Cleveland, Ohio.
October 6	The Duelfer Report was released concluding there were no Iraqi weapons of mass destruction.
October 8	President Bush and Senator Kerry participated in the second presidential debate, a town hall forum, in St. Louis, Missouri.
October 13	President Bush and Senator Kerry participated in the third presidential debate, focused on domestic issues, in Tempe, Arizona.
October 25	Senator Kerry campaigned with President Clinton in Philadelphia.
	The *New York Times* reported that 380 tons of explosives were missing in Iraq.
October 29	New videotape by Osama bin Laden was released.

November 1   President Bush campaigned in Ohio, Pennsylvania, Wis-
                consin, Iowa, New Mexico, and Texas.
                Senator Kerry campaigned in Florida, Michigan, Ohio,
                and Wisconsin.
November 2   President Bush was reelected.

INDEX

Campaigning American Style

CAMPAIGNING AMERICAN STYLE

Series Editors
Daniel M. Shea, Allegheny College
F. Christopher Arterton, George Washington University

Titles in the Series

Forthcoming